Blind!

"In *BlindSpots,* Christian de Quincey pulls back the veil on the thoughtless, delusional ways we too often communicate. It's not just that these shortcuts are wrong, they are also dangerous because they lead to behaviors and beliefs that our fragile species can no longer afford. This very wise, engaging book should be at the top of the reading list of everyone who is concerned about our future."

LARRY DOSSEY, M.D., AUTHOR OF
*ONE MIND: HOW OUR INDIVIDUAL MIND IS PART OF
A GREATER CONSCIOUSNESS AND WHY IT MATTERS*

"In this book, Christian de Quincey illuminates some of the biggest *blindspots* that keep people stuck. Be prepared to be challenged about ideas you probably take for granted. Be prepared to be amused and inspired."

MARILYN SCHLITZ, PH.D., PRESIDENT EMERITUS/
SENIOR FELLOW AT THE INSTITUTE OF NOETIC SCIENCES

"This important book by Christian de Quincey shows that by questioning our own assumptions more carefully we can arrive at a deeper and more accurate understanding of life's complexities. De Quincey brings vitality and excitement to scientific, philosophical, metaphysical, and spiritual issues. I recommend this book for almost everyone."

JEFFREY MISHLOVE, PH.D., DEAN OF TRANSFORMATIONAL
PSYCHOLOGY, UNIVERSITY OF PHILOSOPHICAL RESEARCH

"*BlindSpots* will make your brain hurt, but in a good way, like the after-effects of exercise. De Quincey deftly unpacks 21 ideas that are often taken for granted to reveal why 'deep thought' philosophy remains a vital approach to understanding our complex world. You may agree with some of the ideas and disagree with others, but in all cases you will be invited to reconsider your core assumptions."

DEAN RADIN, PH.D., CHIEF SCIENTIST AT THE INSTITUTE OF
NOETIC SCIENCES AND COEDITOR IN CHIEF OF *EXPLORE*

"In his new book, Christian de Quincey focuses our attention on the ways in which erroneous or flabby or incoherent thoughts have become embedded in our everyday clichés. It is a delight to reflect upon these invisible clunkers in a critical way, and even if one ends up disagreeing with de Quincey, the end result is an improvement in one's verbal expressions; one's language feels brighter, fresher, and more alive."

BRIAN THOMAS SWIMME, PH.D., AUTHOR OF
THE UNIVERSE IS A GREEN DRAGON AND *CANTICLE TO THE COSMOS*

". . . this book will help you think more clearly and converse more fruitfully on a wide range of subjects. *BlindSpots* is an excellent field guide for exploring some of the twenty-first century's most challenging conceptual terrain."

MICHAEL DOWD, AUTHOR OF *THANK GOD FOR EVOLUTION*

"Professor de Quincey has a jeweler's eye for questions concerning the nature of consciousness and its position in the world of nature. I always find his clear thinking and writing a pleasure to read."

ALLAN COMBS, PH.D., DIRECTOR OF CONSCIOUSNESS STUDIES
AT THE CALIFORNIA INSTITUTE OF INTEGRAL STUDIES

"Reading de Quincey's *BlindSpots* is a profoundly liberating experience. All of us absorb beliefs from the culture around us, and we limit ourselves by acting as if those beliefs are true. De Quincey subjects those ideas to his brilliant philosophical critique. We are left with our minds open, free to engage with the world in new and interesting ways. This is my favorite kind of philosophy—philosophy that frees us from limitations and opens us more richly to our participation in the universe!"

ERIC WEISS, PH.D., AUTHOR OF *THE LONG TRAJECTORY*

"A provocative book that challenges many popular assertions about consciousness and the nature of reality. De Quincey encourages us to think for ourselves and base our beliefs on our own experience rather than hearsay or others' opinions. Much food for thought in here for everyone."

PETER RUSSELL, AUTHOR OF
THE GLOBAL BRAIN AND *FROM SCIENCE TO GOD*

BlindSpots

21

Good Reasons
to Think
before You Talk

CHRISTIAN DE QUINCEY

Park Street Press
Rochester, Vermont • Toronto, Canada

Park Street Press
One Park Street
Rochester, Vermont 05767
www.ParkStPress.com

Text stock is SFI certified

Park Street Press is a division of Inner Traditions International

Library of Congress Cataloging-in-Publication Data
De Quincey, Christian.
  Blindspots : 21 good reasons to think before you talk / Christian de Quincey.
    pages cm
  Includes bibliographical references and index.
  Summary: "Examines 21 unquestioned assumptions that cloud our collective consciousness"— Provided by publisher.
    ISBN 978-1-62055-446-3 (pbk.) — ISBN 978-1-62055-447-0 (e-book)
  1. Fallacies (Logic) 2. Reasoning. 3. Thought and thinking. 4. Oral communication. 5. Clichés. 6. Common fallacies. I. Title. II. Title: Blind spots.
  BC175.D43 2015
  110—dc23

                                                                    2015004810

Printed and bound in the United States by Lake Book Manufacturing, Inc. The text stock is SFI certified. The Sustainable Forestry Initiative® program promotes sustainable forest management.

10 9 8 7 6 5 4 3 2 1

Text design by Debbie Glogover and layout by Virginia Scott Bowman
This book was typeset in Garamond Premier Pro, Gill Sans, and Legacy Sans with Helvetica and Gill Sans used as display typefaces

To send correspondence to the author of this book, mail a first-class letter to the author c/o Inner Traditions • Bear & Company, One Park Street, Rochester, VT 05767, and we will forward the communication, or contact the author directly at **www.christiandequincey.com.**

◆

*To everyone who has ever
shone a light on blindspots—
especially mine.*

Contents

Acknowledgments

The ideas for this book came to me over many years and from a wide variety of sources. Whenever I heard or read something that struck me as odd, I jotted a note to myself to investigate the idea further.

Many of these odd ideas, or what I call "blindspots," showed up in conversations I've had with colleagues in academia, from my students, from readers of my books, blogs, and websites, and from fellow philosophers and scientists. I've also seen some of these strange notions repeated over and over in the mass media, apparently without a second thought. And I took note.

I organized my growing collection of "odd notes" into folders on my laptop, and as they accumulated I realized one day I had enough material for a book. Many of these notes grew from remarks someone—a friend, a colleague, a student, a reader—made in e-mails to me. I like to take time to respond and so, in many cases, a dialogue was born. Many of the chapters in this book grew out of these exchanges. Others began as recordings or transcripts of conversations I've had with colleagues in science, philosophy, and spirituality. Whenever I have identified someone by name in these pages, I asked their permission to include parts of our discussions. Others preferred to remain anonymous.

As is often the case, this book, then, is the product of many minds—separated by time and distance, but connected through the magic of modern digital archiving and communications. While most of the people who have stimulated the ideas presented here are my contemporaries, others are voices from the past, writers and scholars who have inspired and influenced my own thinking on these topics.

I cannot name or acknowledge everyone who, now or down the centuries, has contributed, in one way or another, to this book. But I do want to give special mention to a few whose contributions have been particularly significant.

For many years, I have met with close friends and colleagues at my home or theirs for rich and deep conversations. We often record these meetings and sometimes, if we feel we've struck a vein, we get the recordings transcribed and then rework the text to post on blogs or Facebook, or later to weave into articles or books. Two friends stand out: Peter Russell and Eric Weiss, both of whom have contributed significantly to the development of ideas in this volume.

I want to acknowledge Peter Russell because in one of our meetings a couple of years ago on his boat in Sausalito, California, he mentioned his plan to write about what he considered one of the most serious blindspots afflicting the world today: the reality of accelerating change and the relationship between technology and the climate crisis. For as long as I have known him, Pete has researched, lectured on, and written about the looming environmental point of no return—and the need for humanity to "wake up" before we disappear into a "white hole in time." He was one of the first to alert me to the data that highlight the dire situation facing our planet. Clearly, the eco-crisis is a crisis of consciousness.

When I told Pete I was working on this book, he reminded me of our conversation and that he, too, was planning to write a book with the title *Blind Spot*. I had completely forgotten that meeting. We agreed there would be room for both books—they would be very different and, in fact, could complement each other. I look forward to reading Pete's when it appears. In the meantime, inspired by another lengthy dialogue we recorded, I wrote a piece called "Final Exit," a version of which shows up here as the epilogue, while Pete published his version as a long essay on his website.*

---

*Check out Peter Russell's essay "Blind Spot" at www.peterrussell.com/blindspot/blindspot.php.

Besides the ecological crisis, Pete and I have spent many hours exploring the nature and potentials of consciousness. We both share a deep interest in, even passion for, bridging science and spirituality. He was a physics student at Cambridge under Stephen Hawking, and also one of the earliest teachers of transcendental meditation (TM). As you will see later, while we agree on many things, one area of disagreement (or at least so it might appear on the surface) is the issue of choice. Whereas I tend to assert the reality of free will, he doesn't think it exists—not as we usually understand it. He sent me an e-mail with a draft of ideas he was mulling over on this topic. I responded in detail, and the edited result of that exchange shows up here as a dialogue in chapter 15, "Fate or Free Will?"

Thank you, Pete, for all the wonderful hours we have spent together pushing the boundaries of thought, often until we both fell into long, deep silences.

Eric Weiss, another friend and colleague who has profoundly influenced and enriched my thinking—especially about Whitehead's philosophy—also shows up here. See, for instance, our dialogue in chapter 1, "Being and Nothingness." Like Peter, Eric also shares a passion for integrating philosophy and spirituality. I have spent many delightful hours probing Eric's brilliance for nuggets he mined from four of his favorite scholars: Alfred North Whitehead, Sri Aurobindo, Jean Gebser, and Ernst Cassirer.

One of the greatest joys I experience from our rich philosophical conversations happens when our ideas diverge. Even when the disagreement involves some arcane metaphysical issue (as it most often does), our deep respect for each other guides us to search for some underlying common ground where we do agree. Then we follow the trail of implications to identify the point of divergence. Invariably, we discover it results from either some obscure semantic difference or an unconscious shift in perspective. We like to do philosophy by *looking for what is right* in the other's position (if only most philosophy were done this way!).

Thank you, Eric, for our many enriching conversations and for sharpening my knowledge and understanding of metaphysics.

I also want to thank Dawn Carter, a former student, who exhibited exceptional insight and wisdom as she debated me on various topics— in particular, the relationship between intentionality and healing, as recorded in chapter 10. Thank you, Dawn.

Finally, I thank my students from John F. Kennedy University, the University of Philosophical Research, and the Holmes Institute—many of whom exposed some of the more intriguing blindspots discussed here. Over the years, their term papers, e-mails, and conversations have prompted responses from me that eventually became part of this book. I thank all of you for your participation in my courses and for challenging me to think more clearly, and at times humorously, about these often-difficult ideas.

Of course, without my publisher, Park Street Press, this book would not be what it is. Thanks to Jon Graham, my acquisitions editor, for, once again, recognizing enough merit in my manuscript to want to publish it. I am grateful for Peri Ann Swan's design aesthetic and to Inner Traditions' marketing wizard John Hays. I cannot wrap up these acknowledgments without also thanking Chanc VanWinkle Orzell, my project editor, and my line editor, Lynne Ertle. Thank you all.

PREFACE

Speaking in Clichés

Scientists do it. Philosophers, too. So do authors, journalists, and other media gurus. Religious and spiritual teachers do it, and then influence millions of followers to do it. Everyone, it seems, *speaks before thinking*—communicating in clichés. We all carry these "thought viruses," infecting almost everyone we come in contact with. If you stop and pay attention, you can probably recognize common cognitive gremlins flowing from your own lips from time to time.

I call them *blindspots*—ideas we assume make sense, but a few moments' reflection reveals how absurd they really are. We all have them: gaps or knots in how we view and think about the world—about life, mind, space, time, energy, information, healing, free will, reality, belief, self, relationships, evolution, artificial intelligence, God, science, spirituality, metaphysics . . . or anything else.

Think about it: How often do you read or hear something that, at first, seems right, but deep down your gut screams "NO!"? Logic and sheer common sense further convince you "it's just not possible."

Over the years, I've noticed these cognitive blindspots in books, blogs, websites, TV shows, movies, classrooms, and casual conversations. And I keep wondering: Why do so many people (especially those who should know better) speak before thinking, spreading ideas that make no sense, yet fool us into thinking they do?

This book takes on some of the more outrageous culprits:

- **The universe exploded from nothing in a big bang.**
  (Miracle of miracles . . . What exploded?)
- **We create our own reality.**
  (How come, then, we don't always get what we want?)
- **Everything ends sooner or later.**
  (But remember: Every end is also a new beginning.)
- **Nobody knows what consciousness is.**
  (Pay attention: How do you know anything at all?)
- **The future is now.**
  (If so, then nothing new could ever occur.)
- **Time is an illusion.**
  (Well, in that case, how does anything ever happen?)
- **Living in the now is just not practical.**
  (When else can you live?)
- **Obviously, brains create minds.**
  (Run that by me again, step by step: Just how do feelings and thoughts come from "dead" meat?)
- **Everything is energy.**
  (How often have you heard that? Of course, it leaves out the most immediate fact of our existence . . .)
- **Healers use the energy of consciousness.**
  (Big confusion about space, time, and the power of intention.)
- **Everything is information.**
  (Really? What about meaning, intention, purpose, choice?)
- **Everything is connected to everything else.**
  (Is there any other option?)
- **Humans are special.**
  (The most dangerous, self-serving myth of all.)
- **Life is either divine creation or random evolution.**
  (Have I got a surprise for you!)
- **Everything is determined by fate or physics.**
  (Do you choose to believe free will is an illusion?)

- **It's all in the mind. Consciousness is everything.**

  (All right then, let's see you walk through a brick wall.)
- **Quantum physics proves consciousness creates reality.**

  (Ah, if only it were so. How can any science tell us anything about consciousness?)
- **Rocks have consciousness, too.**

  (Well, let's not get carried away or confuse heaps and wholes.)*
- **Everything is alive.**

  (Have you ever seen a dead animal? Notice anything different?)
- **Everything is ruled by scientific laws.**

  (What if the universe changed its mind?)
- **God transcends his creation.**

  (So many blindspots. Best to keep this one for last.)

DEPTH ALERT

Throughout this book, I try to keep everything as simple as possible as I dive into profound questions about "life, the universe, and everything." However, in some places, I feel it worthwhile to go a little deeper and draw on philosophy or science to clarify important points. I'm aware that some readers have a kind of "allergic" reaction to ideas that push the boundaries of their thinking, and so I have included a Depth Alert here and there to identify sections you might want to skip—or, better, to take extra time to *think about* and engage with the ideas. It's up to you.

Even if you do gloss over these sections, you needn't worry about

---

*If the reference to "heaps and wholes" is unfamiliar, here's what it's getting at: The distinction is a simple way to name a quite complex philosophical issue. The technical terms are "aggregates" (heaps) and "individuals" (wholes). As we will see, rocks, railroads, or rainbows, cans, cars, or computers, hills, houses, or hammers, for example, are aggregates of otherwise disconnected parts put together by external forces. They are heaps. Organisms are whole individuals in which all their parts are interdependently interconnected. Organisms are self-organizng wholes, and they grow and evolve guided by their own internal motivation.

missing out. Precisely because many of the ideas explored here are likely to be unfamiliar and challenging, I have deliberately repeated key points at various places and in different chapters. As a teacher, I have found that people often "get" an unfamiliar idea when it's presented to them from different angles. Think of it as a kind of "intellectual triangulation." The more times you are introduced to a counterintuitive idea, the greater your chances of "grokking" it. Repetition with variation helps the mind see deeper.

So, enjoy exploring these common blindspots, and see how your thinking changes along the way.

1

Being and Nothingness
"Everything Came from Nothing in the Big Bang"

Life is full of mystery. No doubt about that. And, even though we live in a universe humming with unsolved enigmas, we can still rely on two certainties. The first is:

Something exists.

While that might seem obvious, many philosophers consider it a profound puzzle. But a little reflection reveals that it's one of two certainties every one of us shares (not death and taxes, by the way). The other certainty is simply this:

Existence comes with consciousness.

Let's begin with the first certainty—*something exists.* (I'll come back to the second certainty later.) Put on your thinking cap for a moment. I'm going to ask you to do a little experiment. You don't need any special tools or equipment—just your imagination and a willingness to think a little deeper than people usually do.

Okay, imagine you are holding a big empty glass jar. Now, put your hand in and pluck out something—*anything.*

What? You can't! Why not? Because, you say, there's *nothing* in there to take out. (For the purpose of our thought experiment, we'll ignore the invisible air and pretend it's a pure vacuum.) Well, of course you can't pull anything out—because, as you rightly insist, *you can't get something from nothing.*

Precisely. It's the same when it comes to the origin of the universe. Some people, including quite a few prominent scientists, believe that the universe began in a big bang that erupted from the void—something, *everything,* from nothing. It's just like your glass jar—except, in this case, there wasn't even a container to "hold" the nothingness.

Nothing means "no thing," the complete absence of any existence whatsoever. Zilch. Zero. How, then, could *anything* come from pure nothingness? That's the first blindspot we'll look at—and it will help us get a grip on some of the other blindspots we'll expose along the way.

WHY YOU CAN'T
GET SOMETHING FROM NOTHING

German philosopher Martin Heidegger once famously stated that the most profound question in all philosophy is some variation of, "Why is there something rather than nothing?"

Although he was not the first to ask that question, it's not surprising he did. After all, his highly influential book *Being and Time* probed deeply into the foundations of metaphysics, inspiring existential French philosopher Jean-Paul Sartre to write *Being and Nothingness.*

Phrasing the question another way—*How does something come from nothing?*—exposes a fallacy in a statement often heard from scientists and religious folk alike: *Everything came from nothing in the Big Bang,* or the religious version, *Everything was created from nothing by God.* Already, these claims make two huge assumptions: one, that *nothing* ever existed, and two, that something *did* (or could) come from it.

Let's dispose of this absurdity right away. As we will see, once we begin to think clearly about this blindspot, many of the others covered in this book will likewise turn out to be absurd—and for similar reasons.

In a text like this, it's important to clarify our key terms. So, without getting into deep and complex metaphysics, I'll just offer some working definitions:

"*Something*" simply refers to the fact that at least one entity exists. More generally, it refers to the existence of *being* itself.

"*Nothing*" (or "nothingness") refers to the state of "nonbeing," complete and total void, blankness, true emptiness, with zero potential, possibility, or actuality.

Blindspot: For those of you familiar with modern physics, this excludes the so-called quantum vacuum because it's not *really* a vacuum or void at all—in fact, in the guise of the fundamental zero-point energy (ZPE) field, the "vacuum" overflows with unimaginably vast amounts of energy, the exact opposite of "nothing." It's what ancient philosophers called the *plenum void*—nothingness full of everything. Of course, anything that's full of anything (or even has just one tiny something) cannot be truly "nothing."

Okay, so *nothingness* means just that: "utter emptiness." And, in case you're wondering, *from* means "out of" or the "source" of something. How, then, could *nothing* be the source of *anything?* In fact, even the idea of nothing as a "source" makes no sense. If "nothing" was a source, then it would not be *nothing*.

"Something coming from nothing" would mean that from a state of utter blankness, emptiness, void, nonexistence, or nonbeing (true nothingness), some object or subject comes into existence. But how could that happen?

BEING AND NOTHINGNESS

Philosopher Eric Weiss and I frequently have dinner together and spend hours in friendly dialogue about some of philosophy's deepest issues. Recently, one of our conversations went right to the heart of the matter. Here's a snippet of that conversation:

> **EW:** *Modern thought tends to start with nonbeing rather than with being. Heidegger, for example, suggests that the most fundamental question of philosophy is, "Why is there something rather than nothing?" I think it's rather odd to assume that the*

idea of nonexistence needs no justification. After all, the most
immediate given fact is that we do exist.

I agree; the idea of nonbeing does require justification. Given that being
is, and nonbeing isn't, not only are we required to "justify" the idea of
nothingness, we can't even conceive it! We can name it, but in doing
so, we make it *something,* and the "nothing" we wanted to name forever
eludes us.

> **EW:** *To modern philosophers, if nothing at all ever happened,*
> *that would be natural. Why should we accept that "nothingness"*
> *is the most natural state of affairs and that being or existence*
> *needs justification? Isn't that what Heidegger's question implies?*

I don't see it that way. The assumption is not that nothingness is the
"natural" state of things, but that it *could* have been—and if that had
been the case, existence itself would never have happened. The fact that
something exists, instead of nothing, is profoundly mysterious simply
because of the possibility that it could have been otherwise. But that
possibility doesn't make nothingness more "natural" than something.

> **EW:** *According to modernism, because things are happening,*
> *that needs an explanation.*

What cries out for explanation—even though it is unattainable—is why,
given the possibility of nothingness, there is something after all. "Why
is there something rather than nothing?" surely is the most profound
metaphysical question. If ever nothingness had been the case, then it
would have forever remained the case, and the counterfactual question,
"Why nothing rather than something?" could never have arisen.

> **EW:** *I think this may be an interesting case of* asymmetrical
> complementarity: *Being and nothingness imply each other*

conceptually. They form a complementarity, like "up and down," "life and death," or "wave and particle." In many cases, such complementarities are symmetrical—each carries the same existential weight. However, in this case, we have an asymmetrical *complementarity, in which "something" is the senior partner.*

Yes, only because something does exist can nothing even be conceived as a possibility. The reverse could not happen. Something, therefore, is "larger" or more fundamental than nothing because something implies the possibility of nothing. But nothing (if it ever really had been the case) could not ever imply the possibility of something—of *anything*.

Just imagining the possibility that nothing *could* have been the case—but isn't—gives me goose bumps. We've already won the cosmic jackpot. Here we are! Everything else is existential gravy.

WHY DOES THE UNIVERSE EXIST?

Famed cosmologist Stephen Hawking (often called the "new Einstein") once posed the question, "Why does the universe bother to exist?"— another variation of Heidegger's "big" question.

But why would Hawking even assume there *could* be an answer to this? Here we are. We exist. Our universe exists. For us to even conceive the question, *something has to exist.* There's no way around that. Now that it's here, the universe (i.e., all of reality) could not *NOT* exist. If it didn't exist, the question couldn't be asked.

Blindspot: Once something—anything—exists, there could never have been a time when there was *pure nothing.* If there ever had been *nothing* (void of all possibility and actuality—complete and utter blankness), there would have been no possibility for anything to have ever existed. Pure nothing simply cannot produce or create something. If it did, it wouldn't have been *pure* nothing.

Something must always come from some other something. Therefore, we can be certain that there never was a "beginning" to existence. Hawking's question is meaningless. It may sound profound, but actually it is absurd. We have no way of making sense of it using language, reason, or logic.

Here's another question: "Why is there something rather than *everything?*" In other words, why don't *all* possibilities manifestly exist? Ponder that.*

---

*Clearly, not *all* possibilities can be realized at any moment—otherwise everything would have already happened! So *something* is actively selecting from among the determinants of the past as well as from among the current set of presenting possibilities, in the new moment of *now*. And that "something" must be *consciousness* because it takes some level of *awareness* to detect possibilities; to evaluate them based on some value, purpose, or aim, and then to *choose* accordingly.

2

Reality

"We Create Our Own Reality"

I often hear people say "we create our own reality"—as if it's an obvious truth. Yet I doubt the folks who say this have thought it through. It might sound nice and "New Agey," but why speak in clichés?

Blindspot: I see two problems with the statement: First, there is no such thing as "our own" reality (just as well), and second, because reality existed billions of years before we came along, how on Earth (or anywhere else) could we create what has created us?

Thanks to pop-science movies such as *What the Bleep Do We Know!?* followed by *The Secret,* people confuse what happens in quantum experiments with what goes on in their own lives. Yes, in physics, consciousness "collapses the quantum wave function" by turning a set of possible outcomes into a single actual outcome. In other words, consciousness has the power to influence the physical world. Well, you don't have to be a quantum physicist to figure that one out. We all make choices every day to move our bodies in ways that affect the world around us. No doubt about it: Consciousness is causal.

But that's a far cry from claiming "we create our own reality." We don't. We don't create reality (it gets along quite nicely with or without us, thank you very much). And we certainly don't create "our own" personal reality. Nope.

We participate in co-creating reality.

That's a very different statement. First, it acknowledges the power of consciousness to create. Second, it acknowledges that all sentient beings make choices and contribute to creation at every moment. We all get to vote in the Great Cosmic Democracy. But we don't get to decide the outcome. That's up to the Cosmic Collective.

We live in, and contribute to, a common, *shared* reality, not "our own" individual reality. If we did create and live in "our own" reality, as many folks claim, how could we ever communicate or relate? For communication and relationships to occur, we must exist in a commonly shared reality.

Think about it. If we really did create our own reality, *everyone* would be creating his or her own world. And that would mean either (1) *all* realities would be independent of each other, which would not permit interaction or communication, and we know that is not the case; or (2) all realities would be mutually contributing to a common reality, which is the case in our own and communal experience. So, clearly, we do not simply "create our own reality." We *participate* in creating the reality that everyone (every sentient being) exists in.

However, while we don't create our own reality, we do create our own *experience* or *perspective* on the one, shared world. Reality remains intact, whatever our perspective and experience of it happens to be.

The idea that we create our own reality is a dangerous oversimplification and does not serve the New Age movement (or anyone else). Much more aligned with what we know from science and spiritual traditions is the idea "we *participate* in co-creating shared reality." A lot more is going on than we either know or have control over.

Now think about this: People who like to say "we create our own reality" are most often the same people who like to talk about "oneness" and "unity." Do you see how these two claims contradict each other? If there truly is "oneness/unity," then how could seven billion of us (and that's not counting the gazillions of other sentient beings we share the world with) create our "own" (i.e., individual and private) realities? If we all created "our own reality" we'd have billions of different realities, leading to cosmic fragmentation, not unity.

Clearly, we live in a shared reality. If everyone went around creating his or her reality, we'd be creating chaos and pandemonium. (Hmm, come to think of it . . .)

CREATING OUR REALITY

You say that our thoughts or beliefs do not create our experiences. Well, in my life, thoughts can and do create my experiences. Ideas and beliefs create emotional as well as somatic responses, which are very definitely experiences. Besides, our stories about a situation cause us to behave in a certain way because we believe the story we have created. For instance, let's say we believe someone is our enemy; then, very likely, we will begin to behave in ways that eventually elicit a behavior from the other person that is not warm and fuzzy, reinforcing our story that this person is not our friend—yet another way we "create our reality."

Intentions and visualization are examples of other ways we "create reality" with our stories. These stories facilitate the creation of a reality we desire. It is well known that even though they are "only" thoughts, they are powerful tools for manifesting goals and desires.

So it could be said that we create our reality by our thoughts. And to create the reality of our choosing, we simply need to change our minds—granted, easier said than done. This requires an awareness and desire to change. However, there are lifelong, or lives-long, habits to change, habits we do not even know we have. Once aware of our habits, we need to stay awake and aware, and consciously choose to change our thoughts. This is beginning to sound suspiciously like a spiritual practice, isn't it?

So, if indeed we are creators, why not create the reality we want? It's as simple as changing our minds!

Blindspot: I think you are making the all-too-easy error of confusing *interpretations* with experience. Thoughts do not, and cannot, create experiences. Thoughts can "influence" or "color" experiences, but whether or not we have thoughts about them, experiences happen *inevitably.* There is nothing we can do to stop having experiences (as long as we are sentient beings).

Yes, it is true that ideas and beliefs—our "stories"—may shape and influence emotional and somatic responses. But remember, emotions have two components: the *felt sense,* or bodily sensations, and a *cognitive* component, or interpretations. So, yes, thoughts can, and do, generate the *interpretative* component in emotions, but they do not create the felt sense or experience. *Feelings come first.*

Influencing or shaping emotions is not at all the same as *creating experiences.* Our thoughts can and do affect the *form* of our experiences, because they act as filters or lenses for our experiences. But those filters or lenses are our *interpretations.* Meanwhile, the flow of experiences and feelings continues regardless of whether we engage in thinking or beliefs.

So, again, bottom line: Thoughts or beliefs influence the *form* of experiences, but they do not, and cannot, create the *fact* of experience itself.

You also seem to think that intentions are forms of thoughts or beliefs. I disagree. Intentionality is an expression of our creative will, and usually happens best when we get thoughts and beliefs out of the way. (I have a chapter on this in *Radical Knowing.*) We most certainly do not "create reality with our thoughts." As I've noted above, that is a common New Age myth. We do, however, drastically limit and block out experiences of reality with our thoughts and beliefs—and so the reality we actually experience in the moment is often radically reduced and filtered. We do *determine,* not create, our particular experience of reality with our thoughts and beliefs, but by no means do we *create reality* with our thoughts. Thoughts and beliefs *distort,* not create, reality.

Changing reality is not "as simple as changing our minds." This is especially true if by *minds* we mean our "thoughts" and "beliefs." Changing our beliefs or thoughts just won't do it. We need to get beyond our beliefs altogether—that's what I mean by "experience beyond belief." When we learn to live from our direct experience, rather than from our thoughts and beliefs about reality, we undergo a profound transformation in consciousness. When that happens, our relationship with reality dramatically and subtly shifts. It's not that we change reality, but by changing our relationship with reality we transform our *experience* of reality.

Reality is a co-creative process, involving the creative contributions of all sentient beings. It is the ultimate democracy! We can contribute to the way reality unfolds and changes, but we fool ourselves if we think *we create it*—doubly so if we think that we can create reality with our thoughts and beliefs. Changing our experience of reality is a far cry from *creating reality*. That is perhaps the most naive and potentially dangerous slogan to come from the New Age movement.

Belief, Reality, and Flat Earth

I do believe that if one person thought the Earth was round, another thought it was flat, and another thought it was triangular, it would indeed be all of those things in each individual's reality. I have no idea what another's person's universe looks like; I only know what mine looks like—and in my universe, the world is round, and those who believe it is flat are "wrong."

Blindspot: First, this view falls into a very common pitfall, shared even by professional philosophers and scientists, who should know better. It's a confusion of *epistemology,* or how we *know,* and *ontology,* or the nature of *reality.* Yes, different beliefs or thoughts might yield different *experiences of* and *knowledge about* reality (epistemology), but that doesn't mean *reality itself* (ontology) is *different.* "What it *looks* like" is epistemology; "what it *is*" is ontology.

And this raises another issue: It is one thing to "believe" or "think we know" something; it is something very different to actually *test* what we believe or think we know. We can test to see if the world is round or flat and decide the issue that way. That test has already been done to the satisfaction of billions of people. So to say that "flat Earth" is just as valid as "global Earth" doesn't hold up. It is not just that those who believe in a flat Earth are wrong in "your universe"—they are wrong *in reality,* according to the most unbiased experiments set up to test this.

Belief and Reality

Doubting our beliefs is fine. But I would prefer to say that I recognize my beliefs as transient expedients with a limited shelf life and limited range of usefulness. Oh sure, I believe them. But they can also be discarded and discredited on a moment's notice, once I decide to "go deeper." But in the interim, we need something like our beliefs to write and talk about, don't we? There is not much to say about raw reality, is there?

I take your point. We would do better to treat our beliefs as transitory expedients. But I question when you say, "Oh sure, I believe them." My point is that if we believe our beliefs we give them added, and unwarranted, weight, usually with no awareness or willingness that someday we might let them go. If you view your beliefs as transient (a good thing), then I'd say you do not *believe* your beliefs. You *have* beliefs. Not the same thing.

In my experience, people who believe their beliefs (turning them into dogma) are not prepared to "discard and discredit them on a moment's notice." Believing our beliefs is tantamount to mistaking them for truth. By contrast, by just having beliefs and noticing them we can hold them lightly as "likely stories" and remain open to change and correction.

And, yes indeed, we do need "something like our beliefs" if we wish to write or talk—most of the time, but not always. Remember, I said we can't help having beliefs—our minds do it naturally, and for practical purposes, as "shorthand memos" to help us navigate our way through the world. All writing and cognition almost always involve interpretations of our experiences—there is no getting around that. However, it seems to make a great difference when people are aware of the following automatic dynamic:

Experience → Interpretation → Belief → Dogma (believing our beliefs) → Action

Once people are aware of this dynamic, it is useful for them to develop the presence of mind to continually refer back to their experience, rather than always thinking, talking, writing, and, more important, acting from interpretations, beliefs, or dogma.

Believe it or not, we can think, talk, write, and act without interpretation, or at the very least with minimal interpretation, when we learn to *feel our thinking,* rather than merely think our thoughts. We can directly give voice to our experience, for example, when we utter authentic exclamations or when we speak from the "heart" of silence. In Bohmian Dialogue, which I teach to groups around the world, people have an opportunity to realize that it is possible not to *talk about* "raw reality," but to actually *speak* reality (see chapter 13 in *Radical Knowing*). It's a much greater challenge, I admit, when we sit down to write.

Blindspot: I'm asking people not to mistake their beliefs (or anyone else's, including mine) for truth. Unfortunately, this is what so often happens in religion and science, and in the rest of our lives.

Feeling Comes First

If I understand you correctly, you are saying that every thought begins with a feeling—that is, feelings and experience necessarily precede thoughts, and thoughts are derivatives or reflections of feelings. Feelings, therefore, are primary modes of knowing, and thought is secondary.

While I wouldn't necessarily disagree with this, it seems to me it's only one half of a circular equation. For example, it's increasingly recognized in psychology, cognitive psychology in particular, that behind every affect and emotion is a hidden thought. Core beliefs influence our thinking, and thinking determines (or influences or leads to) feelings.

For example, if a paranoid person believes that people in authority are by definition evil, then encounters with his boss are likely to lead to feelings of hostility, suspicion, and the like. In this situation, feelings of hostility and suspicion are clearly derivative of a preconception that authority is evil. The belief/thought precedes the feeling/experience. This has led to the conviction, prevalent in psychology today, that by changing negative, self-destructive, disempowering beliefs, people feel better! This notion is at the heart of cognitive behavioral therapy, which began with Albert Ellis's pioneering work in rational-emotive therapy (RET), and is probably the most common form of therapy employed by psychotherapists in the current era, being one of the few backed up by credible studies and data.

The point is that the relationship between feeling and thinking seems to be a complex, circular feedback process.

I'll try to clarify why I say that "feelings come first" and why the circularity you (and others) think happens between feeling and thinking is based on a misunderstanding.

Blindspot: First, I point out that both in evolution and in individual development, feeling (sentience) is present long before conceptual thinking or language arises. Clearly, both in evolution and in our own personal development, feelings come before ideas or words. Hard to imagine anyone seriously disagreeing with that. For example, as newborn infants, we all had feelings—sensations of touch, feelings of warmth or cold on our skin as well as drives such as hunger, fear, and pleasure—long before we had our first thoughts (silent language).

Next, I don't deny that our *interpretations* (thoughts) of our experiences or feelings do *influence* (shape or color) subsequent feelings. But interpretations *do not create* experiences or feelings. Experiences happen all the time, every moment, and we don't have to do anything for them to happen. In fact, we couldn't stop having experiences even if we wanted to. So experiences don't need to be created by thoughts or thinking—experiences and feelings occur with or without thoughts. That's why it is a mistake to say "thoughts create feelings," and it's why in *Radical Knowing* I say that feeling is the primary mode of knowing. Thoughts and thinking are secondary. There is no circularity of creation. No thoughts would exist if feelings or experiences didn't exist, but the reverse is not true.

I agree that "core beliefs influence our thinking," but I would not agree that "thinking determines feeling" or that "thinking leads to feeling." Yes, thinking may influence (i.e., color or even trigger) certain feelings, but that is not the same as "thinking *creates* feelings." Thinking may act as a kind of filter for feelings, but the fact that some or any feeling is occurring happens with or without thinking. That's my point. I want people to focus on *feelings uncolored by thoughts or beliefs*. Interestingly, that's what Ellis's RET also aims toward.

Your example of the paranoid person actually supports what I'm saying. It is full of implicit *interpretations* of feelings or experiences— and we should not mistake our interpretations for the feelings themselves. There is no such *feeling* as "hostility" or "suspicion."

By "feeling," I mean, literally, the sensations coursing through our bodies (tingling nerves, beating hearts, rapid breathing, sweaty palms, etc.), and these are not, by themselves, either hostile or friendly, suspicious or trusting. They just are what they are. *And then we interpret them.* So, I would not agree that the studies and data you cite refute or contradict my essential point. The problem is not with our feelings— it's with our interpretations or beliefs. Remember the sequence:

Experience → Interpretation → Belief → Dogma → Action

Yes, it is true that thinking precedes feeling in an ongoing sequence: We have an experience, we think about it, and then we have another feeling. But we should not make the mistake of confusing *sequence* with *causality*. Just because a thought may precede the appearance of a new feeling does not mean that the thought created or generated that feeling. It may "color" it, yes, but not create it.

I'm aware that the point I'm making involves a subtle awareness (not merely an intellectual distinction) of the relationship between the ongoing flow of experience and the automatic interpretation of experiences that our egoic minds engage in. For many people, especially those not familiar with meditative practice, recognizing this crucial difference between experience and interpretation can be a challenge. It is especially difficult, it seems to me, when people are committed to the belief that our beliefs have the power to create our reality, as is so often proclaimed in New Age circles.

My current work is an attempt to expose or challenge that kind of reflexive, but unreflected, New Age naïveté, and to focus people's attention back on the source of all our beliefs—which is our ongoing in-the-moment experience. That's where transformation occurs, not in our thoughts or beliefs. It's why spirituality is so much more valuable than religion.

ALL IN THE MIND?

In the province of the mind, there are no limits. Everyone is master of her or his own neurological experience. According to semiotics, our minds contain the universe by the simple act of comprehending it. I'm interested in how you view this statement, because it seems that in your philosophy the universe contains the mind but not the reverse— although both are interconnected and inseparable. Is that correct?

I am not a big fan of semiotics as an approach to philosophy or understanding reality. It certainly falls short when we want to tackle the Big Questions such as the origin and nature of the universe, of matter, of mind. Semiotics is all about language and symbolic forms. But, clearly, the universe—both mind and matter—existed for billions of years before any humans came along with our symbols and language. So to say that the universe is contained in the mind (usually meaning the *human* mind) makes no sense to me. How can something be wholly contained in one of its own products or creations?

While I agree that we have no idea what, if any, are the limits to consciousness (again, I'm not talking about just *human* consciousness), I'm not inclined to go as far as the claim that each of us is master of our own neurological experience. Yes, no doubt, we have a lot more power over the contents of our experience than we are led to believe by modern education, science, and culture. Spiritual traditions have taught us that for millennia.

Neuroscience and New Age Beliefs

However, the idea that we alone are the masters of our own neurology overlooks the fact that besides our power of choice, we are also creatures of habit, mental and behavioral, and are greatly determined by events external to us.* All kinds of events extraneous to our nervous systems are constantly impinging on and impacting our neurons and brains. We are inevitably and inextricably enmeshed in a matrix of influences of all kinds—social, cultural, developmental, evolutionary, ecological, cosmological, and so on. We have little or no control over when, where, and how these affect us—including our state of mind.

Yes, we do have *some* say in how we respond to whatever impacts us; we always have the power of choice. However, we don't have the power to decide which *options* are available to us to choose from. For the most part, our *options* are determined. Choice, then, creatively selects among the given options and possibilities.

---

*However, as I point out elsewhere, external determination is not the whole story. We also always have a spark of *choice*—a creative existential spontaneous act—that can and does interrupt the incoming flow or pressure of determinism from the past. Choices do change the course of fate and help create the future.

The idea that we are masters of our own neurological experience is reminiscent of the claim that we create our own reality (see the debate earlier in this chapter). As I've already said, I think that New Age slogan is mistaken on two counts:

First, there is no such thing as "our own" reality, as though each of us exists in our own isolated bubble world. That clearly cannot be the case; otherwise, we could never communicate with each other. Yet we do. Obviously, then, we all exist in some *shared* reality, not "our own" reality.

Second, we simply do not have the power to "create reality." That, too, is pretty obvious if we stop to think about it. Reality existed for billions of years before any of us came along. In fact, if reality had not existed before us, how on Earth did we ever come into being?

Co-creating Shared Reality

Now, while I think the idea that "we create our own reality" is both simplistic and mistaken, I do acknowledge what I take to be the deeper insight it is trying to express. We do have power—a lot more power than most of us believe—given that choice and intention are implicit in consciousness.

However, because we exist in what is clearly a *shared* reality, a more accurate statement would be, as I've said: "Each of us participates in co-creating shared reality." I think that captures the essence of what many in the New Age movement intuit and want to express, while avoiding the logical absurdities of solipsism. We are not "creators" of "our own" reality. We are *co-creators* of *shared* reality.

Every choice we make contributes to the unfolding of the next moment in evolution. In that sense, we participate in the evolution of the Creative Ultimate (God, or the divine, or the cosmos, or whatever you might want to call All That Is). Every choice we make is a "vote" in cosmic democracy. As I said: We get to choose, but we don't get to decide.

Experience beyond Belief

No doubt you've heard it said that "beliefs create reality" or "you are what you believe." I think both of those statements contain a nugget of truth—but both are also misleading.

The deeper truth trying to be expressed is "consciousness creates reality"—or, to be more precise, "consciousness participates in co-creating reality." Yes, consciousness has power. It manifests reality by being aware of possibilities, forming an intention, making a choice, and guiding action.

When people talk about the power of belief, I think they really mean the power of *intention.*

However, this does not mean we shouldn't pay attention to our beliefs. Beliefs can, and often do, restrict our vision of possibilities. Furthermore, many of our most deeply entrenched beliefs are unconscious. Engaging in deep psychospiritual work to uncover long-held unconscious beliefs can be beneficial and liberating. But changing one belief for another does not lead to transformation. For that, we need to cultivate *experience beyond belief.*

Ten Steps to Experience beyond Belief

1. Get clear on what you believe.

2. This often involves doing some deep psychological work to unearth unconscious beliefs.

3. All beliefs—both conscious and unconscious—are *mental habits.* They are ingrained patterns of thoughts.

4. These thought patterns can, and often do, restrict and limit how we think, perceive, and act.

5. By *choosing* a different set of thoughts or beliefs, we can change those patterns, both psychologically and neurologically.

So far, all of this is pretty standard pop psychology. However, some further distinctions complete the circle:

6. Even consciously changed beliefs continue to limit us, although they might liberate us from the deeper constraints of previously unconscious negative beliefs.

7. *Every belief is made up of thoughts, and every thought is an abstraction.* It is a "frozen fragment of consciousness," a "snapshot" of some moment of experience, plucked from the ongoing flow of moment-to-moment reality. We "freeze-frame" experiences because this is a useful way to create mental "maps" that help us navigate our way through life. But the moment we "freeze" an experience by transforming it into a thought, it is already "out of date." It is no longer connected to the new reality of the new moment of experience. Every thought, and therefore every belief, is necessarily to some degree a *distortion* of reality. Now, as it happens, some distortions can be less damaging, or even more useful, than others. That's why people work at changing their beliefs (as many life coaches and New Age gurus teach). However, I am saying that even "good" beliefs still limit us, because they are necessarily to some degree out of touch with present reality.

8. *Pay attention to your experience as it happens in the moment* and use it, rather than your beliefs, to guide your action. Instead of engaging with the world from your *beliefs,* I encourage you to focus attention on your *in-the-moment experience* and to recognize the difference between *belief* and *intention.*

9. *Beliefs have no creative power or potency.* They are made of thoughts and are, therefore, abstractions. They do have mechanical or habitual power to keep us repeating deep-worn patterns of thought and behavior. Intentions, however, are very different.

10. *An intention is a creative expression of consciousness focused on some aim, goal, or purpose.* An intention is, literally, a form of *self-expression.* Rather than operating from abstract beliefs, which limit the self, intention orients the self toward some goal or purpose. *Intentions aim the self at some future possibility.* Beliefs pull

us back toward the past because every belief is necessarily a fragment of consciousness, a "frozen" snapshot of some prior moment of experience.

Intentions involve awareness of *possibilities* and *choosing* to select or focus on one or more possibilities. When we create an intention, we effectively express or project some part of our self out into the world. Intentions arise from, and express, our *experience*. Every intention is an expression of *purpose*.

Intention does not involve "doing." That comes later. First, we create or express an intention (i.e., we form it in consciousness and, perhaps, communicate it to others). Then, we choose and take action.

MANIFESTATION:
THE POWER OF INTENTION AND ACTION

Intention is a nonphysical process that takes place in consciousness. Action involves energy, a physical act. Intention without action is impotent. That's why both consciousness and energy are needed to make a difference. This is also why God (the Creative Ultimate) cannot be "pure" spirit (consciousness). If that were the case, the most that God could achieve would be to create magnificent intentions. But without *action,* intentions would remain forever in the domain of possibilities. With intentions or consciousness alone, God could never manifest anything. Manifestation requires both intention and action or, if you like, both *consciousness* and *energy.*

My point is this: We all have power—through consciousness, intention, and choice—to transform our lives by liberating ourselves from the constraints of belief. However, we are so identified with our beliefs that for many of us it is almost impossible to imagine what it would be like to let them go. Are you willing to let go of your beliefs—particularly those *cherished* beliefs you "just know to be true"?

Try it. At first you might feel disoriented, but I promise you won't die or disappear. My guess is you will feel liberated.

SENTIENT ENERGY

The Seth material by Jane Roberts emphatically states that all energy contains consciousness, that everything in the universe is conscious at some level. This seems to be confirmed by quantum physics, where observation is required for the collapse of the wave function that brings actuality from potential. According to Seth, "The thing perceived is an extension of the one who perceives it." Doesn't this, then, tell us that everything is "made of" consciousness?

I agree with the idea that all energy possesses consciousness. I call it *sentient energy*. But to conclude that this means energy *is* consciousness is to make a simple logical error. It confuses "energy *has* consciousness" with "energy *is* consciousness."

Yes, indeed, "observation implies consciousness." It is true, as far as we know, that in quantum physics an *observer* (and that means some sentient being) is required to collapse the wave function from potential to actuality. But the wave function is a mathematical description for quantum *physical* processes: *a physical object or event is being observed.*

Consciousness is the *subject* observing an *object*. The subject is *non-physical;* the object is *physical*.

However, even though a conscious subject is required for a quantum event to happen, we commit a logical error if we assume that the quantum event is itself *necessarily* "an extension" of the observer.

I agree with Seth's point that *in some sense* "the thing perceived is an extension of the one who perceives it"—but only if it means that some aspect of the observer is incorporated into the being of what is observed. (The reverse is also true: some aspect of what is observed is incorporated into the being of the observer.)

But that does not mean *all* of the object is constituted by the consciousness of the observer. While consciousness may be a *necessary* condition for a quantum event to occur, it does not follow that consciousness is a *sufficient* condition for a quantum event. A quantum event requires *both* subject and object (both consciousness and energy). And these are not identical.

Reality is not exclusively made up of matter, as scientific materialists try to tell us, and it is not exclusively made up of mind or consciousness, as spiritual idealists like to say. On the one hand, a world made up of purely objective "dead" stuff, no matter how complex, could never produce minds and, therefore, would forever remain a world unfelt and unknown. On the other hand, a world of pure consciousness could be *aware* of itself, but it could never *do* anything or make anything *happen*—because that would require energy. We'll look at this again in the chapter on healing. A universe where things happen and are known and felt *must* be a world made up of both energy and consciousness—in the form of *sentient energy*. Happily, that's exactly the kind of universe we actually inhabit.

3

The Universe
"Everything Ends Sooner or Later"

Quick question, probably not easy to answer: Are there good reasons to believe the universe is eternal? If so, what would those reasons be?

Actually, I think at least half of the answer is easy. If we substitute "cosmos" for "universe," then it is impossible to even *imagine* a beginning to the cosmos. It must have always existed. As we've seen, it could not have emerged from *nothing*. Nothing comes from nothing.

Now, if someone prefers to say, "God created the cosmos," my response would be, "Who or what created God?"

Of course the only meaningful answer is that God had no beginning. If God did have a beginning, what could have caused *that* sublime event? This line of thinking inevitably leads to an infinite regress; in other words: no beginning. But if we accept that God had no beginning, why not accept the alternative: that the cosmos had no beginning? For me, in any case, "cosmos" equals "God."

So that part is easy enough. But what about the other half? If the cosmos had no beginning, could it have an end?

Before answering that, I just want to be clear: It certainly seems that the *universe* had a beginning about 13.7 billion years ago in the Big Bang. And by all accounts it is also destined to come to an end, one way or another (either in a "big crunch" or thermodynamic "heat death"). So universes come and go. They have beginnings and ends. Ours is just one in a likely endless cycle of universes within the larger, almost certainly infinite and eternal cosmos.

Current cosmology, incorporating the concept of the zero-point energy (ZPE) field, suggests that all energy, information, and consciousness originate in (or, perhaps more accurately, are *intrinsic* to) this cosmic ZPE field, and we have good reasons to believe that everything returns there eventually—only to be reborn yet again as another universe (or universes). I refer to this as "recycled universes."

Blindspot: What would it mean for the cosmos to "come to an end"? Where would all the energy and information (not to mention consciousness) go? It can't evaporate into *nothingness*. If we say it could, what would that mean? Just as something cannot come from nothing, *something cannot become nothing*. We have no way of understanding such a process or state of affairs—either scientifically or philosophically.

So it all goes on and on and on . . . each time building on the experiences of prior universes.

THE HEAT DEATH OF THE UNIVERSE

According to the second law of thermodynamics, the universe is destined to end forever in a final and eternal "heat death." What is this law, and who discovered it? Sorry if I am being ignorant, but this physics stuff is mostly foreign to me.

The scientist most famously associated with the formulation of the second law of thermodynamics is the Austrian Ludwig Boltzman. Essentially, the law states that in any closed system (e.g., a sealed room, a sealed bottle, your closet, the universe) the natural tendency is for the elements in the system to degrade from order into chaos. In other words, left to themselves, closed systems spontaneously diminish order and organization and increase disorder. The technical term for disorder is *entropy*.

A good close-to-home example is your bedroom closet or kitchen drawer. Now, be honest: How organized is it? If it's anything like mine, it's probably quite disorganized and cluttered. Well, that's *entropy* at work. Unless you consciously choose to *reorganize* the contents of your closet every time you use it—in other words, *add more order*—it will naturally become more and more disorganized over time. You have to choose to inject order back into it to counteract the inevitable rise of entropy, as predicted by the second law. That's just the way things are in all physical systems.

And that includes the universe. According to the second law, the universe as a whole, because it's assumed to be a closed system, is gradually "running down" as energy is transformed into entropy. The dire prediction from this law is that eventually all of existence *everywhere,* not just on Earth, will end in what is called *the heat death of the universe.* When that happens, all organized energy will have turned into chaotic tepid heat, and nothing will ever happen again. Now, isn't that something to look forward to? Kinda cosmologically depressing, eh?

Blindspot: Well, no. Not really. Why? Because the second law refers to purely *physical* systems and takes no account of the fact of *consciousness.* That's a major blindspot. Now, the interesting thing about consciousness is that it can make *choices.* And choices are *creative.* In other words, while physical systems may be subject to the second law and fall into inevitable decay, any system with consciousness can counteract the slide into entropy. And we know from panpsychism* that *all* systems include consciousness—therefore the second law doesn't have absolute rule. Consciousness injects order into systems by making choices, increasing coherence, harmony, and organization. This works for the universe as much as it does for your closet.

---

*Panpsychism is an ancient, and recently revived, philosophy that explains how all matter and energy is intrinsically sentient—that *consciousness goes all the way down* to the most fundamental entities of the physical world. In other words, even molecules, atoms, and subatomic particles have some degree of awareness and choice (see *Radical Nature* for a detailed discussion of this philosophy).

Life itself is a well-known example of systems that run against the grain of entropy. Living systems build up order from their environment—however, we do so at a cost. As we metabolize energy, which we need to do to go on living, we also produce waste (more disorder) that goes back into the environment. So, according to the second law of thermodynamics, life is a cosmic "fluke," an accident, and is constantly fighting a losing battle with death and disorder. Again, this scenario completely leaves out the undeniable presence of consciousness. *We* don't live forever, but the cosmos itself will never tumble into eternal decay. Let's be thankful for "small" mercies!

So, breathe easy. The heat death of the universe is not nigh. And, in fact, it is unlikely to ever happen because of the existence of consciousness.

THE END OF EVERYTHING

In one of your lectures, you mentioned that in the eternal scheme of things when one universe ends, another one begins, and that process continues forever. I have an even bigger question: Is there an end to eternity? I remember some scientist talking about the universe coming to an end. So, which is it: continuation *or* cessation?

First, regarding cessation or continuation, why would you think it's *either/or?* Let me ask you this: Today will come to an end at midnight (or at sunrise, whichever you choose to mark the transition from one day to another). And as soon as today is over (cessation), tomorrow begins (continuation). Do you see that continuation *requires* cessation if anything new is ever to arise?

It's the same with universes. (Think of the lifeline of a universe as a *really, really* long day!) When one universe comes to an end (cessation), a new one begins (continuation). I'm saying that that process of cessation and coming into being continues forever. There's no contradiction. In fact, each implies the other.

Second, I'm quite sure you didn't hear me talk about "the end of eternity"—that would be a meaningless contradiction. The very notion of eternity means "without end," without cessation. Reality, cosmos, nature (whatever you prefer to call All That Is) does not come to an end. How could it? How could reality come to an end? However, our *universe* can, and will, come to an end.

So, what does that tell us? Well, it means that the universe cannot equal all of reality—the cosmos. The universe is one event (a very, very long event of some thirty to a hundred billion years). But no matter how long it is, it is not eternal; it will come to an end (either with a bang or with a whimper, as they say). According to modern physics and cosmology, the universe had a beginning 13.7 billion years ago in a big bang. And, because of gravity and the laws of thermodynamics, sooner or later, one of the following two end states will happen.

1. If the force of gravity is too weak to hold all the countless billions of galaxies together, they will accelerate away from each other, eventually whizzing off at light speed until every galaxy is left alone, isolated in its own lonely region of space-time— effectively sealed off in its own bubble universe. At that point, each isolated galaxy will continue to contract under the force of its own gravity, eventually collapsing into a black hole. Each galactic "universe" will end with a bang.

2. However, if the force of gravity is strong enough to hold all the galaxies together, they will, eventually, begin to slowly move toward each other, gradually gaining speed, until, at some far-distant time, they will fall into one another, ultimately collapsing into one almighty black hole. The universe will end with a massive big bang.

And if, for some reason, the universe manages to escape either of these doomsday scenarios, the final undoing will be the famous second law of thermodynamics. It says that every event that ever happens anywhere, at any time, in the universe burns up some amount of energy. Eventually, far into the future, perhaps a hundred billion years from now, all the available energy in the universe will have been "burned up," or transformed into tepid heat. As physicists know, once energy becomes heat, it cannot be used to do any more work without some other source of available energy to serve as fuel. When all the fuel is used up (turned into heat), nothing more could ever happen again. The universe would come to a silent, eternal standstill. As we saw, this is famously called the "heat death of the universe."

Bottom line: From the perspective of modern science, there's no way out. Our universe will come to an end, one way or another. Charming, eh?

Blindspot: However, that does not mean the end of *everything*. If our universe collapses into a black hole, it will emerge "on the other side" as a white hole—which will be the beginning of a whole new universe, with its own unimaginable and unpredictable sets of "laws" or "habits."

In case you're wondering, science can never predict what a new universe will be like because once anything gets close to a black hole singularity, all the laws of physics, everything we know about space, time, matter/energy, and causality, completely breaks down. It's a whole new ball game.

So, when one universe ends, another new one begins. Cessation followed by continuation. All of this birth and death of universes happens in the cosmos as a whole and continues for all eternity. (Perhaps it takes a break from time to time. Maybe even the cosmos needs a vacation.)

THE REALLY BIG PICTURE

You say we can know for certain that consciousness exists— because even doubting or denying consciousness automatically demonstrates its existence. In other words, we need consciousness to be able to doubt or deny anything. I like that. You go on to say that because consciousness exists, it must have always existed. That got me wondering: Does the same logic apply the other way—if consciousness exists at any time, must it always exist into the future? Can consciousness ever not exist? I was wondering about the very far future and the state of the planet, and if this might imply a potential total death of the human race, including a total death of individual and collective consciousness.

You ask whether consciousness could ever *not* exist. Great question. From the perspective of science, there is no reason why consciousness should be eternal. It could be possible, for instance, that if the entire universe collapsed and disappeared into a black hole, then all the sentience, or consciousness, associated with that energy would also disappear. However, we don't know enough about what happens inside black holes. I doubt that energy is ever actually destroyed—in fact, according to another fundamental law of physics, this time, the *first* law of thermodynamics, *energy can never be created or destroyed.* The most that can happen is that energy gets transformed from one state into another. So even if it were possible for the entire universe to collapse into a black hole singularity, the energy would still be "there." It may not do very much, but it would still exist—and, therefore, from the perspective of panpsychism, its associated consciousness would continue to exist, too.

Blindspot: Just like the second law, the first law of thermodynamics refers exclusively to *physical* systems. It leaves out *consciousness.* And, just as the first law tells us energy is never created or destroyed, the same is true of consciousness. We could call it the first law of panpsychism: *experience is never destroyed.*

So, logically, just as something cannot come from nothing, something cannot become nothing. We're safe . . .

However, you seem to think of consciousness as *human* consciousness—which, as you will discover, I consider a very limited view. Yes, indeed, it is possible for the human race to die off; in fact, we are precariously fouling up our planet to such an extent that we run the risk of making this inevitable. No species lasts forever. It is almost a certainty (but not quite) that the human race will disappear sooner or later.

Even if our species happens to survive for as long as planet Earth does, there will come a time when our sun will consume everything in the solar system. And when that happens: *no more humans or any other species*—unless we manage to colonize other star systems or other galaxies. But even then, sooner or later, all star systems and galaxies will come to an end. Someday, our universe will end. That, too, is almost a certainty.

And there is no conceivable way we can "escape" from here into some other universe. So there will come a time when the human species will no longer exist. If that time comes before the death of the Earth, then other species will be around to carry the torch of consciousness— bacteria, cockroaches, and other animals and plants. But even these other species of consciousness will cease to exist when our planet, and then the universe itself, comes to its end.

How will the universe end? Some scenarios have it imploding in a "big crunch" when the entire universe of matter/energy collapses back into a black hole singularity. But remember that first law: even inside the black hole at the end of our universe, energy will still be there. Current cosmological models include the possibility (if not likelihood) that the black hole at the end of our universe will burst forth as a white hole, creating another big bang—and another universe. So the energy and consciousness of the cosmos continually get recycled.

When we consider the REALLY BIG PICTURE, I'm not sure what comfort we can gain. Yes, consciousness will continue forever, but it won't be *our* human consciousness. Is this good or bad news?

Something to ponder.

4

Consciousness

"Nobody Knows What Consciousness Is"

"Is George Bush conscious?" A few years ago, I began a paper for the *Journal of Consciousness Studies* with that question, and then pointed out: "Well, it all depends on what we mean by 'consciousness.' Are we asking whether he's a zombie, or awake, or spiritually enlightened? I think it safe to say he qualifies in at least one sense. But which?"

Of course, our answer would depend on whether we mean *consciousness* in a philosophical, psychological, or spiritual sense. Philosophically, we'd have to say "yes"—after all, despite his many flaws and shortcomings, W is no zombie. He feels (kind of), thinks (kind of), and has some kind of awareness going on, however dim it might be. We'd even have to say he's conscious in a *psychological* sense, at least some of the time, for example, whenever he's awake, not sleeping or dreaming. However, when it comes to *spiritual* consciousness—meaning not only high levels of awareness but also high levels of ethics, honesty, and compassion—many people would probably give George W. a thumbs-down. (In case you think I'm picking on poor ol' "Shrub," the same could apply to Obama—and, unfortunately, to most other world leaders.)

The point is this: A lot of people would unthinkingly say George W. Bush isn't "conscious," implying he doesn't have consciousness. But clearly that's not the case.

Let's cut to the chase:

What is consciousness? In simplest terms, it is the capacity to feel, know, and create choices. The closest I come to a definition is this:

Consciousness is the intrinsic ability of matter/energy to know, feel, and purposefully direct itself. Any being that has the capacity to *know* or *feel* anything or to make *choices* necessarily has consciousness. In this sense, consciousness is the capacity for awareness and choice.

Here's the bumper sticker: "Consciousness *knows*. Energy *flows*." Consciousness is what knows or is aware of the flowing of energy and *purposefully* directs the flow of energy.

What is mind? In most of my work, I use *mind* and *consciousness* (as well as other terms, such as *experience* and *subjectivity*) synonymously. They all refer to *nonphysical* aspects of reality that involve awareness, feeling, knowing, and choice.

In some traditions, *mind* is often used to refer to our intellectual capacities, the rational, categorizing, or egoic mind. I see that as a special use of the term, and it is not what I refer to as *mind* (e.g., in courses I teach, such as Mind in the Cosmos).

What is intelligence? I define *intelligence* as a sentient being's capacity to create or have a goal and to *purposefully* and *creatively* advance toward achieving that goal. The goal is usually an expression of intention. Achieving the goal is manifestation. Thus, intelligence is the ability to creatively transform intention into manifestation. Or, simply: *Intelligence is the expression of intention.* We will return to this topic in a later chapter when we look at the idea of artificial intelligence.

SWITCHED-ON CONSCIOUSNESS

Over the years, I've attended many conferences on consciousness, and every time I have witnessed scientists, philosophers, and other scholars tangle themselves in knots as they discuss, dispute, and debate this mysterious topic.

It doesn't have to be that way.

Early on, I noticed a recurring problem: Different people use the same word—*consciousness*—to mean quite different things. Some talk about consciousness as the opposite of "unconscious"—

a *psychological* meaning. Others contrast it with the idea of complete *non*consciousness—a *philosophical* meaning.

Now, there's a world of difference between being unconscious and being nonconscious. Being unconscious means having some kind of sentience, or feeling, below a threshold of awareness—think of someone asleep, dreaming, or even in a coma, for example.

Being nonconscious, however, means the complete absence of any kind of sentience or mentality whatsoever—think of a rock, a beer can, or a thermostat, for example.

You don't ever—*ever, ever, ever*—want to be nonconscious because you'd never wake up. However, you do want to be unconscious, at least for a few hours at night to relax and replenish your body and mind.

Just as there's a world of difference between being nonconscious and being merely unconscious, there's a world of difference between the two contrasting meanings of consciousness.

However, scholars, who should know better, continue to frequently mix and confuse these two meanings—sometimes even in the same sentence! The philosophical meaning refers to the raw *fact* of consciousness—its existence. The psychological meaning refers to different *forms* of consciousness—such as cognition, emotion, or volition.

It's so basic. Until we clarify these fundamental differences in meaning, people (scholars and lay folk alike) will continue to stumble and fumble as they try to make sense of consciousness.

Facts about psychological consciousness or unconsciousness (different forms or degrees of awareness) have no bearing whatsoever on the presence or absence of consciousness in the philosophical sense—except in the trivial case that for any *form* of consciousness to exist, consciousness must *already* exist as a *fact*. Yet it's commonplace to see scientists and philosophers refer to data from psychology or neuroscience about the degrees or forms of consciousness as though such data were relevant to philosophical questions about how, or whether, minds emerge from mindless matter.

Next time you see the word *consciousness* in a book or article, or hear someone talk about it, pay attention to which meaning they are using. I bet you will soon discover that most of the time most people are oblivious to this basic difference in meaning.

But now you know the difference. And that puts you ahead of the game.

Quick version: Philosophical consciousness is like a flip switch—it's either on or off. There's no in between. Consciousness is either present or it's not. Psychological (or psychospiritual) consciousness is like a dimmer switch—it can vary from dim unconsciousness to the bright lights of spiritual enlightenment.

Philosophically, the interesting question is: How come the light of consciousness is "on" in the universe? Psychospiritually, the interesting question is: How do we turn up the light?

Are We Not Conscious?

Not only does being aware of these two quite different, though related, meanings of consciousness help cut through all-too-common conceptual tangles and confusions in science and philosophy, the *fact* that consciousness exists, in the philosophical sense, offers a way to bridge the gap between science and spirituality—especially if we accept the idea that consciousness goes all the way down to the most fundamental levels of reality.

In other words, once we accept that consciousness is an integral part of the natural world—not only in animals and plants, but also in molecules, atoms, and subatomic particles—we can see how increases in the complexity of matter in both cosmic and biological evolution can correspond with parallel evolution and increases in the complexity of consciousness, leading to its apex in spiritual enlightenment.

One of my readers challenged me on this point:

You have presented a possible way to reconcile science and religion. In doing that, you consider the evolution of consciousness to be a bottom-up process. May I suggest that consciousness is a top-down process and that for a person to evolve he or she will be going up a preexisting ladder. The higher exists before the lower. Gurdjieff teaches that we are not conscious as we go about our daily activities. This is quite different from your starting point:

> *"The fact of consciousness highlights the shortcomings of both science and religion, and it offers a way out of the seemingly endless debate between evolutionists and creationists."*

Here you are assuming that we are conscious when in fact we are not. We are not conscious of ourselves; we are not conscious of our existence as we go through the day.

Gurdjieff made some important observations about consciousness, but in doing so he confused its two basic meanings.

First, I have no difficulty with the notion that consciousness moves through a process of *involution* (a descent) before it engages in *evolution* (an ascent). In fact, I am impressed by the teachings and thinking of scholars and sages such as Sri Aurobindo and Arthur Young, who have presented engaging and detailed versions of this two-way process. I do write about involution and evolution in my books (e.g., in *Radical Nature,* I refer to the combined process of involution-evolution as *onvolution*—the unfolding of being.)

Blindspot: Next, as I have emphasized above and in many of my other books, we really need to keep in mind the important and fundamental distinction between two very different meanings of *consciousness*— *philosophical,* contrasted with *non*consciousness, and *psychological,* contrasted with being *un*-conscious. Just as there is a world of difference between being merely *un*-conscious (e.g., being asleep or dreaming or in a coma) and being *non*-conscious (the complete absence of any subjective or mental processing whatsoever), the two corresponding meanings of *consciousness* are radically different, too.

My correspondent, like many scholars as well, falls into this consciousness blindspot. When he quotes Gurdjieff, saying we are "not conscious," he is referring to the *psychological* (or psychospiritual) meaning of consciousness. Even unconscious people (or other animals or plants) have some degree of consciousness present *in the philosophical sense*. After all, even sleeping people still have feelings and sensations, which would be impossible if there was a total absence of consciousness, or non-consciousness.

He said: "We are not conscious as we go about out daily activities." But then I ask: *How does he know that?* Even making that statement requires him to have *some degree* of consciousness. We may be *unconscious* most of the time, but we are *never non-conscious*. People wake up from being unconscious, but nothing ever wakes up from a state of *non*consciousness.

So, yes, I agree with Gurdjieff that most people most of the time go through life like machines or zombies—mechanically acting out of habitual patterns. However, the crucial difference between sentient beings and machines is that we can sometimes wake up from our unconsciousness, but machines never wake up from nonconsciousness.

AWARING AND RIPPLES

A recent article in *New Scientist* outlined the possible evolutionary significance of what are called *von Economo neurons* (VENs) and their role in consciousness—a good example of scientists and science journalists confusing the psychological and philosophical meanings of consciousness.

See if you can spot the consciousness blindspot:

The bigger the brain, the more energy it takes to run, so it is crucial that it operates as efficiently as possible. A system that continually monitors the environment and the people or animals in it would therefore be an asset, allowing you to adapt quickly to a situation to save as much energy as possible. "Evolution produced an energy calculation system that incorporated not just the sensory inputs from the body but the sensory inputs from the brain," Craig says. And the fact that we are constantly updating this picture of "how I feel now" has an interesting and very useful by-product: we have a concept that there is an "I" to do the feeling. "Evolution produced a very efficient moment-by-moment calculation of energy utilization and that had an epiphenomenon, a by-product that provided a subjective representation of my feelings."

If he's right—and there is a long way to go before we can be sure—it raises a very humbling possibility: that far from being the pinnacle of brain evolution, consciousness might have been a big, and very successful accident.*

Blindspot: While the interactions between neurons and the environment throughout evolution may well play a role in "shaping" consciousness (which already exists in neurons)—even playing a role in forming the sense of "I," or the ego—none of this points to or explains the simple fact of awareness or subjectivity. I like to call it *awaring* or *aming.* Concluding that subjectivity could be a by-product of purely mechanical or physical "accidents" is an unwarranted jump. Unfortunately, it's a very common leap, made by both scientists and philosophers, from data related to psychological *forms* of consciousness applied to the philosophical *fact* of consciousness. Forms never account for the fact. The fact of consciousness must exist for any of its forms to appear.

If we picture *forms* of consciousness (such as thoughts, beliefs, and desires) as "ripples" in awareness, then the idea that VENs could be responsible for the evolutionary emergence of consciousness is like saying the ripples cause awaring or that awaring is a by-product of the ripples! This is as absurd as saying waves on the ocean cause the ocean and that the ocean is a by-product of the waves. It has it exactly backward!

---

*Williams, "Are These the Brain Cells That Give Us Consciousness?"

Consciousness and Intension

I keep emphasizing that we need to pay attention to a fundamental distinction when thinking about the nature of mind and matter. Mind, or consciousness, is *nonlocated* and unextended—it doesn't exist in space. All matter or energy extends in space; it takes up *some* volume—whether immense spans of space, as in planets, stars, and galaxies, or minuscule amounts of space, as in cells, molecules, and atoms. Just because we can't see something tiny doesn't mean it isn't taking up space. Even subatomic particles like electrons and protons have *some* size.

Matter has *extension.* Mind has *intension.*

In other words, whereas matter is *extensive,* mind is *intensive.* We can measure and quantify the extension of matter/energy, for example, using rulers and other instruments, but we need to *feel* the quality of intension, or the *intensity,* of consciousness.

The more complex consciousness becomes, the greater the degree and levels of intensity. We experience this frequently in our own lives; for instance, while the strength of an emotional reaction or the degree of intellectual concentration cannot be measured or quantified, it can be subjectively and intersubjectively evaluated in terms of its intensity. We *feel* the intensity, or intensiveness, of consciousness, but we measure the extensiveness of matter/energy (how much space it occupies or traverses).

More technically, we could say: When intersubjective relationships within a system of sentient matter become more complex (e.g., in the brains of higher animals), that system possesses greater *intension.* Degrees of *intension* differentiate qualities of consciousness.

Three Forms of Intersubjectivity

Depth Alert: Now that I've introduced the term *intersubjectivity,* let me say a little about this unfamiliar word. Briefly, it refers to the fact that different centers of subjectivity (i.e., individual minds) can and do *connect and communicate*—they are *inter*subjective; they share meaning between each other. This is the foundation of all felt relationships.

In *Radical Knowing,* I identified three different meanings or kinds of intersubjectivity:

Weak intersubjectivity refers to exchanges of signals or symbols, such as words or gestures, through physical media. This is the standard use of the term in science and does not really qualify as true inter*subjectivity.* It is really inter*objectivity.* Measurement is not a form of intersubjectivity because it is the acquisition of objective information about objective things or events—with no direct implied or explicit subject-to-subject engagement.

Moderate intersubjectivity refers to the fact that when sentient beings share meaning or information, they *change* something about each other. This can happen either through standard sharing of information (as in the "weak" interpretation) or without or beyond any exchange of physical signals—for example, when two people engage each other's presence and *feel* the presence or being of the other. This is a true subject-to-subject, or *intersubjective,* connection that transcends the medium of physical exchanges (even though such signals are often involved, too—but not always).

Strong intersubjectivity refers to the idea that when sentient beings engage each other's presence, they don't only change something about each other but actually *co-create* each other. This strong meaning of intersubjectivity is based on the understanding that, fundamentally, we are constituted by our *relationships*—that relationship is primary and individuality is secondary (we will look more closely at this in chapter 12).

Consciousness, Complexity, and Self

Clarifying the relationship between "consciousness," "self," and "self-consciousness" can be tricky. However, when we think in terms of *subjective intensity* and complexity, we can begin to tease apart meaningful distinctions.

"Complexity" can refer to physical systems whose components are related merely through multiple *external* connections, for example, the intricate tangle of wires and circuits in a computer or even the massive tangle of tissues we call our brain. And because consciousness and matter always go together, the complexity of consciousness is *correlated* with the associated physical complexity—for example, the consciousness associated with the nervous system of a worm is "shallower," or less evolved, than the consciousness associated with the complexity of a human or cetacean brain.

But we need to be extra careful about terminology here. We need to leave room for a distinction between "consciousness" and "self-consciousness" (or "self-reflexive consciousness"). While it is true, from a panpsychist perspective, that a worm is conscious, it would be stretching imagination to suggest that a worm (or a cell, molecule, or atom) has *self-consciousness.* And yet it seems meaningful to say that a worm, *because of its sentience or consciousness,* has some felt sense of a distinction between "self" and "not-self"—otherwise, it would be difficult to imagine how the worm's consciousness would function as an aid in surviving and navigating through its environment.

So the mere presence of consciousness would imply an awareness of this fundamental distinction between "self" and "other." Of course, in lower sentient beings, such a distinction would lack any conceptual-linguistic denotation. It would simply be *felt.*

In that case, while consciousness comes with a sense of self, and in this sense any sentient being could be said to be "conscious of itself," we would do well to distinguish between "consciousness of self" (feeling its own embodied boundary) and "self-consciousness" (consciousness reflexively aware of itself).

One way to help clarify this distinction would be to note how "low-grade," or less complex, consciousness implies an awareness of its own *embodied boundary,* whereas high-grade consciousness, associated with more complex bodies, has an additional capacity for self-reflection, for turning the beam of awareness back on awareness itself. In short, low-grade consciousness is *body-oriented,* whereas high-grade consciousness is more *mind-oriented.*

All grades of consciousness possess a raw sense of *subjectivity*—philosopher Thomas Nagel's famous "what-it-feels-like-to-be"—as well as some vague sense of "self-from-other," the evolutionary precursor of the Cartesian ego. But only higher grades of consciousness possess the added ability, or "complexity consciousness," to be self-reflective, to turn the beam of awareness back on itself, where *self has a sense of self.* This ability for self-reflection is, likewise, graded—with some sentient beings having a higher degree of self-reflexivity than others. Presumably, the highest grade is what we call *spiritual enlightenment.*

LIFE AND CONSCIOUSNESS

I agree that something can be alive and not conscious, but I'm not sure that something can be conscious without being alive. If there is a soul or subtle body, it must be "alive" in some sense as opposed to other energies that are inanimate and nonconscious.

You say that something can be alive and not conscious. Well, which meaning of consciousness do you have in mind—philosophical or psychological? This is one example where the distinction in the two basic meanings of consciousness is important. Yes, a living being can be *unconscious* (you and I do this every night), but it cannot be *nonconscious* (unless you accept the reality of true philosophical zombies—creatures identical to us in every physiological respect, including flesh, bones, blood, and brains, but lacking any sentience whatsoever—see my book *Consciousness from Zombies to Angels* for more on this).

If you say it is impossible to be conscious without being alive, then you are saying that only living beings can be conscious. This rules out molecules, atoms, and so forth simply because they do not meet the criteria of being alive—they do not metabolize chemical energy and do not engage in growth and reproduction.

And this view (probably unwittingly) endorses materialist emergence—the claim that nonconscious ingredients such as molecules could combine to form conscious organisms.

If, on the other hand, you decide to redefine *life* in some other way, you would need to clarify what that is. You would need to explain what differentiates a living organism (e.g., you or a dog or a bacterium) from a "living" nonorganism (e.g., a rock, a dead person, a dead dog, or a dead bacterium). Clearly there is a distinction between life and death. How would you account for this distinction if you don't define life in terms of biology?

When you say that a "soul" or subtle body must be "alive," I suspect you are confusing the term *alive* with *aliveness* or *vitality*. These latter two terms refer to the *experience* of aliveness or vitality as distinct from the biological processes that are necessary for an organism to be "alive." Yes, I would say it is possible for sentient beings (in physical or subtle domains) to experience "aliveness" or "vitality" without being alive. A molecule would qualify as one example of this. But even the terms *aliveness* and *vitality* can be misleading here. What we are really focusing on is the *experience of sentience*—the *what-it-feels-like* to be a sentient being.

I'm aware that conflating *life* and *consciousness* is common and widespread (just like the confusion between *consciousness* and *energy,* as we will see later on). But that doesn't make it meaningful or coherent. In fact, the distinction between consciousness and life comes down to exactly the same reason for distinguishing between consciousness and energy: one is subjective and nonphysical; the other is objective and physical.

Blindspot: The distinction between consciousness and life comes down to this: Consciousness is *subjective;* the process of life is *objective.* That is, we can objectively test for signs of life—a beating heart, breathing, active metabolism, flat-lining, and so forth. By contrast, there is no objective test for subjectivity or consciousness—we have no "mind detector."

DETECTING CONSCIOUSNESS

How can we tell that any animals, plants, or anything else has consciousness (aside from ourselves, of course, because we each have direct access to our interior experience)?

This is the perennial *problem of other minds,* as it's called in philosophy. The fact is that we just don't have (and never will have) a "mindalyzer" or "consciousness meter" to detect or measure the presence or absence of anything subjective or nonphysical.

Any truly scientific exploration of consciousness (i.e., subjectivity) will necessarily require a radical shift in the current methodology of science beyond *sensory* empiricism. We will need to cultivate what I call the Four Gifts of Knowing. In addition to the Scientist's Gift of the *senses* and the Philosopher's Gift of *reason* and *language,* we will also need to develop the Shaman's Gift of *participatory feeling* and the Mystic's Gift of *direct knowing* or *intuition* through sacred silence.

Blindspot: To know consciousness in another (another human or another animal, plant, or inanimate system), we need to move beyond the Cartesian notion of isolated individual subjective minds and recognize, as shamans do, that consciousness is *intersubjective,* not merely subjective. Employing this other way of knowing, this intersubjective sharing of *presence,* we can "detect" consciousness in others. Good, sensitive spiritual teachers apply this mode of knowing when working with their students.

CONSCIOUSNESS, EGOS, AND GHOSTS

I heard an interesting theory that after death we exist in a dual state of both collective consciousness and individual ego—everything we've learned in life remains in our memories on the other side. In the Buddhist view, after death comes rebirth until we reach enlightenment. I've been reading up on reincarnation and near-death experiences (NDE), and there's been a lot of profound work on both. Studies indicate that "some" kind of individuality remains after death, though in a large number of NDE reports the experiencer talks about fusing with Cosmic Consciousness—involving a total loss of ego—and then regaining that ego identity either while still "dead" or when returned to the body.

My favorite theory comes in the form of a question: What if life is just a game—Cosmic Consciousness playing a game against itself, setting up its own rules, inhabiting different "pieces," and playing out each adventure of each individual?

I just can't see oblivion as something to look forward to. Losing one's ego doesn't seem like anything to worry about as long as we remain connected to everything. Oblivion just makes everything feel pointless.

First of all, I have no desire to deny or even question anyone's personal experience. However, I am always cautious to distinguish between *experience* and *interpretations* of experience. So, it is possible (not necessarily so) that so-called postmortem experiences do not accurately express or represent what people *actually* experienced as documented in NDE and other "afterlife" reports.

However, I am intrigued by your idea, borrowed from Buddhism, that after death we may exist in a "dual state" of both collective consciousness and some kind of personal consciousness. I need to consider that idea in more depth, but my first intuitive response is that it *feels* right. It could account for the countless reports of "ghosts" and other after-death phenomena.

From the ego's point of view, returning to collective consciousness is tantamount to falling into oblivion. There is little or no solace *for the ego* to know that *consciousness* will survive, but not *my* consciousness. I think that at a "soul" level, we may find comfort in the notion (or experience) of nonpersonal survival of consciousness, but that won't satisfy the ego.

One possibility that I'm inclined to take seriously is that after death the focus of consciousness shifts from egoic individuality shaped by our physically *embodied* experiences to whatever subtle embodiment (subtle energy, astral body, ch'i, prana, etc.) survives the death of the physiological body. Buddhists call this after-death period the *bardo*. We could imagine it as a kind of "echo" of our personality reverberating after death, and that some humans sufficiently sensitive enough can "tune in to" or communicate with such a consciousness, or "ghost." However, in time, even these "echoes" or reverberations die off, and when that happens the individual personality is eventually reabsorbed back into the universal or collective consciousness. All of this is compatible with the worldview of panpsychism ("radical naturalism") that I espouse—and, I think, it is aligned with Buddhist philosophy, too.

Am I Real?

What if, really, there's "nobody home" inside anyone else but me? Even more frightening, how do I know I am really real?

Blindspot: Well, the simplest answer is a question: *Who* is asking? *You* (as an egoic individual) may not be ultimately real, but the *consciousness* that's "pretending" to be you most certainly is. If only Descartes had been a Buddhist!

CHOICE AND CONSCIOUSNESS

I have just reread Radical Nature *and I have a question: In your discussion of free will and choice, I understand you to say that the essence of self is the act of choice or choosing. How does this fit with the Buddhist notion of "choiceless awareness" or the notion of the "Witness" as the essence of the true self?*

Quite honestly, I'm not sure of this. I seem to oscillate, sometimes convinced that choice is essential to all forms of consciousness, and sometimes intuiting the Buddhist view. On balance, though, I'm inclined to come down on the side of "choice" rather than "choiceless" consciousness.

What would be the point of consciousness that was purely witness? How could a purely witnessing consciousness ever direct or purposefully shift attention?

Like most deep issues to do with consciousness, I think we encounter a paradox here: For consciousness to reach the stage of "pure" witness, it needs to make a choice (or a series of choices) to "let go" and simply "be." Achieving "choicelessness" requires an initial act of "choice."

Over the years, as I've meditated on this, I've come more and more to the intuition that really the issue is not choice versus choicelessness but rather *who* is choosing. Yes, I think for individual humans to experience "enlightenment," we need to let go of our personal, egoic, individual will. In doing so, we "relax" into the intersubjective communion of "universal consciousness" (call it *spirit,* if you like). We relinquish personal choice, or perhaps the illusion of personal choice, and open up to the true source of self-agency: the Creative Ultimate. "Our" choices may be manifestations or expressions, *through us,* of choices enacted by the Creative Ultimate.

Blindspot: If choice is not intrinsic to consciousness, how could anything ever happen purposefully or creatively?

CONSCIOUSNESS AND TIME

I think of consciousness as the experience of the numinous, or maybe I equate consciousness with God (beyond all time, space, and form). Yes, as you say, "what happens in consciousness takes time," but what happens in consciousness is not consciousness.

If "what happens in consciousness is not consciousness," well, then what is it? What happens in consciousness could be nothing other than consciousness. Just like a ripple in a pool of water is still water. Consciousness is a process—and every process requires time.

You say you disagree that consciousness is within time possibly because you identify consciousness with experience of the numinous (a sense of spiritual awe). First, an experience of numinosity is just one form of consciousness, an aspect of the psychospiritual meaning. That's a valid, but narrow, view of a much wider phenomenon.

In general, as I've noted elsewhere, *consciousness is the intrinsic ability of matter/energy to know, feel, and purposefully direct itself.* A worm or a molecule has these characteristics, but I've no reason to suppose worms or molecules have numinous experiences.

Even if consciousness did mean an experience of the numinous, that would not mean it would (or could) exist beyond time.

Blindspot: If you take the time to just observe your own consciousness (numinous or otherwise), you will notice that, without a doubt, each moment of experience endures, and is then followed by another moment of experience. All of this requires *time*. How could you have a "moment," or any duration, or a sequence of experiences without time?

If there were a state of reality beyond time, then in that domain nothing could ever happen. How could it? Every "happening" requires time. Yet we know, again without a doubt, that events do happen in consciousness. Therefore, consciousness must happen in time.

Creation Takes Time

Similarly, even if you equate *God* and *consciousness,* that doesn't get us beyond time. Yes, I know, a lot of people claim that God is beyond space and time—but, again, how could that be? If by *God* you mean the source or creator of All That Is (what else could it mean?), then how on Earth (or how in Cosmos) could creation happen without time? How could a timeless being generate time? Creation is an action, an event—and every action or event takes time.

Blindspot: If there ever was a timeless state, it could never have produced time. Why? Because to do so would require some mode or moment of transition from timelessness to time. But any such transition would take time!

If God "creates," "generates," or "produces" anything, that could happen only in time. The idea of creation, generation, or production without time is meaningless.

The Miracle of Timelessness

If God or anything else could create time from some timeless dimension, it would take a miracle. It would be an inexplicable mystery.

Yes, mysteries continue to confound us. They spur us on to look for new ways to know reality. And I have little doubt that no matter how many mysteries we "crack," more will always remain (thankfully).

Blindspot: But mystery is not the same as miracle. Mysteries can be solved—by further study, new information, and coherent interpretation of the data we receive. In short, mysteries can, at least in principle, be explained. That is not so with miracles. By definition, miracles cannot be explained. If we could explain them, they would cease to be miracles. Miracles are gaps in explanation, indications of our ignorance.

Now, this does not mean that miracles never happen. But it does mean that if they do happen they cannot be explained—and that puts them beyond the reach of science and philosophy.

It also means that if miracles happen, they, too, must occur in time. Every "happening" takes time. Think about that.

MIRACLE OF EXISTENCE?

In Radical Nature, *you challenge the idea of consciousness emerging from a purely material world. You point out that such an emergence of something radically new from nothing would be a miracle. This makes sense to me, and my own lived experience is that the whole world is conscious somehow. But isn't the presence of consciousness as an inherent aspect of the universe just as miraculous? Why it is more difficult to accept the emergence of consciousness than to accept that some form of consciousness has always been present in the universe? After all, isn't the sheer fact of existence (even mere matter) an awesome miracle?*

Here's my view: *Something* exists. That's a given. We know this *for certain* because here we are, experiencing embodied beings. Given "something rather than nothing," the next fundamental question is: *What is the ontological nature of existence?*

You may not wish to skip over the seemingly "miraculous" fact that *something exists* because, after all, it could have been otherwise—it could have been that nothing exists or ever existed. But this is really an inconceivable idea because it takes an existing mind to even try to imagine such a possibility. We cannot really imagine true *nothingness.*

I agree, experiencing the *fact of being* is awesome. And to the extent that it is beyond explanation, you could say it is "miraculous." But, really, there is no other conceivable option—now that we know we are here, that being exists. Whatever is fundamentally "given" not only is beyond explanation but doesn't *require* explanation, which involves causal sequences, and *nothing* could not have caused *something.* Therefore, something must have *always* existed. So, *in that sense,* the fact of being is not a miracle. We are blessed with the inescapable fact of being.

And so, our question is not *Is existence a miracle?* but *What is the fundamental nature of existence—its ontological makeup?* Well, we know it must include consciousness because here we are contemplating it. Any materialist philosophy that claims consciousness "emerges" from wholly nonconscious matter/energy slams into the "hard problem" of understanding how mindless stuff could ever produce minds, and tumbles into an unbridgeable "explanatory gap." Ontologically, then, materialist emergence is a nonstarter.

Blindspot: Therefore, because (1) we know *for certain* that consciousness exists now, and (2) it could not have emerged from a state of reality that didn't possess at least some minimal consciousness, we can logically conclude (3) that *consciousness must have always existed*. There really is no coherent alternative.

THE TAO OF CONSCIOUSNESS AND ENERGY

As I was walking the beach this morning (a wonderful thing to do while contemplating the mysteries of existence), I was thinking about your discussion of consciousness and energy, and how you challenge the idea of "pure" spirit. The image of the Taoist yin/yang *symbol came to mind. I was considering how it shows that the seed of one is in the other. The analogy came to mind of pure spirit being in matter and matter being in pure spirit. I wondered: Is consciousness what moves each into the other along a spectrum of being?*

Here's where the Philosopher's Gift of precision in language comes in useful: If, as you say, "pure" spirit is in matter, and if this is always the case, then reality actually consists of "spirit-matter." In that case, reality is never "pure" spirit—it is always both spirit and matter (consciousness and energy), or unified *sentient energy*. Similarly, if matter were in "pure" spirit, then in fact there would be no "pure" spirit because it would contain some form of matter or energy.

This is the position of panpsychism, and it's why I challenge the idealist notion of *pure spirit*—meaning "pure consciousness." Pure spirit could never do or create anything. The best it could do is form intentions, but without energy it could never take any *action* to make things happen. "Pure" spirit, in that case, would actually be impotent (and that does not seem like a good job description for a divine ultimate!).

Blindspot: When you talk of consciousness "moving" into both spirit and matter, I think you may be falling into the very common pitfall of envisioning consciousness as some form of energy. Movement means a transition from one point in space to some other point in space. And consciousness doesn't exist as a thing (or a "field") in space in any way whatsoever. Consciousness is not an object. It is what *knows* or *experiences* or is *aware of* objects (of energy). Only energy, which is objective, can move through space. Remember: Consciousness *knows*. Energy *flows*.

Also, I'm not sure why you make a distinction between consciousness and spirit. Ontologically, they are the same kind of reality—*nonphysical,* not existing in space. If you think that spirit is not consciousness (or not *only* consciousness), then what else does spirit possess in addition to consciousness? Have you thought about that?

Having said all this, I want to also acknowledge your insight and the circumstances in which it arose—walking on the beach! What a wonderful way to engage the wholeness of mind and body and the environment. I share your enthusiasm for the Taoist *yin/yang* symbol. It is full of wisdom. You are quite right: *yin* and *yang* do contain the seeds of their opposite. So what could this mean in relation to consciousness and energy (or spirit and matter)?

I propose that what we call *spirit* is the Tao, containing within itself both *yin*-consciousness and *yang*-energy. And the "dot" or seed of *yang* within *yin* represents graphically the idea that consciousness is never "pure"; it is always grounded in some *yang*-energy. Likewise, the "dot" or seed of *yin* within *yang* represents the insight that energy is never "pure" or insentient but always possesses some form or degree of consciousness.

To think of consciousness and energy shading into each other on a spectrum is to misunderstand the nature of consciousness and energy. They cannot transform one into the other. What is physical can never become nonphysical, and what is nonphysical (consciousness) can never become physical (energy). Nevertheless, they always go together, always mutually implicating each other.

Think of the shape and substance of a ball: We would not say that the shape and the substance form a "spectrum"; that would be absurd. Shapes never transform into substances, or vice versa. Yet every shape is always the shape of some substance, and every substance always has some shape. They are inseparable; they form a unity, but they are never identical. You cannot reduce one to the other (we'll come back to this later).

It is the same with consciousness and energy. One is the source of intention and purpose (consciousness); the other is the source of action (energy) and matter. Together, intention and action result in *creation*. In this sense, what we call *spirit* (Tao) is both intentional and energetic; it is *creative* and expresses its creativity through *purposeful action*.*

What Is Consciousness For?

In Consciousness: An Introduction, *researcher Susan Blackmore asks an intriguing question: Is consciousness an extra ingredient in addition to the matter of our bodies? In other words, she wonders:* What is consciousness for? *What function does it serve in evolution? Why did it evolve?*

Blackmore doesn't address this, but the question, "what is consciousness for?" is loaded with materialist and mechanistic assumptions. It implies that everything must be explicable in terms of "functional fit," as though the only important and significant aspects of existence are those parts that fit together like cogs in a wheel. If there is no *observable* (i.e., *measurable)* change in behavior to explain the reason for the existence of something, then its existence is a mystery and questionable— according to modern science. Blackmore even goes as far as claiming that consciousness is an illusion. Really? Who or what is having the illusion—and *how?*

Blindspot: I disagree with this view of things. I do not accept that only what can be observed or measured, or explained in terms of functional

---

*In his landmark book *The Reflexive Universe,* renegade cosmologist and mathematician Arthur Young identified the quantum of action as the ultimate monad of universal spirit.

fit, is important or significant. Blackmore may not realize it, but her question *presupposes* materialism. The question is an attempt to squeeze consciousness into the restrictive criteria of objective matter/energy. But consciousness is not at all like that.

If we want to know what consciousness is "for," we need to approach the question on its own terms. And when we do, we see that there is another kind of "fit," a very different set of explanations. I'm talking about *experiential fit:* What is the *meaning* of my existence, who am I, and how do I relate to others? How do I *experience fitting into my world?*

The simple answer to Blackmore's question is: *Consciousness is for experiencing meaning, purpose, and value.* It is for *knowing* and *choosing* among a range of alternative possibilities. It is for creating *intentions.* And when we engage these capacities of consciousness, not only does life become much more enjoyable and interesting, it becomes more healthy—and that is of immense survival value.

When I first heard Blackmore and others pose this question, I thought it was some kind of scientific in-joke. The function and purpose of consciousness are obvious enough to anyone who pays attention: *Consciousness is necessary for awareness and choice*—for *intelligence,* for guiding actions that help us survive and thrive.

Consciousness is for *thriving* as well as for surviving. Einstein summed it up well (I paraphrase): Not everything that can be counted, counts. And not everything that counts can be counted.

CONSCIOUS EVOLUTION

Zombie evolution wouldn't vary from natural selection because, by definition, zombies look exactly the same, act the same, and say the same kinds of things as we do. There wouldn't be any observable distinguishing characteristics for natural selection to work on between conscious beings and zombies.

Blindspot: In effect, this is a restatement of Blackmore's view and is similarly off-track because it assumes natural selection is purely about *functional fit.* But ponder this: What survival value might *experiential fit* confer on species? Does it make any difference that individuals and species *experience fitting into their world, enjoy* their existence, find *meaning,* have *purposes* and *value,* and *choose* among possibilities? I think it makes a big difference.

Surely even materialists must recognize that *choices* (which determine actions) make an enormous difference in the survival of species. And because zombies cannot make choices, their evolutionary path would, almost certainly, be very different from beings who do have consciousness and make choices.

For one thing, lacking any capacity for *conscious evolution,* it is highly likely that zombies would evolve far more slowly than beings who make choices that enhance their evolution.

When Is Consciousness?

Because science cannot account for consciousness, how can it offer any credible explanation for where consciousness comes from, where it exists, and where it does not?

Blindspot: Given its methodology of *sensory* empiricism, plus the fact that consciousness is *nonlocated,* science cannot—and *could* not—tell us where consciousness is. Consciousness doesn't exist *anywhere.*

One day, I hope, scientists (and the rest of us) will wake up to the fact that asking "where is consciousness?" is the wrong question. Instead, better to ask (many times a day): "*When* is consciousness?"

Of course, the answer is: *now.* Always now. And this leads us to our next topic, time, and a whole new set of blindspots.

5

Time

"The Future Is Now"

Have you ever tried to capture and hold a special moment? Ever tried to freeze-frame time, only to discover you can never grasp it? The present moment is elusive—here now, then gone as soon as it arrives. The fickle finger of time pushes on, indifferent to our desires or fears. Omar Khayyam expressed it well:

> *The Moving Finger writes: and, having writ,*
> *Moves on: nor all thy Piety nor Wit*
> *Shall lure it back to cancel half a Line,*
> *Nor all thy Tears wash out a Word of it.*

And yet time does seem to be elastic. Ever notice how it slows down when you are waiting for a kettle to boil? Or how it zips by in a flash when you are really enjoying yourself? How does time speed up or slow to a crawl, yet the clock on the wall ticks away at its regular rate?

Time remains one of our deepest mysteries. It has inspired and frustrated philosophers, scientists, psychologists, and spiritual teachers the world over. Philosophers, in particular, have argued over the nature of time since . . . well, since time immemorial, and scientists have turned it into a dimension of space. (Thanks, Einstein!)

Some folks even say time doesn't really exist—it's just an illusion. There is only *now,* including past and future. One thing seems clear: *Somehow, time and consciousness are intimately connected.*

THE PARADOX OF TIME

We know it intimately, yet when asked to define it, time leaves us scratching our heads. Even more than *consciousness,* attempts to define *time* pull us in circles. Time, it seems, cannot be precisely explained, expressed, or defined in language.

Try a little experiment: See if you can come up with a definition of time that does not depend on a word that itself depends on the notion of time. I suggest it cannot be done.

For example: "Time is the difference between *before* and *after.*" "Time is what *flows* from *past* to *present* to *future.*" "Time is the *succession* of *moments* or *events.*" "Time is *duration.*" "Time is *change.*"

All the italicized words above require an understanding of time for their meaning. The very nature of time appears to be tautological—it requires itself for its own definition—and, therefore, resists precise, clear definition.

Nevertheless, time is so central to our experience and way of life that it seems too important to leave uninvestigated.

So, what *is* time? If we can't define it, how can we know it? Perhaps we can indicate it or approach it along a *via negativa*—by describing what it is not, by pointing out its opposites, or its absence.

Without time, the world would be utterly static. Nothing could *happen* (we might say, whimsically, that time is the "hap" in "happening"). Yet even a totally static universe is unimaginable without enduring, and duration involves a sense of time. Even an eternally static universe must endure and therefore must be threaded on some fiber of time.

The Future Is Now

Blindspot: We cannot meaningfully say, "The future is now." Besides the contradiction of tenses, we must decide, "Which future?" Do we mean the *next second* or *fifty billion years from now?* If we mean that *all* futures are *now,* then we are effectively saying there is no distinction between any future moments. The next minute is no different from a moment fifty billion years hence. It amounts to saying the future has no future.

The same is true for every past moment that once was *now*—right back to the Big Bang. There would be *no difference* between the past, the present, and the future. In other words, *NOTHING EVER HAPPENED!* But for this absurdity to be possible, we would have to say that no time ever existed. Without time, what meaning do the words *past, present,* and *future* have?

If the notion of time is to preserve any meaning, a fixed relation between "before" and "after" must exist. If what was once "before" (in the past) were to become "after" (the future in relation to that past), then language breaks down and those words lose all meaning and usefulness.

Has Everything Already Happened?

This presence we call consciousness *was there before we were born and will still be there after we die. In silence, we can let go into the flow of Love and become Love itself. In this state, the qualities of pure consciousness are revealed and experienced fully. We sit, just being, our full potentiality totally activated, and we become the pure dynamic silence, boundless, brimming with infinite creativity. We are perfect balance and invincible power. As Deepak Chopra says about this state: "You can eavesdrop on the cosmic mind." What I mean is that all of our potential plus the entire activity of the cosmos is at a still point that feels dynamic but is not yet actualized in the world—like experiencing a mature tree and its qualities just by experiencing the seed's potential. Everything is there and on some level already accomplished, and it is all at a perfect still point.*

Blindspot: Philosophically, I have difficulty with the idea that the "still point" of consciousness means all activity of energy is also stilled. The fact is, reality includes both what is *actual* and what is *potential*. Even if we could somehow have full knowledge in consciousness of all potentialities and their probable trajectories of unfolding, those events that are *already actualized* would continue to dynamically unfold and evolve. In short, I don't think a quiet mind translates into cessation of activity in the physical world. I think it means that the still mind is now able to open up to a great deal more information about what is actually happening in the world.

I also find it difficult to get my head (or intuition) around the idea of "block time"—where past, present, and future exist all together—where, in effect, *everything has already happened.* If that were the case, then *nothing new would ever happen again.* And that just doesn't match my experience (or logic).

So, here again, I'm making a distinction between consciousness and energy: Consciousness is what *knows* or *is aware of* energy (summed up in the bumper sticker "Consciousness *knows*. Energy *flows.*"). That is, consciousness is what knows or is aware of the various ways and combinations in which energy flows through the universe. Consciousness is the source of intention and knowledge. But besides intention (in consciousness), events also *happen*—that is, energy or action is present and real.

Pure consciousness, at best, could create pure intentions, but it could never manifest or actualize anything. For manifestation to happen, for potential to become actual, we also need *action,* or *energy.* The best intentions in the world never amount to anything if not backed up with action. I often say to my students that Ultimate Reality, or God, could not be *pure spirit,* meaning "pure consciousness," because all such a god could ever do would be to generate wonderful intentions, but never manifest or actualize anything. For that, God also needs *energy.* Therefore, if we use the term *pure spirit,* it cannot mean just "pure consciousness"; it must also include energy. That's why when I use the term *spirit,* I often mean "sentient energy" or "purposeful action." The sentient, or purposeful, component is nonphysical consciousness, and the energy, or action, part is what we know as physical energy.

About the acorn and the oak tree: Yes, the grown oak is implicit in the potentials of the acorn. However, no acorn ever grows into an oak *without interacting with its environment*. For an acorn to become an oak, *action* is needed to translate the acorn's potentials into the actuality of an oak tree. In other words, *manifestation requires both time and energy*. Nothing ever happens (or could ever happen) without energy—and because energy involves action, it necessarily requires *time*. A world without time or energy would be a world of pure static possibilities. (What a boring world that would be!)

THE ARROW OF TIME

Time implies, even requires, *duration*. In other words, time consists of *moments,* not timeless *instants*. Each moment endures, or "smears" itself out in time. Unlike instants, moments are *continuous*—they *flow into* each other, in *one direction*.

Duration *extends* into the past (and preserves it), but it does not *flow* into the past. Its direction is future-oriented; more accurately, it *creates* the future, because there *is* no future yet for it to flow into—an image similar to the notion of the inflationary universe that does not expand into empty space but creates more space as it goes.

Our lived experience of time defies the limits of language. Time is indefinable, the present moment forever ineffable. The best human minds can do, it seems, is to reach deep inside the psyche for metaphors that may communicate something of the essence of time, bypassing the intellectual faculties and touching a nerve of emotion or intuition.

Communication about time is a poetic affair, not a matter of technical discourse. In my work (particularly in the forthcoming third book in my Radical Consciousness trilogy, *Radical Science: Exploring the Frontiers of Consciousness*), I show how time is intimately related to consciousness and cannot be divorced from an experiencing subject. All efforts to objectify time yield a lifeless shell, an abstraction. Time and consciousness flow together.

To know time, it must be experienced.

A DIALOGUE ON TIME

At the Wisdom Academy, I teach a course on the nature of time. To ease our way into this puzzling but fascinating topic, we start off with two books that present different perspectives on this puzzle: *Deep Spirit* and *The Power of Now*. What follows is based on a dialogue with one of my students as we delved deeper into the mystery of time.

In The Power of Now, *Eckhart Tolle reminds us of this fact throughout his book: There is no past, no future, only now—a new presence, a new creation. In reality, there is only now; time exists only in my mind.*

My favorite philosopher, Alfred North Whitehead, offers a different perspective. He explains how the past very much influences the present; *now* is the "growing tip" of the past. In fact, there could be no *now* without the past. If you doubt this, then pay attention to how much of your present life is still influenced by events you experienced as a child. *The past is always with us.*

However, Whitehead and Tolle agree that the past is *fixed and unalterable.* You can never go back and change it, though you can change your "story" about the past and how you react to it in the present. Whitehead refers to the past as "stubborn fact." And, although the present is deeply influenced by the past—every moment carries the entire history of the cosmos—the present is not fully determined by the past. Every *now* also contains a "spark" of creativity and choice. This adds something new to the mix from the past and opens the present to the next moment when something novel occurs (the future).

Whitehead would also agree with Tolle that the future does not exist—not yet, at least. How could it? By definition, the future refers to events that have not yet occurred. If they had already happened or were happening now, then they wouldn't be "future." They would be part of either the past or the present.

Blindspot: For Whitehead, because the past "pours into" the present and shapes it, the past is part of the *actual* world—*of what is actually real.* Of course, the present is also real and actual and adds something new to the input from the past: The present is always surrounded by a "halo" of possibilities or potential.

Experientially, psychologically, and spiritually, Tolle's focus on *now* makes a lot of sense. However, *philosophically* it is not as robust or as rigorous as Whitehead's treatment of process, the flow of the past into the present. I write about this in *Radical Nature,* in the chapter "Past Matter, Present Mind."

> *Tolle distinguishes between* mind *and* consciousness. *For him, consciousness means presence or awareness. Like Tolle, I think of mind as the seat of our thought processes, our past experiences, our acquired cultural mind-set, our emotions. The mind feeds on stories about our past. When we are in the state of no-mind, however, we are free from the illusions of past and future.*

Good point. *Psychologically* (as distinct from philosophically), our awareness of the past is most often distorted by memory and by our stories. Our psychological *interpretations* of the past are, as Tolle says, "illusions" that feed the egoic mind.

Blindspot: Nevertheless, the past is still very much with us, and it shapes and influences us in very real ways. Just watch the healing process of a wound, either physical or emotional. A scar is a remnant of some past injury—an example of how the past remains with us.

Psychospiritual progress goes hand in hand with our ability to let go of our stories—by not believing our interpretations of past events. Much better, I find, to pay attention to *feeling* how the past shows up in our bodies and present experience.

When we are not thinking, judging, analyzing—not stuck in the mind—we are not being held hostage to meanings or reactions acquired from our past. We are more alert and present to what is. In this sense, the mind can be an obstacle to our development. But the mind is also evolving together with the body and spirit. We are all one, and no part can be ignored.

I agree. And I would add that "what is" includes the present influence of the past. The past lives on in our bodies—in all our tissues, not just our scars.

Tolle's key message is that there has been no past, there is no future, there is only now. Immediately I respond: "What do you mean 'no past'? I remember it. It has shaped who I am. No future? I am planning for it."

Ah, yes . . . but the future doesn't exist, not yet. In fact, that's why you are *planning*. But planning takes place right *now,* in the present.

Blindspot: The future is a new present that *will be*. And when it happens, that new present moment will also be shaped by the past and—this is crucial—also shaped by the *choices* made in the present from the options or possibilities that also exist at every moment. Thus, the present moment consists of the "presence of the past" *plus* a "halo" of present possibilities—as well as the *choice* that selects and actualizes possibilities at every moment. The past does not determine which possibility will be chosen to contribute to the next, new moment. Choice is never determined by the past; otherwise, it would not be choice. *Choice is creative.* And creativity, or creation, always involves choice.

Memories also take place in the present, and this, essentially, is Tolle's point. However, he overlooks that for a memory to exist in the present moment, it must *retain* some information or impetus from the past.

We allow past situations to determine our present. I faced a difficult situation ten years ago, and when I address it only in my mind it stays in the mind and in the body.

You are right: We do often allow our past to determine our present. However, we do so by giving up our god-given power of choice to manifest a new future from present *possibilities* combined with the residue of the past. When we exercise choice, we are no longer fully determined by the past. From the perspective of Tolle's teaching, a key question is this: Who is this "I" who chooses? *Who chooses?* That's the $64 trillion question at the heart of all spiritual traditions. Clearly (or perhaps not so clearly) the chooser is *not* the ego.

Blindspot: The ego, or "mechanical mind," runs on habit and is fully determined by the past. The ego operates like a machine. It is never creative. This tells us that something other than the ego is present in consciousness at every moment. We might call it *Self.* Can we say, then, that "Self chooses"? Yes, that seems to make sense. But that just pushes the question back a step because we still need to ask: *Who or what is Self?* Pretty soon we hit the limits of thought, language, and imagination. And so we turn to meditation, to silence, to no-mind, to "emptiness," in which the answer reveals itself.

Ultimately, it seems to me, the answer to "who chooses?" must be the Cosmic I (the Creative Ultimate or what spiritual traditions call the Divine Source). The Creative Ultimate expresses itself through each sentient being in a cascade of "little choices" at every moment—creating what I like to call the Great Cosmic Democracy, in which every sentient being gets to choose, but does not decide the outcome.

Bumper sticker: "We all get to vote, but we don't get to decide." In *Deep Spirit,* I write: "Intelligence seeks expression."

6

And Time Again

"Time Is an Illusion"

Living in the now requires an understanding of time. In reality, time does not exist. It is an illusion—except to the mind. There is no time in consciousness or being.

Blindspot: Given what I said earlier, you won't be surprised to hear that I don't agree that "time does not exist." I am often puzzled when people claim there is no time, that it's just an illusion. My first question is: *How long did it take you to realize there is no time?* Followed by: *How long does the illusion last?*

Sometimes a student will tell me, "But I have experienced timelessness in meditation—so I know time is an illusion."

"How long did your experience of timelessness last?" I ask. Oops! Usually, that "clicks."

Why, I wonder, do so many people want time to be an illusion? I guess it has to do with our ego's fear of growing old, dying, and death. After all, egos want to live forever.

Even so, a desire for eternity is not the same as a desire for timelessness. Eternity is the exact opposite of timelessness: it is time without end.

If they still don't "get it," I go on to point out that if time didn't exist, then nothing could ever happen—including any shift from an experience of timelessness to an experience of time passing (or vice versa). The point is that even an experience we call "timeless" still has some *duration*. It begins, endures for a while, and then ends. And duration means that time is spread out from the past, through the present, on its way to the future.

Isn't it meaningful to distinguish between events that *have happened* (past), events that *are happening* (present), and events that *have yet to happen* (future)? Not only is this meaningful, don't we structure our entire lives based on this distinction? In other words, we treat time as *real*. In fact, I would say we have no other option.

Every experience *endures*—if not from moment to moment, then for at least the duration of a single moment. And the idea and experience of a "single moment" in the present implies, and requires, the existence of previous moments in the past. Otherwise where did this present moment come from? And why is any moment different from any other moment? *Differences in moments require time*—in fact, *are* time.

In *Deep Spirit,* I address this issue in chapter 26, "An Experiment with Time." During a shamanic session, the protagonist Dara Martin hears this poem:

> *It takes time to greet the birth of each new dawn;*
> *time for day to meet the dark of every night,*
> *time for night to dream into the deep.*
> *It takes time for Father Sun to send us light;*
> *time for light to nurture Mother Earth,*
> *time for Mother Earth to bring forth life.*
> *It takes time for every womb to grow its seed;*
> *time for life to find its place in death,*
> *time for death to find its place in life.*
> *It takes time to sing the stories of the past;*
> *time to open up for what's to come,*
> *time to close each story and let go.*
> *It takes time to venture from the path of grace;*
> *time to right the wrongs we give and get,*
> *time to be forgiven and forget.*
> *It takes time for stars to spin from ancient dust;*

> *time for all creation to return,*
> *time and time again, for all we know.**

The poem appears in the story just before Dara "meets" Whitehead in a dream. The philosopher works with Dara to clarify the meaning and the *experience* of time:

"It is really quite simple. Just pay close attention and you'll see what I mean." Whitehead raised a hand in front of Dara.

"Every experience comes into being and lasts for a mere blink of time. Isn't that right?" He snapped his fingers. "No sooner has it appeared, than it's over. Complete. Expired. Slipped into the past." He snapped his fingers again, pronouncing each syllable carefully.

"Of course, Whitehead is correct," Dara thought. "The present moment is elusive. You can never grasp it. It's here, then gone. Everyone knows this."

Whitehead continued: "What hardly anybody notices, however, is that matter is expired experiences." The Victorian philosopher's voice deepened, alerting Dara that what was coming next was crucial. "Matter, you see, exists just a moment ago." He paused, then emphasized: "Matter is what used to be 'now.'"

Dara struggled with the idea that matter is in the past. But Whitehead insisted that this was an important point to grasp.

"What we know as matter is really layer upon layer of past moments of experience. Matter is the way the past persists into the present." He paused, then repeated: "Past matter."

"But, in sharp contrast, every fleeting moment of now is alive with experience. Isn't that right?" He smiled at Dara. "It is the easiest thing in the world to test this: Just sit or lie quietly and observe the passing of time within."

Immobile in the single dimension of time, it was indeed easy for

---

*de Quincey, *Deep Spirit,* 175–76.

Dara to do nothing but pay attention to the flow of experiences coursing through him.

"Yes," he said, "I feel it. I live in the present, and the present is alive. My past, even my immediate past of just a moment ago, is gone, dead. This is where I live, only in this moment do I exist."

"Present mind," Whitehead emphasized. "What else do you notice?"

"Even though my past is gone, it somehow still lives in me, as if my present self scoops up my past experiences and draws them into me over and over with each passing moment."

"That's quite right. Truly, the past does live on in the present. That's the only way it can live on." He paused. "It's as simple as that."*

For most of my life I've believed that all just is.

Blindspot: But is "is" static or dynamic? Is "is" "*is-ing*"? Is *being* in the process of *becoming*? Is your experience of "I am" really more an experience of "*am-ing*"? If time or process were just illusory, how come we were ever born, how come we grow up, fall ill, heal, age, and die? How come there are seasons? How come anything can ever move, change, or grow? How come generations of people (and other animals as well as plants) succeed each other? *Even the denial of time takes time!*

While it is true that we always live in the present moment, *now,* and experience is always *now,* we also experience *different* experiences. We experience a *succession* of experiences. In other words, we experience *now* existing as a fleeting moment in an ongoing flow of time—this *now* is different from prior, expired *nows* and from all future *nows* that have yet to happen.

And yet so many people report an intuition of something *timeless*. This, I think, accounts for the immense resonance and popularity of Tolle's *The Power of Now.* So how do we account for these seemingly incompatible intuitions?

---

*de Quincey, Deep Spirit, 178–79.

Let me preface my response by noting that, in the end, I don't think language or concepts are sufficiently up to the job of clarifying the nature of time or timelessness. But they can help—at least a little.

Do We Move through Time?

Do we move through time or does time move through us? In other words, is time a line along which (or through which) people, objects, and even space move, or is time itself a moving point?

We can think of time in two ways: (1) as a succession of instants or moments and (2) as a point-instant or fleeting moment moving from past to future. In short, we can picture time as a line (a succession of instants or moments) or as a moving point. When we think of time as a succession of moments, it is clear that the idea of past, present, and future makes sense. That's how we know there is a succession—some moments have already happened, some are happening, and some have yet to happen. From this perspective, time seems undeniable.

However, from within the perspective of time as a passing instant—a moving point we call *now*—that point-instant is all there is. Everything that exists, everything we are aware of, everything we experience, *happens now*—including all our memories and anticipations. That *now* is itself timeless. All knowledge of the past and possible futures "exist" *now*. Reality happens *now*. Experience happens *now*. Therefore, the best way to know reality is by experiencing our experience as it happens *now*.

From this perspective, *now* is a gateway to eternity. It takes either a lot of practice through meditation or a powerful input of grace to have all our attention and experience focused on the *now*. If we succeed, as the mystics have reported, we access an experience of "stepping out of time" into a realm of timelessness. As far as I can tell, this experience of transcending time goes hand in hand with the experience of transcending the *ego,* or the sense of an individual self.

And here's a profound paradox: *The experience of timelessness takes time.* The apparently self-contained, timeless moment *now* occurs in a *sequence of nows.* The point of time occurs in a *succession* of points. It's a version of Zeno's paradox. If each now-instant were truly timeless, there would be no way for any two instants to ever connect. Memory would be impossible. Movement and change would likewise be impossible. Yet we do remember prior moments, and we do experience movement and change. Even the experience of timelessness has duration.

Psychological and Ontological Time

Blindspot: It seems that one way to make any sense of this perennial conundrum is to recognize the difference between *psychological* time, meaning our experience of time, and *ontological* time, or the inevitability of duration, the plain fact that reality endures from moment to moment. If reality per se didn't endure, it would stop, vanish, cease to exist.

In certain states of consciousness, we may "tune out" or "transcend" our awareness of time, our experience of duration, and then we say we experience "timelessness." However, even while we are unconscious of the passage of time, reality itself continues to endure. It must. Sooner or later, if we don't die in the meantime, our state of consciousness shifts and we again become aware of the passage of time. At that moment, our psychological experience of "timelessness" reconnects with the ever-ongoing ontological stream of duration, and once again we experience time passing from one moment to the next.

> *When referring to the mind, Tolle mentions two types of time, clock time and psychological time.*

Ah! Just as I was saying—with one exception: I would not equate "clock time" with *ontological* time. Clocks don't measure *time;* they measure increments of *space.* Next time (no pun) you see an analog clock, watch the second hand closely. Notice how it tick-tocks its way through small increments of space, between the digits. The hands on a clock measure movements through small *distances;* they do not measure time. In fact, time cannot be measured; it can only be experienced. But that's another conversation . . . and one of the few points where I disagree with Einstein.

Blindspot: Psychological time does not necessarily match ontological time. In other words, our experience of duration can speed up or slow down, but the unfolding of ontological time flows according to its own regular tempo. Whether we are paying attention or not, ontological time still flows on. Even people in comas, assuming they have no experience of time passing, also grow old and die.

> *I think there is no past, but the mind will keep us remembering, reliving, regretting something we think has happened. I still think the past is an illusion.*

Are you implying that no past events ever really happened? Were you never really a young girl? Did you just imagine that you got out of bed this morning? I am just imagining that I'm responding to something you wrote or said some time ago? And are you *now* just imagining that you are reading my responses, and that, in fact, I never really did respond?

Blindspot: Do you see how easy it is to lose all sense of reality if we deny the reality of time? *Things do happen.* And, in most cases, the things happening now are related to or caused by events that previously happened. *The present is inexplicable without the past.*

> *We might think some action should be taken, such as a phone call to reestablish ties or a visit to clear up what we perceive as a misunderstanding. To do this effectively, we need to forget the past—or our perception of the past—and to be lovingly present when the connection is made.*

Blindspots: This is a *psychological* issue and not even directly related to "psychological time." You are talking here about *attitude,* about shifting consciousness at the level of values. "Forgetting" some hurt or wrong someone has done to us, whether real or imagined—so we can be more fully present, loving, and compassionate next time we meet them—does not nullify the reality of time. In fact, it reinforces the reality of time. First, it takes time to forget or to suppress a memory, or to forgive—to shift our attitude or focus of attention. Second, it takes time between the original event (the hurt or wrong) and the next, new meeting. Forgiving or forgetting what someone did to us in the past does not eliminate or stop the passage of time.

> *More often than not, all we can do is put the event out of our mind; the degree of difficulty in doing this will depend on how closely we have identified with the mind. The future is part of this same process. The mind takes over; we plan and anticipate, fearing what is in the mind.*

Blindspot: I don't see this as an issue about the nature of time. It is an issue about psychological identification, of a willingness to let go, to forgive, to detach from certain memories. I don't see how any of that negates the reality of time.

Yes, we might let our imaginations run away with us and imagine all kinds of problematic things that might happen in the future. But just because our worst fears or cherished hopes don't come to pass—just because the future does not turn out the way we anticipated—does not mean there is no time or that no future will eventually happen. Even if we are wildly off the mark in what we imagine or anticipate, *something* will still happen at the appointed hour. The universe will not just suddenly vanish and everything come to a standstill. *Something will always happen—whatever the particular contents of our minds.*

This is not to deny the value of checking our imaginations and not letting our fears and projections run away with us. As a psychospiritual practice, this can be very useful. And that is part of the value of Tolle's book: It helps us focus attention back on the present moment, and in doing so we minimize (or, if we are more fortunate or skillful, actually eliminate) psychological distresses caused by our rampant imaginings. But none of this implies or requires the elimination of time.

Being in the *now* does not take us out of time. It just concentrates our attention on the present, rather than being caught up in our memories of the past or our anticipations of the future. Being *present* is a psychologically useful practice. It enables us, or even *empowers* us, to make more informed choices as we become more mindful of how the past shows up in the present and of the possibilities that exist in the present, opening the way for us to choose a different future, aligned with our values and aims.

This, I think, is the value and meaning of the "power" of now: We are empowered to choose more mindfully, with greater awareness of what actually exists—including the inevitable and unavoidable pressure of the past and the ever-present presence of alternative possibilities.

Being present roots us more firmly in reality, including the reality of time—both psychological time as experienced and ontological time, duration flowing from one moment to the next, *no matter what our psychological state happens to be.*

Remembering and anticipating seem impossible to stop—as if I am holding on to a belief I identify as "me." I need to drop this identity, connect with my true being, and live in the present moment. This will happen only when I have a shift in consciousness. This state of being is always available, but we have to realize it at each moment, and it takes practice.

Blindspot: Do you see that the psychological (or psychospiritual) benefits of this practice—focusing attention in the present moment—do not eliminate time or make it illusory? It is one thing to be so focused in the present, *now,* that we detach from our habitual ways of thinking determined by our past and from our fears and imaginings about some possible future, and in doing so liberate ourselves from all kinds of unnecessary mind-induced suffering. But none of this means that time ceases to be real. Just because we shift awareness and no longer attend to the flow of time (to the distinctions between past, present, and future) does not mean that time stops or that it never existed. Acknowledging the psychological benefits of focusing attention *now* does not affect the ontological flow of time.

Sooner or later, though, even the most accomplished mystic shifts back out of that intensely focused state, where *psychologically* there was no awareness of the passage of time, and finds him- or herself once again experiencing *duration*—the ontological difference between events that have happened, events that are happening, and events that have yet to happen. Whether we allow awareness of this temporal distinction to snag us, hooking us back into being overly concerned about past events (which are beyond our control) or about future events (over which we might have some limited control)—thereby causing us unnecessary mental upset or suffering—is up to us. But in no case does it transform time into an illusion.

Our ability to choose where we focus attention in time—on the past, on the present, or on the future—is a useful psychospiritual skill that can have important social effects. But it does not interfere with the fact that time continues to exist no matter where we happen to focus our attention.

We are all living day to day; that's a given until we die. But the question is: How am I living? When I'm with a friend, am I listening to her, or am I thinking how I will respond when she finishes talking? My cat is sitting on my lap, but where am I? Mentally, sometimes I'm someplace else. It is not long before she realizes I am not there, and she leaves my lap. More and more each day, we need to take time to stop and be present, to connect with who we are. We will find that the more we are present to what we are doing, the easier it is, and the more positive and effective the work becomes.

Without a doubt . . . and this is what Tolle is advocating. I think his book is immensely valuable as a "manual" for reminding us of the importance of living with our awareness focused in the present. It is *psychologically* and *spiritually* relevant and valuable.

Blindspot: However, he does not sufficiently or clearly distinguish between time as a *psychological* process and time as an *ontological* process. As a psychospiritual teacher, he is right on target. As a philosopher—for example when he says time is an illusion—he leads readers astray by confusing psychology and philosophy.

> Tolle says: "The accumulation of time as the psychological burden of the past and future greatly impairs the cells' capacity for self-renewal. So if you inhabit the inner body, the outer body will grow old at a much slower rate, and even when it does, your timeless essence will shine through the outer form, and you will not give the appearance of an old person."
>
> Later he makes an important distinction between two levels of pain: that which we create now and pain from the past that we still carry in our mind and body. He teaches that when we realize the past does not exist, we can begin to work on letting go of pain.

Blindspot: Note that here Tolle is explicitly referring to our *psychological* relation to time and its impact on our biology. This is a perfect example of confusing psychology and ontology. His *psychological* analyses, which are quite accurate as far as I can tell, do not warrant the *ontological* conclusion that time does not exist. He has shifted from the role of psychospiritual teacher to metaphysician, and he seems ill-equipped to make that leap.

In *The Power of Now*, Tolle lacks a clear distinction between understanding time as a *psychological* process and time as an *ontological* existential reality. When he slips from spiritual teacher to metaphysician-philosopher (for example, by declaring that time is an illusion), he overlooks some important nuances that have value even within the psychospiritual domain.

One reason I assign *Deep Spirit* and *The Power of Now*, and recommend reading them in sequence, is precisely because of their different treatments of, and perspectives on, time.

7

Now

"Living in the Now Is Just Not Practical"

How practical is living in the now*? Recently, I cared for my late husband, who had Alzheimer's disease, and he certainly lived in the* now *while I was living in the past (helping him to recall), the present (coping), and the future (anticipating next steps). In the case of Alzheimer's, it certainly seems as if living in the* now *is not a functioning, healthy way to be. Yet, in your work, you emphasize the importance of experiencing our experience in the* now *and not living from our beliefs or memories.*

What is memory? In one of your lectures, you describe quantum reality as "bubbles" popping in and out of existence every moment. The "spray" from each popped bubble is the past, which carries over into the next bubble moment. Is memory, then, the spray from one quantum moment of experience to the next? Do we have remnant sprays that help us to learn?

These are important questions. In process philosophy, *memory* is literally reexperiencing past experiences *right now*. It is the "spray" of expired experiences reexperienced in the present moment. Another way to think about it is that memory is "feeling the pressure of the past as it streams into the present." Memory, of course, is also selective. We don't remember everything that ever happened. We remember and select according to our aims and values.

And, yes, without the "spray" from the past, or memory, we wouldn't learn anything.

Your biggest question, however, is: How practical is living in the *now* (especially in light of your own personal experience with your husband's Alzheimer's)? I think living in the *now* is crucially important and practical. However, as implied above, *now* is never disconnected entirely from the past; the past constantly streams into and informs the present.

Blindspot: In other words, some kind of memory is always present, even in Alzheimer's patients. It is possible, however, for neurological reasons, that memory may have difficulty rising to the level of *conscious, self-reflective* awareness, as in Alzheimer's patients. The point is that living in the *now* does not mean ignoring or avoiding what we have learned from past experiences. It just means that we don't live exclusively or predominantly with attention focused on past or future events or experiences. Instead, we let the present moment of experience inform and "light up" the "spray" from the past with new information about the *current* state of reality, which we access through experiencing our experience *as it is happening*. This is a highly practical practice to cultivate.

I have not had much direct experience with Alzheimer's patients, so what I am about to say is speculative: It seems to me that the *now* of Alzheimer's differs in profoundly important ways from the *now* of mystics or spiritually enlightened beings, and indeed from master martial artists or sportsmen or -women or people confronted with a deadly crisis. As I noted earlier, with Alzheimer's, the flow of expired experiences into the present moment ("memory") has been drastically disrupted so that memories do not easily rise to conscious awareness. It is not that memory is not present, but that *access* to memories is seriously impaired. While you, as caretaker, were not only present to your husband's condition in the present (you had to cope), you also were aware of your own memories, including the memory of the memories he used to have, and you also had a functioning *imagination* that allowed you to project or anticipate possible futures.

Perhaps one way of looking at the difference is this: Alzheimer's patients have lost, or have significantly reduced access to, their *personal stories,* composed of their beliefs and memories. Healthy people with functioning brains have the option of living from our personal stories (our beliefs and memories) *or* living into a "space of possibility" (a clearing of "everything/nothing") through the creative potency of *intention* and *choice.*

In my work, I aim to raise awareness of this distinction: We have options *beyond our stories.* That does not mean giving up our stories or pretending we don't have them. It simply means that we don't mistake our stories for actual reality or think we are limited to, or determined by, the narrative trajectory of our stories (our beliefs and memories). The present is not wholly constituted by the past. The present always also contains a spark of creative choice that enables us to express intentions to be aware of and to select new and different possibilities, leading to novel and unpredictable outcomes. *Creativity.*

I'm saying that in addition to the "spray from the past" we also have the "spark in the present." We are both "spray" and "spark." Alzheimer's patients seem to have difficulty accessing both "spray" and "spark." They are often, to one degree or another, lost in a twilight world of recent short-term memory.

THE PULSE OF PROCESS

Depth Alert: Time is both discrete and continuous: *Continuous* in the sense that every moment builds on, and, in a sense, contains, the entire history of the universe—the past flows into the present. *Discrete* in the sense that every moment arises anew and is not completely determined by its past—because every *now* is *experienced* by a *subject* who chooses from among the objective events flowing in from the past and from among the infinite domain of eternal objects or possibilities.

A fundamental tenet of process philosophy is that every actuality is *experiential.* That is, experience (subjectivity or consciousness) is intrinsic to the nature of being or becoming. And because of this intrinsic element of *subjectivity,* no actual entity is ever fully accounted for, or fully determined by, its objective past. In other words, unlike the claim of scientific materialism, actual entities (e.g., atoms, molecules, cells) are not "vacuous," devoid of subjective experience. This intrinsic, always newly arising subjectivity in every actual occasion is what accounts for the "quantized" pulsating character of process.

Blindspot: Something new must come into being at each new moment, with each actual occasion; otherwise nothing different could ever happen. Without novelty, there could be no creative advance.

Like Whitehead, I'm more with the ancient Greek philosopher Heraclitus than with his contemporary Parmenides: "The only constant is the constancy of change." And this "constancy of change" requires a discrete pulsation of moments that are, nevertheless, continuous.

The present is never wholly different from its past. But it is always, in some respects, *different.*

I often say it this way: The past is always flowing into the present—that is, the present could not exist without the past (continuity). But the present is never wholly determined by the past; the present is the "growing tip" of the past—always adding something undetermined and new (discreteness).

In process metaphysics, reality (made up of *actual entities*) is both "quantized" and "continuous"—because *reality pulses* into being from moment to moment.

8

Brains and Minds
"Obviously, Brains Create Minds"

Let's say you taste a scoop of your favorite chocolate fudge ice cream. We watch your brain in an fMRI scan and, lo and behold, neurons associated with taste and pleasure (and maybe some momentary guilt) immediately light up.

All of this is visible and detectable. But no matter how finely and deeply someone looks at your brain, he or she will never find your *experience of taste or pleasure* (or guilt). No surgeon, no scientist . . . no one . . . will ever discover in your brain cells what it *feels like* when you enjoy the taste of chocolate, or any other experience. That's a *first-person* event, and it belongs to you alone.

Even if the neurosurgeon stepped beyond the bounds of good scientific protocol and lopped off the top of your skull (with great care and compassion, of course) and licked your brain (yuk!) . . . even then, he or she would not be able to access your experience of chocolate. The scientist could experience only his or her taste (a little salty, like caviar, perhaps).

Neurosurgeons, like all physicians and scientists, work with matter and energy, with *physical* objects. But your experience is not an object; it is not made of matter or energy.

NO METAPHYSICAL FREE LUNCH

I've been debating your views on panpsychism with a friend who's a materialist. He believes that consciousness emerges from the complexity of the brain. He claims that if the "whole" (e.g., a person) is conscious, that does not prove its "parts" are also conscious (which is what you claim). He says it is a fallacy to ascribe consciousness to the parts just because the whole is conscious. He gave an example of baking a cake where the parts (ingredients) do not equal the whole. Something new emerges in the cooking.

Then he topped off his argument by saying that we can't even prove that the "whole" (a human being or any other animal) is conscious. So, if we can't prove the whole is conscious, why would you claim that the parts are conscious? As I see it, the problem is: How do we scientifically demonstrate that matter has mind or interiority?

Blindspot: Your questions get right to the heart of the mind-body problem and what's called the *fallacy of emergence.* At this point, you won't be surprised to hear that if we begin with *nothing,* then that's all there is forever—*nothing!* Quite simply, you can't get something from nothing. How would it be possible?

So let's say we do have *something* to begin with—the Big Bang packed with unimaginably dense amounts of energy. But according to materialism, this energy is *wholly* physical, *wholly* objective, *wholly* nonconscious. It doesn't have even the slightest trace of interiority or subjectivity.

Let's call this State of Reality A—it's *wholly* physical.

Now fast-forward about 13.7 billion years: Some of that energy has condensed into the matter of galaxies, stars, and planets. And on at least one of those planets, matter has evolved to become so complex that it produces life, nervous systems, and brains. So far so good. No problem with the grand outlines of that story. It is standard scientific cosmology.

But we know for certain that besides the matter of nervous systems and brains, something else also now exists—*consciousness.*

Let's call this State of Reality B—it's physical and *nonphysical.*

State of Reality A is utterly different from State of Reality B. The first is *purely* physical (has absolutely no consciousness), while the second possesses something nonphysical (it does have consciousness).

Brains and nervous systems are physical (exist in space, are objective, and measurable), but consciousness is *nonphysical* (has no physical characteristics whatsoever—does not exist in space, is subjective, and cannot be measured). Where did that nonphysical consciousness come from?

THE FALLACY OF EMERGENCE

Materialists (or anyone) cannot explain how *purely* physical components could produce something *nonphysical*. That would be a metaphysical impossibility. It would require an *ontological* jump—from one state of reality (*wholly physical*) to a completely different state of reality (physical *plus nonphysical*).

Blindspot: In other words, if you begin with wholly physical parts, that's all you ever end up with. No matter how complex or evolved the physical parts become, they can produce only complex *physical* systems. It is utterly inexplicable how consciousness or mind could "emerge" from wholly nonconscious ingredients. That's the *fallacy of emergence.*

Materialists are fond of pointing out that emergence *does* occur, and they are right. They point to many instances of emergence in nature supported by solid scientific data. For example, a standard comparison is that water emerges from the gases hydrogen and oxygen. The gases H and O do not possess liquidity, but water does. So, they say, the phenomenon of liquidity *emerges* from wholly nonliquid components. There was no trace of liquidity in the gases, but with water there is—*something new emerges.* They think this example supports or even proves their case. But they are wrong. It does nothing of the sort.

Here's why: The gases of H and O (like all gases) are physical. *But so is the water!* Both gases and water are *ontologically* identical: they are both physical. So although it is true that a new property, liquidity, emerges, it is still a *physical* property. In this example, we get something physical (water) from nothing but physical components (gases). No mystery there.

This is an example of *physical emergence,* and it is explicable by science. It does not pose a metaphysical problem. Same with baking a cake. Yes, something new emerges (a solid cake) from mushy ingredients. But both cake and ingredients are *physical* and *objective* (all are made of physical atoms and molecules).

Big Mystery

Blindspot: This is not at all the case with consciousness. As we know, mind, or consciousness, is nonphysical—it doesn't exist in space and has no physical characteristics. When materialists claim that consciousness emerges from the complexity of the brain, they are proposing that *something* nonphysical *emerges from nothing but physical components.* That would be *ontological emergence* (not merely *physical emergence*), and it is inexplicable.

Ontological emergence, a completely new kind of reality, is not at all the same as mere physical emergence. It is a profound metaphysical problem without a solution.

As you've heard many times already in this book: *You can't get something from nothing.* Even though the materialists don't begin with absolutely "nothing"—after all, they have the energy and matter of the universe to begin with—nevertheless, they still have a major problem. According to them, there was *nothing* nonphysical present at the Big Bang and for billions of years after. Then, *somehow,* there was—consciousness. Big mystery.

To repeat: You can't get "something" nonphysical from parts that had *nothing* nonphysical—*no matter how complex they become.* That's the fallacy of ontological minds-from-brains emergence.

No Proof of Consciousness

Then there's the objection that "proving" consciousness in the whole doesn't "prove" consciousness exists in the parts. Two problems with this: First, science cannot *prove* anything; most of all it cannot "prove" the presence of consciousness. Second, if the parts didn't already possess some trace of consciousness, then where the heck did the whole organism's consciousness come from? It's the problem of mind-from-brain emergence all over again.

Blindspot: Let's look at the first problem: Like I said earlier, there's no such thing as a "consciousness meter," no "mindalyzer" to detect consciousness. Because consciousness is subjective, it is undetectable, and therefore it is not measurable.

However, scientists (or anyone) cannot "prove" the existence of even *their own* consciousness! So proof of consciousness is a nonstarter; it's a red herring. We don't need to "prove" consciousness exists. We *know* it does in our own case from direct, immediate experience. We can be *absolutely certain* of our own consciousness. Anyone who doubts or denies consciousness thereby automatically and inevitably *demonstrates* its existence. As we've seen, only creatures with consciousness can "doubt" or "deny" anything.

Now to the second problem: For the sake of argument, let's suppose it was possible to prove that a whole organism (say a human) has consciousness. Would that also "prove" that his or her parts (cells, molecules, atoms, subatomic forces, quanta, etc.) would also possess consciousness? I'm saying the answer would have to be a resounding "yes" based on the argument of the fallacy of ontological emergence.

If the whole is conscious, then whatever it consists of must also have some degree of consciousness, too—*all the way down*. Otherwise, we face the problem discussed above: How would it be possible to get consciousness (in the whole organism) from *wholly* nonconscious, nonsubjective parts (atoms, molecules, cells)? That, too, is a nonstarter. And that's why materialism is a flawed metaphysic.

Materialism faces a real problem: It relies on the claim of *ontological emergence* (a jump to a radically new and different state of reality), where mind emerges from mindless matter. Such an ontological jump is utterly inexplicable. It would require a *miracle*. (A *miracle* is an event without any possibility of *explanation*. Instead of explanation, miracles presuppose some supernatural intervention—see below.)

Blindspot: To put it bluntly: In order to be true, materialism requires a miracle, but miracles are precisely what materialism denies are possible. In short: *In order to be true, scientific materialism must be false!* A troubling state of affairs, indeed!

Bumper sticker: "Consciousness is free. But it's not for nothing."

The Miracle of Emergence

For many years I have struggled with the concept of consciousness. My working definition is: "I am aware, and I am aware that I am aware." Additionally, I am able to span time in my thinking, one of the attributes of consciousness. While I find panpsychism appealing because it doesn't require supernatural forces, I wonder if this worldview is truly valid. I have been in the materialism camp for a very long time, and I don't understand why emergence implies supernatural forces. Emergence is an outcome that cannot be predicted in advance, but that doesn't make an emergent outcome the result of supernatural forces.

You are by no means alone as you struggle to come to terms with the topic of "consciousness." Re: your working definition . . . I would say you are referring to a quite special and advanced form of consciousness— *self-reflexive.* Long before beings evolved to the stage of being able to be "aware of their own awareness," the world teemed with beings that were simply and merely aware (conscious). That is, such beings (worms, cells, molecules, atoms, and so forth) could *feel* something about the world they inhabited and could make *choices* among various options and possibilities.

In my work, I say that *consciousness is the intrinsic ability of matter/energy to know, feel, and purposefully direct itself.* The capacity for self-reflexivity comes much, much later in cosmic and terrestrial evolution and (at least on our planet) is correlated with the development of advanced nervous systems and brains.

Now to your specific questions about panpsychism and emergence. There are two kinds of emergence: (1) When something emerges from precursors that are of the same *ontological* type—for example, something physical emerges from prior physical ingredients. As we saw, water emerging from gases of oxygen and hydrogen is a good example. (2) When something emerges from precursors of a radically different ontological type—for example, the idea of nonphysical consciousness, or minds, emerging from physical brains.

The first kind of emergence is fully explicable (if not always in practice, then in principle). However, the second type of emergence (getting something nonphysical from purely physical stuff) is entirely inexplicable—and will always remain so. There simply is no way of conceiving how one kind of reality (e.g., physical) could ever give rise to a completely different kind of reality (e.g., nonphysical). No one has ever even begun to imagine or explain how such an ontological jump could ever happen. It would require a miracle (a supernatural intervention). Remember: A *miracle* involves an event for which there is no explanation and no possibility of an explanation. Miracles are *gaps* in explanation. If we could explain it, it wouldn't be a miracle.

There simply is no conceivable way to explain how such an ontological jump could ever happen. If there was no prior trace of anything *nonphysical*, then it is inconceivable for something nonphysical to emerge from whatever came before. *Something cannot come from nothing.*

In short, physical things or events can evolve only into other physical things or events. Purely physical things cannot give rise to something *nonphysical*.

◈

CHEMICALS AND CONSCIOUSNESS

I'd like to hear your opinion on this problem for those of us who believe that matter and spirit or consciousness are one and never has one existed without the other. Given that matter could never give rise to spirit or consciousness, how do we imagine that the chemicals that first made up the universe after the Big Bang, or whatever was there at the beginning, had consciousness? Could free-floating atoms have consciousness, and what exactly would that mean? Or was the consciousness at the start of the universe a product of the relationship between the chemical and material products that first made up the universe, and if so, how so? I'm afraid that the only way I can envision the relationship is dualistic— to say that there is consciousness separate from the initial matter of the universe and somehow guiding it, and yet that is the position I want to avoid. Any thoughts on this would be appreciated.

Let's take each question, one by one . . .

1. Did post–Big Bang chemicals have consciousness?

In *Radical Nature,* I present a lengthy defense of panpsychism—the view that consciousness goes all the way down. That means not only do cells have sentience, but so do molecules, atoms, and subatomic particles. So, yes, individual molecules and atoms *must* have some degree (and some kind) of "molecular" and "atomic" consciousness. I say "must" because we are made of those chemicals and if we have consciousness, then *whatever we are made of* must also have consciousness. Otherwise, we are faced with the insuperable problem of trying to explain (in vain) how nonphysical minds could have "emerged" from purely physical brains. As I show in detail in *Radical Nature,* that is a nonstarter—and perhaps the biggest blindspot among modern scientists and philosophers (and much of the lay public, too).

2. Could free-floating atoms have consciousness, and what exactly would that mean?

As noted above, yes, free-floating atoms must also have consciousness. I sometimes point out that there is no such thing as a special human atom ("Hu") in the periodic table of the elements. Every kind of atom found in our bodies exists elsewhere in the universe. If carbon atoms, for example, predominate in human and other animal cells, and we are conscious, then those atoms must also have some degree of sentience, too. Why? Because, as we have seen over and over, *you can't get something from nothing.* You can't get nonphysical minds from brains made of purely physical atoms with zero sentience. Mindless matter cannot ever produce minds.

Furthermore, because no special "sentience atom" exists—no atom specializes in sentience—therefore, if *any* atom has sentience, there's no reason to doubt that *all* atoms also have sentience. It makes no difference whether the atom of carbon (or oxygen, hydrogen, nitrogen, etc.) is part of a molecule that is part of a living cell or is free-floating; it would still have sentience.

Blindspot: Again, because consciousness goes all the way down, the subatomic electrons, protons, and quanta have their own complement of consciousness, and the atoms they compose would inherit that consciousness, just as we, as whole animal organisms, inherit the consciousness of our constituent cells. This means, therefore, that atoms and their constituent subatomic particles have some capacity for awareness, or feeling, or for "prehending" their environment (to use Whitehead's phrase).

Not only that, it means that atoms and subatomic particles *make choices.* Every atom, like every actually existing entity, is surrounded by a "halo" of possibilities (think "quantum probabilities"). At every moment, it has a variety of options available for how it will move or behave in the next moment, including whether it joins up with other atoms to form a molecule. It can *actualize* one of these possibilities only by *making a choice* (the collapse of the quantum wave function). Of course, the range of options available to an atom are incomparably more limited than options available to complex multicellular organisms like us. That's why, for all appearances, the choices that atoms make seem so mechanical, determined, and predictable—because, for the most part, they are. But not completely. *For no apparent reason,* single (and even sometimes complexes of) quantum or atomic events "act out" unpredictably—spontaneously producing apparently random quantum jumps that can actualize some highly unlikely and unpredictable probability.

The "randomness" of quantum events (including free-floating atoms), I propose, is a misinterpretation of the inherent *unpredictability* of quantum events. Exactly the same unpredictable behavior can be accounted for if we assume that the quantum is not acting randomly but is actually *choosing*. To an observer, there is no way to tell whether the unpredictability of a quantum event is due to chance or choice.

If we assume (as standard materialism does) that quantum events are purely random, then there is no way to ever account for the fact that we are made of quanta and we make choices. Just like consciousness (and for the same reasons), *choice goes all the way down*. If we want our fundamental metaphysical assumptions to cash out, then "quantum choice" explains much more of the world we actually experience than the alternative of "quantum chance."

3. Is the consciousness at the start of the universe a product of the relationship between the chemical and material products that first made up the universe, and if so, how so?

Consciousness cannot be the product of chemical interactions or relationships—unless those chemicals, molecules, and atoms *already* had some degree of consciousness to begin with. Otherwise, it would be "emergence" all over again, along with the unbridgeable explanatory gap and the infamous "hard problem" of explaining how minds could emerge from brains.

4. The only way I can envision the relationship is dualistic—to say that there is consciousness separate from the initial matter of the universe and somehow guiding it, and yet that is the position I want to avoid.

In panpsychism, consciousness and matter are *inseparable*. One never exists without the other. Matter is always "ensouled" and mind is always "embodied." One way to think of this, and a way to avoid the specter of Cartesian dualism, is to recognize the ultimate "stuff" as *sentient energy*. The materialists almost had it right: Yes, energy is fundamental—everything that exists is made of energy. However, they got it wrong when they assumed (and then insisted) that energy is essentially *insentient*.

Blindspot: When we recognize that energy inherently and natively "tingles with the spark of sentience," we have a more holistic monism. Sentience and energy form an inseparable unity. All energy comes with a capacity to *feel* and to *choose*. However, unity does not equal identity. Unity still allows for *distinction*. So, while inseparable and always forming a unity, consciousness and energy remain *distinct*. Neither can be reduced to the other. That's what I mean by: "Consciousness *knows*. Energy *flows*." Consciousness is what knows (is aware of, or feels) the movement or flowing of energy through our bodies and the world.

I have described consciousness as *the innate ability of matter/energy to know, feel, and purposefully direct itself.* While this still involves a *distinction* between consciousness and matter/energy, it does not imply an ontological dualism nor a materialist (or idealist) reductionism. Here's another bumper sticker: "Distinction does not mean separation." Just because consciousness and energy are distinct does not mean they could ever be separated (as in Cartesian dualism).

You say that consciousness and energy are always linked together and therefore always part of the same whole. And if they are always linked together, aren't they just the same thing? Where would you find energy but not consciousness, or vice versa?

Yes, indeed, consciousness and energy always go together (as I've emphasized many times in my books, blogs, and other online posts). They are inseparable. They form an indivisible unity. So, yes, wherever we find energy, we can also be sure consciousness exists, too.

Blindspot: But while energy exists in space (it flows and moves), consciousness does not have that kind of spatial existence. It exists as *awareness* of space and objects in space. But consciousness is not itself an object.

Through my work, I aim to help people get beyond habitual ways of thinking about consciousness as though it were some kind of object, some kind of "thing" made of energy. It's not. It's what *knows* things.

In my writings and lectures, I also point out a very common logical error: Just because two items form a "unity" does not mean they are the "same." Here's another bumper sticker: "Unity does not equal identity." Yes, consciousness and energy are inseparable, but that does not mean they are identical. Think of the shape and substance of a rubber ball. Now, if I ask you to separate the shape from the substance, you can't. Squeeze and twist the rubber, and the shape of the ball changes, but the substance stays exactly the same.

So, even though shape and substance are inseparable, clearly they are not the same (because you have changed one, but the other remains unchanged). Well, in a similar way, consciousness and energy always go together, forming an inseparable unity, but they are not identical. Consciousness and energy are *inseparable yet distinct.*

One more time: "Consciousness *knows.* Energy *flows.*"

IS CONSCIOUSNESS A QUIDDLEQUOT?

I have not researched enough to feel I can adamantly rule out the possibility that energy and consciousness are not the same, though I think it is likely they are not. Nor am I confident that we understand the nature of either mind or the physical world well enough to make that a statement of fact.

Blindspot: It's a statement of *logic,* not fact. Remember, philosophy is not about discovering *actual facts*—it is about identifying and clarifying *possibilities,* and then relating possibilities and ideas (such as consciousness and energy) in ways that are coherent, are consistent, and avoid internal contradictions. The logical "truth" that consciousness is not a form of energy does not mean that *in actual fact* consciousness is not a form of energy. For all we know, it just might be; or it might be a lump of green cheese, or a quiddlequot. But if it is, we have no way of making any *rational* sense of that.

Here's the logic, using Descartes's definitions of matter and mind:

1. *Physical* entities (all matter and energy) have extension in space.
2. *Nonphysical* entities (all mind and consciousness) have no extension in space.
3. Therefore, physical events or things are radically different from nonphysical events or things—that is, energy and matter cannot be the same as consciousness and mind.

It's that simple.

However, when we access other states of consciousness, reality shows up different—often radically different—and it may not (most often does not) conform to the constraints of rationality and logic. Why should it? Why should the vast, complex, and subtle universe be constrained by the rules of human-generated grammar or logic? Reason does not reveal reality. It reveals what we can coherently say or think about reality.

Other ways of knowing can, and do, reveal very different kinds of reality than what mere logic and reason can deal with. But such revelations are not to be *thought* about, or *conceptualized*. We cannot think coherently or write about them in ways that make sense within descriptive or explanatory language. But—and here's the point to keep in mind—*if we do wish to think, or talk, or write about consciousness and energy, we do need to adhere to the rules of logic and grammar.* And when we do, we will find it makes no sense at all to talk of consciousness as a form of energy.

Is that the truth? Who knows? Reason certainly doesn't. But reason can point us in the direction of the "most likely story."

9

Energy
"Everything Is Energy"

How often have you heard people say, "Everything is energy"? Perhaps you have even said it yourself. After all, isn't that what the great Einstein told us with his famous equation $E = mc^2$—all matter is just a form of energy? Well, yes, that is what he said.

However, if you happen to be one of those folks who like to believe that you, and everything around you, is just "pure energy," I suspect you are not thinking things through clearly enough—you are blindsided by a very common blindspot.

> *Quick question: If something other than energy exists in the universe, what is it and how was it formed?*

Quick response: The "something" other than energy in the universe is, obviously, *consciousness!* Right? You *know* you are conscious without a shadow of a doubt. And even if you do doubt your own consciousness, you have automatically demonstrated it—because only a creature with consciousness can doubt anything.

Now, given that consciousness exists *as a certainty,* the next question is: Is consciousness a form of energy? The answer to that is "no," for reasons I've given above (and in much greater detail in *Radical Nature* and *Radical Knowing*).

You will hear me say this many times, in different ways: Consciousness is the capacity to *know, feel,* and *be aware of* energy in any of its forms. Consciousness is the *subject* that knows any object (both physical objects made of energy and nonphysical objects, such as thoughts, beliefs, and ideas). Every experiencing subject (consciousness) is nonphysical and, therefore, cannot be any kind of physical object (energy). So, while consciousness is necessary for energy to be known, consciousness is not itself a form of energy.

That's how we can know *for sure* that there isn't only energy in the universe. The universe is *known*. And that requires consciousness. What *is known* is energy. What *knows* is consciousness.

Consciousness and energy are inseparable—they always go together *all the way down*. Like energy, consciousness always existed, so it was never "formed" in the sense of coming into being from nowhere or nothing, or from a state of reality that didn't possess some form of consciousness (or energy).

The core of my philosophy is that reality consists of *sentient energy*. In other words, energy is natively and intrinsically sentient, experiential, conscious. Energy comes with consciousness already "built in."

Blindspot: Yes, our bodies are made of energy, but, as you well know, we are not just our bodies. We also have *minds.* Therefore, we are not just energy (the ability to move and act). First and foremost, we are also *sentient* beings, capable of forming intentions, experiencing meaning, feeling possibilities, and choosing between options. This is *consciousness,* and it's very different from matter or energy.

To drive home the point: Energy is *physical*—it flows through space; consciousness is *nonphysical*—it doesn't exist in space at all.

No one has ever detected consciousness (or ever will) anywhere in space—including inside your brain. Even the most skilled neurosurgeon, working with state-of-the-art PET or fMRI scans and probes, can inspect only the fine details of your neurons and synapses, sparkling with electrochemical events. These are all physical.

So, no . . . consciousness is not at all like energy.

Energy flows through space and can be detected and observed with our senses and their technological extensions. Energy is objective.

Consciousness does not exist in space—it is *nonlocated*. It is the capacity to know, feel, and be aware of anything, including space and the objects and energy that move through space. It is subjective.

Once more, the bumper sticker: "Consciousness *knows*. Energy *flows*." Be careful not to confuse them.

Is Subtle Energy Consciousness?

What if consciousness is nonphysical energy? In Radical Knowing, *you say "consciousness does not work like a machine—it is not a form of energy, and does not exist in space." I guess you are saying energy exists only in the physical domain?*

That is what I'm saying: Energy is physical. And "physical" means anything that occupies space, anything that has extension, such as matter or fields of energy. I talk about this in some detail in both *Radical Nature* and *Radical Knowing*. To summarize, we have two options:

1. Consciousness is a form of *physical* energy.
2. Consciousness is a form of *nonphysical* energy.

That's it. There are no other options. If energy is physical, that means it occurs in space; it can be detected and measured. This is what physicists work with all the time.

If, as you suggest, we say that consciousness is nonphysical energy, then we need to explain how nonphysical energy differs from physical energy. I don't know of anyone who can explain this difference. If we say that nonphysical energy does not occur in space, is not detectable, or is not measurable, then we need to ask: How do we know it exists? And why do we call it *energy*? The word *energy* is borrowed from physics and means a capacity or force to move an object from one point in space to another point in space.

Now, this does not deny that *different kinds* of energy can exist—including *subtle* forms (e.g., ch'i or prana as identified in Eastern traditions). But if we read what the Chinese or Indian sages tell us about these forms of energy, they *are* detectable, by healers, for instance, and they do talk about such energy moving through *space.* So even subtle energy, although not detectable by Western scientific instruments, still has a field effect in space.

Therefore, in that sense, even subtle energy is a form of physical energy—it is *subtle* physical energy.

Blindspot: However, subtle energy is very different from *consciousness.* Consciousness does not occur in *any kind* of space whatsoever. Consciousness is *nonlocated,* not just nonlocal. It has no extension. It is not detectable by any kind of instrument; consciousness can be "detected" only by other consciousness.

Consciousness is a capacity for *knowing,* for *feeling,* for being *aware* of something. Energy is a capacity for exerting a force. Consciousness is what *knows* the flow or the force of energy. That's a fundamental difference.

DISEMBODIED CONSCIOUSNESS?

From reading your books and blogs, I would say you are on a mission to get scientists to understand the new paradigm. Your colleague Eric Weiss writes in fine detail about the Doctrine of the Subtle Worlds, saying: "These other worlds are not physical and they operate according to laws different from those that govern the physical world. They are, nonetheless, objectively real." Is this, then, the world of disembodied consciousness where entities such as souls and spirits hang out and where people have out-of-body experiences? If so, how does this fit with your teaching that consciousness and energy (or mind and body) can never be separated?

Eric and I both share a mission to "get scientists to understand the new paradigm" where consciousness is intrinsic to reality. And we both acknowledge the existence of *subtle energy* (e.g., ch'i, prana, mana). Subtle energy, just like gross physical energy, exists in *space.*

Blindspot: In out-of-body experiences (OBEs), consciousness does not become "disembodied," floating free of all embodiment. How could it "float"? No, in such experiences, consciousness shifts its *locus of identity* from the physiological body to some subtle body. Consciousness remains embodied. It's just a different kind of embodiment.

Consciousness needs some form of energy to *act.* Intentionality (an event in consciousness) is impotent to do anything without also being embodied in some form of energy to make things happen. Consciousness forms intentions; energy acts and carries out the intention in response to the meaning or purpose created in consciousness.

Creativity requires both intention and action. If either one is missing, creativity cannot occur. If there were only "disembodied" intention (consciousness), nothing could ever happen. And if there were only energy without intention or purpose, all action would be random or determined. We need both, and both must always go together for a real world to happen and evolve.

Consciousness and energy, intention and action, are inseparable—but also ontologically distinct. Energy exists in space; consciousness doesn't.

CONSCIOUSNESS AND ENERGY

It may be that consciousness itself has no power or energy but in some cases works along with individual power, group power, cultural power, or the power of archetypes to create certain impacts on us as individuals and as groups.

Depth Alert: This is an important insight because it raises the profoundly challenging idea that consciousness is causal—that *somehow,* something *nonphysical* causes events to happen in the physical world. This idea is challenging for two reasons: First, it flies in the face of one of the cornerstones of modern science—the law of conservation of energy (we met this earlier, when talking about the first law of thermodynamics, p. 30). How can something nonphysical (and not itself energy) produce effects in the physical world? If consciousness is causal, then one of the foundation stones of modern science is seriously undermined. (Of course, the very existence of consciousness is a profound problem for modern science.)

Second, while science *must* deny the causality of consciousness (to protect the conservation law), very clearly our own everyday experience seems to provide abundant evidence that consciousness is, indeed, causal—that consciousness, through intention and choices, *does* produce effects in the physical world. (I intend to move my fingers to type these words, and lo! my intention makes my fingers move! The big mystery is *how?*)

Here's the key issue: Clearly, certain states or qualities of consciousness (e.g., intention and volition) do *seem* to have power to produce effects in the physical world. Undoubtedly, consciousness does *seem* to be potent. But *how?* It is very tempting to assume that the potency of consciousness means it possesses some kind of energetic capacity. How else could it *do* anything? But this assumption is actually held in place by a kind of "physics envy." We assume that all causality must involve exchanges of *energy,* just as the laws of physics state. But perhaps there are other ways of understanding how consciousness can be potent without assuming that it is either energetic or causal. That's what I explore in my books.

Blindspot: In a nutshell: Reality consists of *sentient energy*—that is, energy is *intrinsically* sentient. Energy has consciousness built in right from the get-go. Consciousness and energy *always go together.* They are inseparable. They form an indissoluble unity. But they are not identical. They remain distinct aspects of reality even though they are inseparable. Remember the example using the shape and substance of a ball: You cannot separate them (they form a unity), but shape and substance are not identical. You can change the shape while the substance stays exactly the same. Clearly, if one changes and the other doesn't, they cannot be identical. Yet they remain inseparable. Analogously, the relationship between consciousness and energy is that they form an indissoluble unity, but they are not identical. Consciousness is not energy. Energy is not consciousness. Energy (in any of its myriad of forms) is *what* consciousness knows. Consciousness is always the *subject* that knows. And what it knows are the *objects* in our world.

Consciousness and energy *always* go together because consciousness is *inherent* in energy. In other words, energy has the native capacity to know, to feel, to be aware. But this ability to know, feel, be aware *is not itself a form of energy*. It is the *knowingness* inherent in energy. Therefore, consciousness is potent because it *directs the flow of energy* through the world. Or, if you prefer, energy directs itself because it is intrinsically sentient and has the ability to choose. *Sentient energy is purposeful.* This view can account for both the causality of energy exchanges and for the apparent causality of consciousness. It avoids the problem of violating the law of conservation of energy by positing consciousness *"within"* energy.

FORCES OF NATURE

Nature is often described as the forces and processes of the material world. I say that a force has no mind of its own, yet it is directed by the mind.

Yes, nature is often described as "forces and processes" in the material world. But what are these "forces" and "processes"? They can be nothing other than *energy*. And what is "material" or "matter"? It, too, is *energy*. Therefore, it follows that nature is energy.

And to be consistent, because forces are energy (the *same* energy that makes up matter), and because matter/energy is intrinsically sentient (it has a mind), logically we can conclude that *forces do have sentience.*

"*Force*" is just another term for energy. If we accept that energy is sentient, that it has a mind, then we must conclude that a force *does* have a mind of its own. The mind within a force is what directs that force. That's what *sentient energy* means.

Blindspot: Even though consciousness and energy are very different, and we risk falling into "physics envy" whenever we use energy talk to describe mind or consciousness, we can still use the dynamics of energy as *analogies* or *metaphors* for understanding aspects of consciousness. We just need to remember that metaphors are not literal. The following section offers an example.

EGO AND ENTROPY

I was thinking about the scientific concept of dissipative structures—how living organisms capture energy (order) from their environment and then export entropy (disorder or waste) as part of the process of growth and becoming more complex. This got me thinking: Our egos try to capture just what works for us and to "export" (project) what doesn't work. But, it seems, "We have a problem, Houston," because nothing can really be "exported"—we're all still one. What are your thoughts on this?

"Egoic entropy"*—now that's a tasty nugget for thought. Great insight. It makes sense that the ego tries to organize ("control") the world by capturing what "works" (organized energy), and that it would try to export, through projection, what doesn't work—disorder (egoic entropy). And then the clincher: The ego has an *Apollo 13*–size problem because, ulti-

---

*"Entropy" is a scientific term for the innate tendency of complex systems to increase disorder. In simple terms: left to itself, a complex system (your bedroom closet, for instance) will automatically become more and more disorganized—*unless some energy is used to input or restore order.*

mately, since it exists in an interconnected and unified *uni-verse,* there is nowhere to actually get rid of the entropy.

However, if we pursue this line of thinking—the "thermodynamics of the ego"—we would have to conclude that we live in a world where egoic entropy, the psyche's shadow, *necessarily* accumulates in consciousness and *cannot be dissipated.* The most an ego can do is project, or export, its shadow onto some other ego or thing. So, we would end up living in a world where people project their shadows willy-nilly like hot potatoes, all the while *increasing* egoic entropy in the world. Sound familiar?

Blindspot: So, what's the solution? Is there a solution? Well, of course. Standard physical thermodynamics and the science of complex systems completely overlook a crucial factor in evolution that *counteracts* entropy. And this factor is none other than *consciousness* itself—more specifically, the intrinsic ability of consciousness to make *choices.*

Choice is the injection of order into otherwise random processes.

The *creativity* of consciousness through choice counteracts entropy, both in the physical universe and in the inner cosmos of the psyche. Choice neutralizes egoic entropy by increasing order. Choice is the "lever" or "catalyst" that leverages the shadow into the light of awareness.

However, entropy is never completely eliminated by choice. Instead, through choice, consciousness *reorganizes* the system so that what was "shadow" now *works with*, not against, the evolution and integrity of the system. It's a never-ending process—and that's how evolution occurs.

10

Healing

"Healers Use the Energy of Consciousness"

Everything that exists, including the human body, consists of *sentient* energy—energy that intrinsically *feels*. In other words, despite what modern science tells us, energy is not "dead"; it is "alive" with innate awareness and purpose.

Not only is energy sentient, but all forms of energy also vibrate— from high-frequency light waves to lower frequencies in the form of matter. Our bodies are made of different forms of energy and matter with different frequencies. For example, higher-frequency electromagnetic waves emanate from our brains and hearts, while lower-frequency matter/energy forms our blood, flesh, and bones.

Our state of health depends on how the various frequencies of our body resonate together. Think of the body like a symphony of musical notes and chords, orchestrated by consciousness as the conductor. When our frequencies are in balance, we experience the "music of health," and when our energies fall out of balance, we experience the discord of illness. Resonance and harmony are indicators of a healthy living system.

Not only do the foods we eat and the exercise we take affect the state of our bodies, but our thoughts and emotions also affect the energy frequencies associated with different organs—including the brain, heart, lungs, and liver. Every thought and emotion comes with its own "signature vibration" that shows up *somewhere* in our bodies.

Most, if not all, illnesses occur because some thought, emotion, or bodily action produces discord among our energy frequencies. Unfortunately, these "energy knots" get stored in our bodies, deep below the threshold of consciousness. *Every illness is a symptom of unconsciousness.* It follows, then, that healing reverses this process by shining the light of awareness onto unconscious energy knots. That's what *conscious healing* means. You become the "conductor" orchestrating the symphony of your own health and well-being.

Every moment, you are having an experience—and you don't have to do anything to make that happen. *Experience happens automatically.* And then you immediately *interpret* your experience. You have a *thought* about it, usually in the form of self-talk or a story. And then, like everyone else, most of the time you turn "important" thoughts into *beliefs.* That's often when trouble begins—including illness.

This process—from experience to interpretation to belief—starts in early childhood and continues throughout our lives, and it happens mostly unconsciously. That's how we form the mental "programs" that shape—and block—the flows of energy through our system. As we grow up, these mental programs solidify and block the associated energy circuits in our body and brain. Inevitably, later in life we continue to project these deeply ingrained mental habits and energy patterns onto others, especially in our intimate relationships. Whenever we feel ignored by our partner or friends, or our needs are not met, we embellish our story that no one understands or cares about us. We literally relive the same feelings of hurt, sadness, confusion, and self-doubt we experienced in childhood. *Our stories disrupt the natural harmony of our bodies, leading to emotional and physiological disease.*

So, what do we do? Well, if we turn to conventional medicine, we use some kind of physical intervention to restore balance to the body, or we might use some form of alternative medicine to readjust the flows of energy through our system. In either case, we deal only with the physical symptoms. If the root cause—our beliefs and mental programs—are left unaddressed, the illness will either persist or return (perhaps in some other form) to snare our attention over and over.

Blindspot: Working only with the mechanisms of energy, without the intentional powers of consciousness, we cannot bring about healing. Manipulating symptoms can, at best, give some temporary relief. Permanent healing, however, requires getting at the underlying causes, rooted in the complex of energy knots held in place by dysfunctional thoughts, emotions, and physical habits. These causes are always psychosomatic in nature (or, to be more precise, *psycho-somatic-spiritual*). The causes of both illness and healing involve the intimate and ever-present relationship between mind, body, and spirit, between consciousness and energy.

Energy, Subtle Energy, and Consciousness

> *I am taking a class called Energy Models of Healing. Would you define* energy *and* subtle energy *differently? I am interested in your perspective.*

Yes, there is a difference. *Energy* is what physicists work with. It exists in physical space and is the essence of matter, expressed in $E = mc^2$. Energy is the *causal factor* responsible for events in *space*.

Subtle energy (e.g., prana, ch'i, ki) involves the idea (or cosmology) of a "continuum ontology" consisting of multiple levels of reality, as portrayed in one form or another in just about every culture in every age, and generally known as the Great Chain of Being—referring to, for example, gradations between Matter, Mind, Soul, and Spirit.

From the perspective of a continuum ontology, each level has both spatial (objective) and nonspatial (subjective) aspects. In levels above Matter (where the energy of physics exists), the spatial-objective causal factor can be called *subtle energy*. It is "subtle" because it is not detectable by instruments made of matter (e.g., Geiger counters, telescopes, electron microscopes). It is "energy" because it is a causal factor responsible for events happening in subtle space.

For example, in dreams, we experience or observe both *spatial* and *nonspatial* events. In our dreams, characters and objects move about in "dream space" (much more fluidly, of course, than in familiar physical or waking space). These events involve exchanges or interactions of subtle energy—the *objective* events in dream space. However, in dreams, we also experience ourselves as *subjective agents,* as the observing witness or creator of events in the dream. This agent or witness is not one of the objects in the dream and is not locatable in the dream space. It is the *subject experiencing* the dream.

At every level—from Matter through to Spirit—causality comes in two forms: *energetic,* in which events in space are caused by other events in space, and *mental,* in which events are caused by *intention* and *choice.* Energetic events at every level are *mechanistic,* involving transfers of energy from one point in space to some other point in space. Mental events at every level operate through *meaning,* involving an "experienced fit" between the self and not-self, achieved through *intention* and *choice.*

Language is somewhat limiting and confusing here—especially my use of the term *mental.* In this model, "mental" does not simply refer to what happens on the level of Mind (capital "M"). It refers to *any* non-spatial, nonobjective event sourced in a subject's consciousness, or mind (lowercase "m").* Ideally, we need an equivalent adjectival form ("X") of the noun *consciousness:* as "mental" is to "mind," "X" is to "consciousness." Alternatives such as *spiritual* or *soulful* or even *psychic* won't do because they come loaded with other associations. And if we coin a new term, such as *consciousal* or *consciousnessal,* it sounds too weird and cumbersome. Of the current options, *mental* and *psychic* are most common—but, as I said, they have other, potentially confusing meanings. We could, instead, use *subjective,* which I often do. Or, shifting focus slightly, we could refer to nonspatial, nonphysical causality as *volitional,* caused by consciousness, as distinct from *deterministic,* caused by energy.

---

*"Mind" (capital "M") refers to a specific level in the Great Chain of Being (above Matter and below Soul); "mind" (small "m") refers to awareness, mental activity, or subjectivity at *any* level. All levels have both physical and mental aspects. Another way to understand the difference is to think of "mind" as equivalent to *consciousness,* whereas "Mind" is a level of being dominated by intellect or abstract thought.

And so, I would rephrase the paragraph above:

At every level—from Matter through to Spirit—causality comes in two forms: **energetic,** in which events in space are caused by other events in space, and **volitional,** in which events are caused by *intention* and *choice.* Energetic events at every level are *mechanistic,* involving transfers of energy from one point in space to some other point in space. Volitional events at every level operate through *meaning,* involving an "experienced fit" between the self and not-self, achieved through *intention* and *choice.*

Blindspot: Just as energy always comes with consciousness—it is *sentient energy*—subtle energy also always comes with consciousness; it, too, is a form of sentient energy—*sentient* subtle energy. And just as consciousness is not a form of energy, neither is it a form of subtle energy. A common confusion in New Age thinking is the notion that because subtle energy transcends yet acts on (physical) energy, it is consciousness. While it is true that consciousness also transcends yet directs energy, it is invalid to conclude that therefore subtle energy is equivalent to consciousness.

The logical error takes this form:

Premise 1: A does not equal B.
Premise 2: C does not equal B.
Conclusion: Therefore A equals C.

Just because a horse is not a human and a hare is not a human, it does not follow that a horse is a hare.

So, while (1) consciousness is not energy and (2) subtle energy is not (physical) energy, it does not follow that consciousness is a form of subtle energy.

Both energy and subtle energy are *sentient.* But in neither case is the sentience a form of energy. In both cases, sentience, or consciousness, is the ability of energy, both physical and subtle, to feel, to know, and to purposefully direct itself. Energy in all its forms, at every level of the continuum ontology, is intrinsically sentient. It has the ability or capacity to be aware, to feel, to know, and to make choices. But this ability is not itself any form of energy.

This applies up and down the Great Chain of Being.

Okay, so now let's look more closely at how consciousness plays a role in illness and healing.

CONSCIOUS HEALING

From my work as a philosopher of consciousness and the mind-body connection, I understand the role of consciousness in healing as follows:

1. As a result of traumatic life experiences (possibly involving past lives), we suppress the pain, fear, anger, and so forth, as well as the thoughts and beliefs we have attached to some emotion or trauma.

2. These suppressed emotions (and "thought forms") get stored in our bodies—literally in our cells, possibly affecting our DNA— where they form "blockages" to the healthy flow of energy, both electromagnetic and subtle, through our bodies. Blocked energy results in ill health.

3. *These energetic blockages are deeply unconscious* and tend to run (and sometimes ruin) our lives.

4. However, we can focus our attention and awareness on these energy knots in our bodies (emotional) and on our mental programs (psychological)—effectively shining the light of consciousness onto previously dark and hidden shadows.

5. Once energy blocks are illuminated by consciousness, the simple act of awareness dissolves the embodied emotional knots, freeing the blocked energy to flow again. This free flow of energy is experienced as (and, in fact, *is*) healing. Healing, or unblocking

energy flows, occurs when we bring previously unconscious and blocked energy knots into conscious awareness.

6. "Healing," therefore, is not a process of transforming energy into consciousness. Energy remains energy, and consciousness remains consciousness. However, what does shift is our *level of awareness* of the state and flux of energy in our bodies. *We become conscious of what was previously unconscious.* There's a "before" and "after": Before, people are *unconscious* of their energy and its blockages. After, they become *conscious* of their energy, and this act of consciousness unblocks the energy to flow again more freely and naturally.

Intentions and Energy Healing

You talk about how energy has the ability to feel and direct itself. This brought to mind the teachings of the medieval physician Paracelsus. In one of his writings, he talks about how we can use energy or thought forms mindfully to initiate healing. Does that mean we choose, even unconsciously, to work with energies that resonate with our own thoughts?

When I say "energy can feel," I mean energy is sentient; it has the capacity to feel its way through the world. And that means *energy has consciousness.* But there is more to energy than its consciousness. Energy is also *physical;* it exists and moves in space—the only kind of energy recognized by science. Science denies that energy also has consciousness and can *feel* as well as move through space.

In contrast, the philosophy of panpsychism tells us that energy possesses an innate and natural ability to feel and direct itself with purpose. In other words, energy is not "dead" and insentient, as modern scientists generally assume.

Blindspot: When you talk about energy resonating with our thoughts (or "thought forms"), I suspect you may be making a basic, though very common, error—one I've been trying to draw attention to in this book.

Energies can resonate only with other energies. They cannot resonate with thoughts, intentions, purposes, or meanings. Remember, "resonate" is part of energy talk—the idea comes from physics and refers to vibrations, which are *movements in space* (i.e., they are *physical*). But as events in consciousness, thoughts are not physical—like every other form or content in consciousness, thoughts are nonphysical.

When we use intention for the purpose of healing, the intention expressed by our consciousness (embodied in our own energy) *shares the meaning* "healing" with the consciousness embodied in the energy of the patient. When that happens, intentional healing can, and does, occur.

In general, our intentions are constantly affecting and directing the energy swirling all around us—both within our own bodies and elsewhere throughout the world (ultimately, throughout the cosmos). Remember, though, *all* sentient beings express intentions that affect the flow and directions of energy. Therefore, the world is awash with all kinds of aligned and interfering intentions affecting the behavior of energy everywhere—including in our own bodies and in the bodies of others. However, because the energy in our own bodies is self-organizing (formed into hierarchies of subatomic particles, atoms, molecules, cells, etc., where all the levels up and down the hierarchy are intimately connected to form a *unified* organism), our own intentions have a much greater effect on our own bodies than the complex of intentions "swirling" around us. In short, because of the greater intimacy* between our own intentions and our own bodies, our own intentions have a more direct impact on the energies flowing through our own bodies—more potent than the intentions impinging on us from other sentient beings. But other intentions do affect us, nonetheless. It's a matter of degree.

Carl Jung referred to this universal complex of intentions as the *collective unconscious,* which constantly informs and affects our individual

---

*See below for more on the role of intimacy in healing.

minds and bodies. Most of the time, however, these effects remain unconscious—we are not aware of them in waking consciousness. Often, these influences show up in dreams or art or other symbols, and then we can become somewhat more conscious of them. Another way to become conscious of these unconscious influences, of course, is through meditation or psychotherapy.

How Does Intentional Healing Work?

A couple of years ago, I gave a lecture in which I explained why "energy healing" is often really "intentional healing." I pointed out that reported cases of instantaneous healing at a distance cannot involve exchanges of energy because it takes time for energy to travel through space. Therefore, something else must be the agent of healing. Consciousness or intention is the most likely candidate. Picking up on my perspective, a woman from the audience then asked:

> *If every sentient being is choosing at every moment (i.e., expressing an intention), how does a healer's intention "get through" to a specific recipient amid the "blooming, buzzing confusion" of all the intentions swirling around the cosmos? In other words, how could the intention of a healer in San Francisco happen to zoom in on a single individual in, say, Sydney, Australia?*

I responded: When a healer expresses an intention, it can potentially contribute to the restoration of harmony and wholeness anywhere in the world because consciousness is not confined in space. This, of course, includes the cells in the recipient's body in Sydney.

Then the question becomes: When the healer's intention is "directed" to a specific person, how does that person's cells "know" to respond?

Blindspot: It's a question of *intimacy*. Effective focused healing depends on the quality of relationship, or intimacy, between healer and healee.

The closer or more intimate the relationship, the more likely the healing will be effective. By "intimacy," I mean greater shared or common awareness, love, caring, and respect for each other.

In some cases, the recipient may not even be aware of the healer or the intentional healing. Even so, distant healing can be effective because the healer's awareness, intention, or consciousness is sufficiently inclusive to create a deep and intimate connection with the healee, or at least with the cells in the recipient's body—even without the recipient's knowledge.

Healing is all about the quality or degree of connection.

As counterintuitive as it sounds, in some extreme circumstances, intimacy might be the result of trauma or even abusive relationships. It depends on the extent and degree of shared experience. For example, the relationship between a master and slave, or abuser and abused, can be intimate—even though it is pathological for both parties. In such cases, when people are strongly bound in relationship, even pathological, the connections between them can be strong and deep and, paradoxically, could form the foundation for effective "intentional healing," if either party were so inclined.

Intentional healing, then, works most effectively when the relationship between healer and healee is deeply intimate.

INTIMACY AND CAUSALITY

If the causal exchange among organisms is purely physical (and spatial), does that mean that each individual consciousness is separated from having direct contact with all others? That is, can we communicate only through a physical medium?

I don't think causality is ever just physical or just volitional. Both always occur together. Sentience never exists without energy, and vice versa—they form an inseparable unity: *sentient energy.* Nevertheless, it is meaningful to make a *conceptual distinction* between the two terms, or aspects, of the unity.

Similarly, energetic and volitional causality always occur together, in different proportions, depending on the grade of the entities involved; likewise, it is useful to make a conceptual distinction between the two forms of causality.

Whenever anything happens, it involves some transfer of energy through space (mechanism) and simultaneously some degree of volitional causality (e.g., nonspatial sharing of meaning). An interesting exception to this could be an event involving quantum nonlocality, in which no energy is exchanged through space. However, it is possible that while no physical ("gross") energy is transferred through space, in quantum nonlocal events it is possible that transfers of subtle energy could be involved. In any case, and in every case, some volitional causation is involved—unless we question the whole notion of causality and allow for true synchronistic effects.

Blindspot: Consciousness is never "separated" (if this means *spatial* separation) from one being to another. Throughout the universe, all sentient beings are constantly sharing meaning, although the degree, or intensity, of sharing depends on the level of *intimacy* between the sentient beings ("intimacy" being determined by the history or evolution of the components in any sentient system). For example, the molecules and cells in my body share meaning much more intimately and intensely than my cells do with your cells or molecules. That's why it is much easier for me (my mind and body) to heal *me* than it is for me to heal *you*.

Healing involves both exchanges of energy between cells (energetic causality) *and* sharing of meaning between cells (volitional causality). In so-called distant healing, however, in which nonlocal effects are involved, no energy is exchanged between the healer and healee. Because consciousness does not exist in space, the distance between healer and healee makes no difference whatsoever to the efficacy of the healing intention. However, once the meaning is "received" (more accurately, *experienced*) in the cells of the healee and begins to redirect the flow of energy in the recipient's cells, both energetic and volitional causality are in play. That's why intentional, or volitional, healing can produce physical effects in bodies separated by great distances.

Consciousness Is Not the "Vibes"

When talking about "energy healing," you say that consciousness does not "travel" because it does not exist in "space." I agree. But you fall short of saying that consciousness is All That Is. *Doesn't healing happen when we bring another into our field of conscious awareness as if they are part of us?*

If so, then healing is not about meaning—which implies conscious intention or participation. I think intention is very important. But I also feel that someone like Jesus cured without any intention or meaning. He was just vibrating so high that people's energy field changed frequency. I have met teachers like this. They are so high-frequency that they alter reality for others.

You have made some very interesting points here. First, while I acknowledge that the idea "consciousness is all" is a widely held belief, I do not agree with it. I hold that *both* consciousness and energy are real and that they always go together. Consciousness is the ability to *know* (to be aware) and to *choose* (to create intentions). It is not enough just to "know" or to have "intentions." We also need to *act* in order to manifest or realize intentions (this applies to God, the Creative Ultimate, too). And *action* is energy. Without action, or energy, *nothing would ever happen,* despite the best intentions.

So we (the universe) need both. We need consciousness to *know* and to *choose,* and we need the embodiment of energy to *make things happen.*

I invite everyone to pay closer attention to language to see if the words we use actually express what we wish to communicate. For example, you talk of healing as bringing others into our "field of conscious awareness as if they are part of us." While I agree with the general idea, I think using the word *field* is misleading. Fields exist in and are spread out through space. Fields are made of energy, not consciousness. Consciousness is what *knows* (or is *aware of*) fields of energy, and consciousness chooses to direct the flow of energy through the field.

When you talk of healing as "fields" or "vibrations," you are using "energy talk," appropriate for physics, but not for consciousness. Consciousness doesn't "vibrate" because in order to vibrate something needs to exist in space—like a field. Vibrations are movements in space. But consciousness does not exist in space. It is *nonlocated*.

Your point about Jesus is interesting. Yes, it is quite plausible that Jesus healed, at least sometimes, without any specific intention—because, as you say, "he was just vibrating so high that people's energy field changed frequency." That, indeed, would be a good example of "energy healing"—in which Jesus's body (his subtle energy) was vibrating at a high frequency.

However, keep in mind: It is quite likely that the frequency level of a person's body responds to the state of consciousness of that person, and even if energy healing through vibrational resonance happens, it would not account for *instantaneous distant healing*—which is what I'm discussing. I do think that the effective component in distant healing is *meaning* (i.e., participatory shared experience). I will say more about this below.

Distant healing, sometimes referred to as nonlocal healing, cannot be explained as a transmission of energy—no matter how high the vibration. My colleague Dr. Larry Dossey has made the same point: When distant healing is involved, *something else is going on* besides energy exchanges.

And that "something else," I'm saying, is *consciousness*. It's a sharing of *meaning*, not a *mechanism* (transmission of energy through space).

Blindspot: When you say you have met people with "high frequency" or "high vibration," you are using energy talk. This is fine if you are referring to their *bodies* or *energy*. But if you use the same language to refer to a person's *consciousness*, that's "physics envy." You would be using the language of physics to talk about something that is not physical.

I suspect what you really mean is that you have met people whose *presence* is charismatic, peaceful, and healing. I have, too. Given a higher state of consciousness, it is quite possible that their *bodies* also emanate or radiate some kind of higher vibrational energy. But let's not confuse higher vibrations of energy (bodies) with higher states of consciousness. When distant healing occurs instantaneously, we know that nothing "vibrational" is responsible because the fastest anything can travel through space is the speed of light. But, as I have explained, distance is irrelevant to consciousness. People separated by continents (even by galaxies) could instantly participate in sharing the same meaning, such as "heal" or "be whole."

Only *physical* objects (energy) vibrate, and consciousness is not a physical object. I'm inviting us to get beyond the "physics envy" of energy talk and instead use the already very rich vocabulary we have for "mind talk." I know this is a stretch for some (perhaps many) people—our culture has so conditioned us to treat the physical world as the only real world. As a result, people who know that consciousness is real and potent look for ways to talk about it that "sound" scientific, and they default to energy talk. But my point is *we don't have to default to energy talk*. We can give up "physics envy" and instead honor consciousness for what it is—a reality beyond physics.

No amount of vibrations can account for the fact that sentient beings exist who *know* and can *choose*. By themselves, vibrations or frequencies are just measures of physical movements. But consciousness is not physical and cannot be measured. It has a completely different kind of existence from that of objects that exist in space—no matter how high they vibrate. Consciousness is the *subject* that knows and chooses—*subjectivity* is the key characteristic of consciousness.

What's Up with Energy Healing?

I'm a Reiki energy healer, and I've read where you say consciousness and matter always go together. If what you say is true, then I'm wondering how it is possible to send healing energy to another person in a distant place. As far as I know, nothing material passes between people in a healing session.

You are quite right: Nothing material or physical travels through space in cases of distant healing—not even *energy*. (Remember, matter is just a form of energy.)

What is often called *energy healing,* including Reiki, is, I think, more accurately called *consciousness healing* or *intentional healing*—and it works through *shared meaning.*

All energy moves through space. Therefore, according to relativity theory, there cannot be any instantaneous transmission of energy from one part of space (the healer) to some other part of space (the healee). Yet, the literature is full of examples of so-called instantaneous nonlocal healing—in which prayer or intention is correlated with apparently spontaneous and instant healing, even across great distances, for example from the U.S. to Europe or Australia, or vice versa.

Blindspot: When studied under scientific conditions, it is clear that the healing event took place faster than energy moving at the speed of light (hence nonlocal healing). And because energy cannot move faster than light, it follows that no energy could be traveling between healer and healee to account for the healing.

Something else must be going on. And, as I say, that "something else" is *consciousness.* Not energy.

Consciousness does not exist in space and therefore is not constrained by distances (it is not even nonlocal; it is *nonlocated*). It doesn't take consciousness any time to travel from A to B because consciousness doesn't travel—period. It is not in space.

What happens in healing, I suggest, is that healer and healee share, or participate in, the *same meaning:* "heal," or "be whole," or "thy will be done," or "divine perfection," or "let it be," or whatever the intention is. While the healer's intention may be *conscious,* the healee may participate *unconsciously*. He or she may not even know that healing is intended for him or her.

Here's one way of thinking about what may be happening: The consciousness of the healer, always associated with the energy, or body, of the healer, forms an intention or clarifies a meaning, in this case, *healing*. This intention or meaning does not travel through space, and therefore it takes zero time for the consciousness of the healee to participate in sharing the meaning "healing."

The moment the clarity of the healing intention is expressed by the healer, the healee responds to the new constellation of meaning in his or her body. Healing begins. No energy has been transferred from healer to healee; they simply participate in sharing the same meaning. And clarity of meaning, I propose, is how healing works.

What do I mean by "meaning"? It is the *experienced* fit between self and other or between self and environment. If something or someone doesn't fit in, it's a "misfit," and that's another way of describing illness or dysfunction. On the other hand, when we experience fitting in—and this applies to the relationship between our body and our cells, and between our bodies and our environment—we realign with the larger intelligence and processes of nature all the way down.

And that, I think, is how healing happens. It is the restoration of natural balance and integration between various elements or parts of the universe. It happens through meaning shared in consciousness, not through exchanges of energy. In other words, healing happens through *meaning*, not through *mechanism*.

Circles of Meaning

We all belong to circles-within-circles of meaning—from our own bodies all the way to the cosmos as a whole (see figure 10.1 on p. 118).

The important question for most of us is whether or to what degree we *feel* or *experience* fitting in to our circles. If we don't feel we fit in, or belong, our life lacks meaning. To the extent we experience fitting in or belonging to our circles, our life has meaning. The

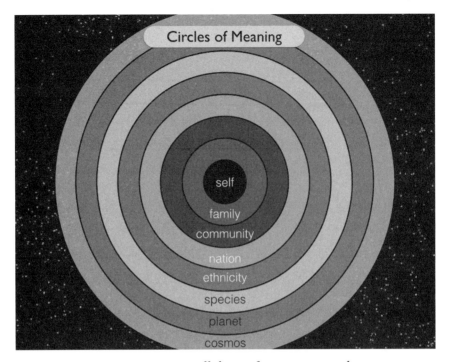

Figure 10.1. How well do you fit in to your circles?
Name your own circles, if you prefer.

experience of fitting in at every level is a useful way to think about enlightenment.

I want to end this chapter by going a little deeper into this topic of energy healing—or, more accurately, *intentional* healing—because the topic is fraught with confusion and misunderstanding, both within the mainstream scientific-medical establishment and within the alternative healing community.

In the following pages, then, I will summarize a dialogue with one of my more astute students, Dawn Carter, and will expand on some key points already covered in this chapter. I think intentional healing is such an important—and seriously misunderstood—phenomenon that it is worth drilling down to some of the finer details to clarify what's likely going on.

If you happen to be allergic to philosophical thinking, you might want to skip over this section and go straight to the next chapter. I've included this discussion precisely because it does go deeper.

INTENTIONAL HEALING

Dawn: I tried the best I could to explain distant consciousness healing to my partners, but I met strong resistance (as I expected). How would I test the reality of this type of healing? I've met people who claim they can heal a burn this way, but none will put it to a real test. If they really could do that, it would be a huge *finding, with the potential to change the world. But they refuse to do this under controlled conditions, and in cases where they tried, they failed (no one has won skeptic James Randi's million-dollar dare).*

I mentioned the placebo effect, and my friends said that works because your own consciousness, thoughts, and neural pathways create the changes in your body. And, to them, this is very different *from affecting someone else's consciousness and neural pathways.*

Another objection: If you have the ability to affect someone's consciousness in such a way that it heals that person, then you would also be able to "read their mind" or, at the very least, be able to experience that they are conscious. But how would you test this?

Do you know any indigenous cultures that did distant healing? If so, which ones? This is the only *part of your worldview I don't agree with; it's the only thing that stands out as illogical. Not that we have to agree, but I really want to explore it openly. On some level, I* want *this form of healing to be true, but I just can't see it based on the evidence to the contrary and no evidence of this from our ancestors.*

CdeQ: You ask which indigenous cultures have practiced this. In my understanding (though not in their terminology), indigenous shamanic healing is essentially *intentional* healing, not "energy" healing, as many Western New Agers interpret it. I think that's the purpose and function of *rituals.* They prepare the mind for alternative states of consciousness that facilitate "sharing meaning," and this allows and enhances the healing process. All intentional healing is "distant" healing in the sense that it involves consciousness, and consciousness does not operate through space. Therefore, distance—near or far—is irrelevant. This applies whether the healing takes place within one's own body or in someone else's body.

I understand why someone could accept that consciousness can be a potent healing (or destructive) influence on the cells of one's own body but not that same kind of influence could happen "at a distance." However, my point is that *all* intentional healing is distant (nonphysical) healing—whether it's just a couple of millimeters away or half a world away. It makes no difference whatsoever. How could it?

The "placebo effect" is no less mysterious than distant healing: How does your mind influence or affect your own body? This is another version of the famous "hard problem" discussed over and over in modern philosophy and attempts to solve the mind-body relationship. If you think of your mind in terms of "energy talk," as if some "force" travels from your mind to the matter of your cells, then that just does not fit what we know about the nature of consciousness—it's not made of energy. *Consciousness is what knows or feels and purposefully directs (sentient) energy from within.*

In the panpsychist model, the consciousness of an organism (its "dominant monad") expresses the intention "be healed" or simply "heal," and the consciousness of the recipient cells shares or participates in this meaning, and then those cells *purposefully* direct their energy to move in ways that restore physiological balance to the organism or some part of the organism. Here's the crucial point: *It makes no difference whatsoever where those cells are located.* They could be in your own body or in the body of some other organism. However, as we will see below, the degree of intimacy between healer and healee can and does affect the *potency,* not the *possibility,* of healing.

Blindspot: The mistake I think your friends (and perhaps you) make when doubting or rejecting distant healing is that you are probably still defaulting to "energy talk" and "energy think"—as if some force needs to travel through space for the healing to occur.

I think it's right to assume that if consciousness can heal "at a distance," in someone else's body, then we should be able to know if someone else was conscious. That is the *only* way to solve the infamous "problem of other minds"—the only way to detect consciousness is through *consciousness*. No physical test exists for detecting the presence (or absence) of consciousness. However, the problem of other minds is a problem only if we accept the Cartesian notion of separate, isolated egoic minds that have to exchange some signal in order to communicate with each other. However, from the perspective of *intersubjectivity,* we are constantly creating each other, and therefore we are in part constituted by each other (see *Radical Knowing*). In other words, part of who I am is part of who you are, and *that's* how I can know that you are a sentient being.

I wonder why you think it is "illogical" for healing to occur at a distance. Why would your intention be confined to what happens in your body? Remember: *Consciousness is nonlocated.* It doesn't exist in space at all. Why, then, should distance be a limiting factor? The real question, it seems to me, is *why doesn't healing occur all over the world* (indeed throughout the universe) when someone expresses an intention for healing? The answer, I think, is that a multitude of other counter intentions, expressed by self-centered egoic minds (i.e., minds focused on their own satisfaction), cancel or block each other out. And so healing gets lost in a blizzard of conflicting intentions.

The point you raise about the placebo effect is valid and worth exploring. However, I think process metaphysics helps us understand why intentional healing is not limited to the relationship between one's own mind and body.

When we view the world in terms of *process,* instead of *substance,* we can see that the processes in your body (in your cells and organs) share a level of *intimacy* ("internal relatedness") with your host organism that they do not have with the cells of other bodies. Yes, it is easier to heal oneself with one's own intention than it is to heal another—but the latter is by no means impossible. Your relationship with events happening in your own mind-body is much more intimate than it is with events in someone else's. That's why it is easier (*much* easier) for you to lift *your own* arm through the power of intention than it is to induce a psychokinetic effect and move someone else's arm solely through the power of your mind. But this is a consequence of the status of *internal relations* and *shared history* ("intimacy") and not an effect of distance.

The details of this explanation require an understanding of Whitehead's process metaphysics. Too much to go into here. But I hope you get a glimmer of the direction in which the solution lies.

Bottom line: *Intentional healing works because of intimacy between those involved.*

INTIMATE HEALING

Dawn: *My partner and I had a lovely conversation tonight regarding healing. Having read your response, it turns out now that he doesn't reject the possibility of distant healing but was missing some crucial information, which you provided.*

I'll give you an outline of our conclusions, followed by more questions.

The information you sent regarding intimacy was very useful. It explains why we have not seen very many examples of healing working. Based on what you have said about distant healing, here's what we have come up with:

> ### Conclusion 1: Shared meaning requires intimacy, and the lack of intimacy feels like distance.

You explained how the relationship *(the level of* intimacy*) between body and mind makes the placebo effect work. The placebo effect has even been demonstrated in rats. It makes sense that our bodies would have a deeply intimate relationship with our own* *minds, and therefore our minds are able to effect huge changes in our bodies. The placebo effect is a proven phenomenon.*

If we take that same idea and apply it to the Australian aborigines' ability to "know" when a tribe or family member died hundreds of miles away, but inability to notice a boy dead in the backyard in an urban setting, then we see that the level of intimacy has a direct effect on the body's ability to "know" and translate that into anything meaningful (shared meaning).

Tribal people really had no need for a long-distance method of healing. They were very intimate with each other, and they shared meaning through their rituals. Hence the shaman could heal his people but would not be as successful in healing someone outside the tribe.

So, again based on your insights, our conclusion here is that what we are calling distant *healing is actually* intimacy *healing expressed through shared meaning. Without intimacy, shared meaning does not exist; therefore, there is little or no healing effect.*

How much intimacy do you think typically transpires between a Reiki healer and her patient? Probably not much; and even if some positive effects do happen, whose consciousness created the effects—the healer's consciousness or the placebo effect of the patient's own mind?

Conclusion 2: Intention must be followed by, or enriched with, shared meaning, which requires intimacy.

Conclusion 3: A physical response to the shared meaning has to happen in order for change to happen (healing).

In order for intention to be received and incorporated, a catalyst for change is needed—shared meaning through consciousness. And once the shared meaning is understood or felt, it paves the way for an appropriate physical response to follow—and there has to be a physical response or nothing will change. Where consciousness knows, energy flows. Body follows mind.

Conclusion 4:
Intention and shared meaning are very fragile.

It is important to note the fragile nature of intention and shared meaning, more so in today's society, but also in tribal societies so sadly eradicated. It doesn't take much to squash it into little tiny bits and pieces.

The following list compares the differences between today's Western view of healing and "yesterday's" indigenous views (adapted from Honoring the Medicine: The Essential Guide to Native American Healing, *by Kenneth "Bear Hawk" Cohen).*

WESTERN MEDICINE	INDIGENOUS MEDICINE
• *Focuses on pathology and curing disease.*	• *Focuses on health and healing the person and community.*
• *Investigates disease with a "divide-and-conquer strategy," looking for a microscopic cause.*	• *Practices teleological medicine: "What can the disease teach the patient? Is there a message or story in the disease?"*
• *Is reductionistic: Diseases are biological, and treatment should produce measurable outcomes.*	• *Regards maladies as complex: Diseases do not have a simple explanation, and outcomes are not always measurable.*
• *Considers the intellect as primary. Medical practice is based on scientific theory.*	• *Looks at the "big picture"— the causes and effects of disease in the physical, emotional, environmental, social, and spiritual realms.*

- *Fosters dependence on medication, technology, and other* physical *or mechanistic solutions.*

- *Focuses the health history on the patient and family: "Did your mother have cancer?"*

- *Believes intervention should result in the rapid cure or management of disease.*

- *Emphasizes adversarial medicine: "How can I destroy the disease?"*

- *Regards the physician as an authority.*

- *Considers intuition as primary. Healing is based on spiritual truths learned from nature, elders, and spiritual vision.*

- *Includes the environment in the health history: "Are the salmon in your rivers ill?"*

- *Empowers patients with confidence and awareness, and provides tools to help them take charge of their own health.*

- *Considers patience to be paramount. Healing occurs when the time is right.*

- *Views the healer as a health counselor and advisor.*

Following your insights, the bottom line for us is that distant healing cannot happen without intimacy. And the farther away you get from intimacy between your own mind and body, the less likely you will be able to effect a change in anyone else's mind or body. In line with your teaching, I'd also say that "distance" is energy talk *and "intimacy" is* consciousness talk. *So, the better phrase (in my mind) is "intimacy healing" rather than "distant healing." Distance doesn't play a role in consciousness healing.*

CdeQ: Thanks for your very thoughtful response. I see you really do "get" my views on intentional healing. Even though consciousness is nonlocated (not affected by distance), I still think the phrase "distance" or "distant" healing is valid. You are quite right, it is not that consciousness works *through* distance (through space), but that the *physical* effects of the healing do occur at a real distance from the source of the intentional healing. In fact, it's *because* of this phenomenon ("healing at a distance") that we know the healing is not primarily "energetic" but occurs through a sharing of meaning and intention in consciousness.

Nevertheless, of course, energy is involved, too. That's what is affected or changed by the intention and shared meaning in consciousness. As the meaning changes (from "illness" to "healing") within the cells of the recipient,* that shift in intention and meaning *purposefully redirects* the matter/energy of the recipient's cells in ways that bring about healing. What happens, I suggest, is that the meaning "healing," sourced in the healer's nonlocated intention, is instantaneously *felt* or *experienced* by the consciousness in the cells of the recipient. This shift in meaning then redirects the energy of the host's cells to move in ways that restore physiological and metabolic balance to bring about an increase in health and well-being.

Blindspot: The point to remember, though, is that the healing does not take place because *energy* has been *transmitted* from one person to another. Nothing has been "transmitted." Nothing has traveled through space, which is the only way energy can work. As I keep emphasizing, distant healing is not even nonlocal, it is *nonlocated*—it doesn't occur in or through space at all.

Of course, when the healing is physiological, the effect does take place in someone's body, which is located in space. Typically, we know that healing has occurred by monitoring its *physical* effects. Healing can also be predominantly *psychological* or *emotional,* restoring balance in soul or spirit, in which case there would be no measur-

---

*Just to be clear: The suggestion that cells share meaning and, based on that, redirect their energy does not imply that cells have any *cognitive* understanding. That would require sophisticated symbolic language, and we have no reason to suspect that cells have that level of sophistication. However, every sentient organism has an innate ability to *feel,* and that is how cells share meaning: they *feel it*—they intersubjectively *experience the experience* of the healer's intentions.

able effects or changes to test according to the methods of standard science.*

Like everything else in consciousness, "intimacy" is unaffected by distance. I can be more intimately related and connected with someone in China, for instance, than with my neighbor next door (I live in California). Intimacy is constituted by *internal relatedness* (i.e., "shared meaning" and "shared aims, purposes, and intentions"). Because the cells and other matter of my body share a long history of mutual influence and shared meaning, I am much more intimately related to processes in my own body than I am to what goes on in someone else's body. It is much easier, therefore, for me to effect intentional healing in my own body than in someone else's. But that is not to say it can't be done. It's just, typically, more difficult. However, it is quite possible that certain people (e.g., shamans and other healers—including authentic Reiki healers) are so much more attuned to the world around them that they have a much higher threshold of intimacy with other bodies, both human and nonhuman, and can, therefore, be much more effective in healing others *even at a distance*.

---

*The difference between spirit and soul refers to different levels in the Great Chain of Being. Essentially, Spirit and Soul are two distinct levels in the Great Chain (others being Mind and Matter). Briefly, in many traditions, Spirit is assumed to exist beyond space and time, completely unconditioned and unconstrained, whereas Soul is the first manifestation of Spirit and occurs in the dimension of time. In other words, souls exist in time but not in space (see, for example, Arthur M. Young's *The Reflexive Universe*).

11

Information

"Everything Is Information"

Remember the good old days before the Internet and e-mail? Life was simpler. You could switch off the light, leave the office, go home, and relax for the night. No obsessive checking your iPhone. No YouTube, Facebook, Google, or Twitter to enthrall you. No compulsive tracking or updating blogs. No late-night browsing for bargains on eBay or Amazon. You had downtime. Remember that?

Remember when it all seemed more sane—and safer? Plentiful fresh, wholesome food. Abundant clear, clean water. Breathable air. Cheap gas. And a beautiful big wide world of pristine mountains, forests, rivers, lakes, and oceans to explore. Alas, no more.

Today, the world is exploding with food riots, communities are parched for potable water and gasping for clean air, while others burn up bank balances to feed insatiable SUVs. And pristine nature? Forget it. Even the remotest places on Earth are polluted with plastic and poisoned with countless consumer chemicals.

Yes, we may long for the good old days before the information revolution—when life was far less complicated and more relaxed. Faced with big problems, people mostly knew what to do. It was easy enough to find the right answers. Not now. The recent global financial collapse is just a harbinger of what can happen when blind trust in information technology runs so deep and wide that the true seriousness of the situation is lost in the digital sinews of transnational computer networks. The challenges are huge and mind-numbingly complex. All around us, everywhere we look, we face the long, tangled tentacles of one global crisis after another: Environment. Economics. Education. Housing. Health. Hunger. Religion. Fuel. Food. Air. Water. War. And, of course, weather and climate change.

CRISIS AS A WAY OF LIFE

Faced with a crisis, smart people find out what went wrong and what to do to fix it. But today the problems are so vast, so deeply intertwined, that even our best minds seem to be at a loss. The irony is stark: Blitzed by information overload, we are inspirationally challenged.

It's a common complaint: We have more information than we know what to do with. Yet what we have may not be enough to get us out of the predicament in time.

Blindspot: The problem, though, is not really information—either lack of it or too much of it. The problem is lack of *wisdom*. We have turned our backs on the plain old common sense that comes naturally with the gift of consciousness. We pay more attention to digital data than to the qualities of mind needed to manage our immensely complex information systems.

Not only do we feel the pain personally, but the entire economic system is in jeopardy. In our data-dependent corporate culture, the worst executive sin is to say, "I don't know." Information at our fingertips is the Holy Grail, and if you don't have it, then bluff it. Managers and politicians are afraid of being found out. Because nobody knows it all, everybody devises spins and stratagems for disguising and protecting their vulnerable information gaps. Corporate life thrives on second-guessing what the other guy knows—if he (and "he" could just as well be "she") doesn't know that you don't know, and you don't know that he doesn't know . . . then who'll ever know that nobody really knows?

One reason for the epidemic of ignorance and pretense in the worlds of business and politics is, I believe, that corporate executives have embraced digital technology as a substitute for the human mind. Information systems have changed our working lives in fundamental ways, yet millions still hardly understand the first thing about computers. Why, for instance, do politicians accept touch-screen voting, when the software is so vulnerable to hacking? New technology has taken them—and the rest of us—into a new age where data manipulation is the new designer drug, flowing like supercharged electronic blood through the digital veins of the World Wide Web and its global network of ISP servers. It runs our lives.

To be sure, information technology quickens the pace of business. It helps keep the competition at bay. It gives executives that warm, sexy feeling called "the competitive edge," promised so loudly by the marketing hobnobs from computer and software companies. They can feel it in their fingers, yet in their guts many feel a gnawing uneasiness. The latest software update is just another fix. Gotta have it.

The Myth of Progress

Blindspot: Beyond the drive for ever-enhanced data efficiency lurks the implicit assumption that progress is good. And information is essential for progress; ergo, information is good. But information must be managed: Enter computers and networks of information technology. Ergo, information technology is good. To many people, especially those earning a living from information technology, this last statement is taken for granted. However, we would do well to question it.

Information technology may be turbo-driving business and the rest of the world headlong into chaos—blind and oblivious to its impact on the greater ecological systems in which it is embedded. Surprisingly, it strikes many people as counterintuitive that information technology is *far more* environmentally destructive than the impacts of smokestack industry. Our local and global computer networks are utterly dependent on industrial technology for extracting, processing, and transporting the raw materials needed to build the networks. Hidden behind the clean and crisp design of your new laptop or cell phone stomps a massive ecological footprint—spewing toxins into air, land, and water. Bottom line: Information technology is pure economic and ecological overhead.

What is true of information technology is true for the business world and modern lifestyles in general. The problem with information—getting it and using it—is that it *costs*. Entropy—a basic law of physics that tells us nothing ever happens without a cost—is now a cliché in the business world: "No free lunches"; you don't get something for nothing. It's the sort of corporate graffiti executives are fond of. Everybody seems to be scrambling for a piece of the pie, before it's all gone.

The scenario, simplified, runs on two assumptions: First, progress is good and, therefore, desirable. Second, progress should be measured in material gain. Following the logic, we are compelled to pit human ingenuity against the forces of nature.

We manipulate the raw material of the environment into more and more products—manufacturing order out of chaos. That's the definition of progress. And how do we build order? By gathering, generating, communicating, sharing, and acting on *information*. Order is built up by corralling and concentrating the flow of energy and information from the environment and shaping it to suit our needs. Well, so be it—difficult to argue with that.

But remember entropy? There's a price tag for every lunch—*we have to pay for the order and information*. The buildup of material order through the constant drive for development of next-generation products *necessarily* dissipates increasing quantities of waste and disorder into the environment. We pay for our order and information by polluting our rivers, lakes, oceans, and land and the air we breathe. That inconvenient truth is no longer so easily dismissed.

Souled In or Sold Out?

Blindspot: Another glaring assumption, conspicuously overlooked in the information colonies—the Silicon Valleys, Glens, Glades, Beltways, and God-knows-where-else the information revolution is hatched—is this: Underlying the drive for material progress is the belief that *brute matter is all there is.* Dead stuff. Atoms colliding in the void. The paradigm of scientific materialism. Notice the dichotomy and contradiction here—a kind of metaphysical schizophrenia unconsciously driving the world of business and politics. On one hand, the ideal of progress flows from a divine mandate: "Go forth and multiply; fill the Earth and subdue it." On the other, fulfilling that mandate relies on the methods of secular science. Behind the religious impulse is a concern for the spiritual well-being of humans; behind science is the assumption that what matters is only what you can measure. The digital dances with the divine.

Each shares the idea that *humans are special*—because we alone have souls (religion), or because we have unique brains and intelligence (science)—and this gives us the right and the might to take whatever we want or need from the world around us. *Progress.*

But then we have a double price to pay. The advance of our information-addicted civilization is paid for not only by polluting the physical environment but also by degrading the spirit of humanity, our system of values—by *polluting consciousness.*

Values, such as compassion and empathy (not just for humans but for other animals, too), are compromised in exchange for the accumulation of material wealth and the eternal pursuit of the almighty dollar. Not only have we "sold out" on nature, we have forgotten how to be "souled in."

Without a parallel paradigm shift in human consciousness, in our value systems, the information revolution will be worse than meaningless. It will so degrade both our physical and psychological environments that we will self-consume in a globalized "heat death" eons before that inevitable fate befalls the solar system. The looming environmental collapse is just a symptom of a much deeper and widespread psychospiritual malaise.

Unless information technology (and by extension, the entire domain of business, economics, and politics) is geared to what Brazilian educator Paulo Freire called "authentic liberation,"* it will increase psychic entropy in the form of alienation from nature. If the purpose of information is progress, and progress means transforming our world, it sets humanity *against* our environment, rather than seeing us as part of a single coevolving interrelated system.

True authenticity comes with the realization that people are integral subsystems within the nested systems of nature. Unless information and information technology serve *self-transformation,* we will continue to increase our alienation. Real progress liberates human potential and fulfills our coevolutionary promise within a complex ecosystem.

BEYOND THE INFORMATION REVOLUTION

More than an information revolution, then, we need a *consciousness revolution.* (That Sixties slogan just won't go away!)

Ultimately, why do we need information? To help us work better. Why do we work? To help us cope and survive; to help us generate order and organization as we face the unrelenting forces of nature. We work to ward off decay and chaos. And, yes, information helps us manage that task. But information technology will not be sufficient to pull us through.

Blindspot: Humans are living examples of teleological systems. We think and act with purpose. Information without intention is like a thermostat without a governor. We need to align technology with *intentionality.* We need to develop and evolve—not only by focusing on the external world of nature but also by turning the beam of consciousness on consciousness itself. In this way, information transforms into wisdom.

The information model—high-tech as a paradigm for business and

---

*Freire, *Pedagogy of the Oppressed.*

human development—sells us short by turning the human-technology relationship on its head. Instead of creating systems that stimulate our highest capacities, we end up reducing people to the status of information processors. Instead of creative stimulation, we settle for mechanical simulation. We become virtual instead of virtuous.

There's another problem. Digital technology elevates the importance of *memory*. Information is stored as data to be accessed and retrieved on demand. But life is more than memory. Life sparkles with *experience,* with *feeling,* with *creativity.*

Too much emphasis on memory—digital or neural—blots out the live current of experience that animates people interacting with each other and with the world around us. When memory dominates, intentionality is obscured, and *we forget the driving purpose behind whatever we are recalling.* We lose our humanity in a storm of facts.

The high-tech model turns people into information processors *for something else*—whether it's sales goals, the corporate bottom line, market share, or industry leadership—not *for themselves.* But it is the nature of all living systems to be "for themselves," to maintain their self-identity, to protect their defining boundaries, to enhance their own well-being. When people work "for the organization," without also ensuring sufficient self-growth, they become self-alienated, and they lose their driving purpose. In time, both individual and system fall prey to dysfunction and entropy.

A Consciousness Revolution

Dysfunction creeps into organizations when people are valued more for what they know—for their information content, for their *memory*—than for who they are. Yet the greatest value someone can bring to an organization is his or her *experience*—not "experience" in the sense of "accumulated knowledge" (i.e., "memory"), but experience as the vital flow of consciousness and awareness, the source of human choice and creativity . . . in short, the *self.*

Only when the self is welcomed, accepted, and valued can a memory for facts and information be of any long-term value to the organization and the individual. The exponential growth of data storage and exchange is inversely proportional to the cognitive, creative capacities of human beings to absorb and integrate information. The more we are exposed to the daily blizzard of digitized facts, the less we are meaningfully informed. Our mental bandwidth is not up to the challenge. The full, life-enhancing value of information can be realized only if coupled with evolution in the consciousness of the person exposed to the information storm. Growth in external, mechanistic information processing requires a corresponding internal development in consciousness—in our ability to create and express *meaning*. More than information processors, *we are meaning processors.*

Blindspot: Without an expansion of consciousness, our minds will remain vulnerable to information overwhelm. With expanded awareness, we may grow to include and integrate more details from the field of information and learn to recognize more meaningful patterns. Expanded awareness enables individuals to more easily single out specific elements from the background context, to perceive relationships, and to reflect and act on them purposefully.

A preoccupation with information inhibits creativity and stifles intentionality by isolating the person from the world. Consciousness, as Freire pointed out, is a "problem-posing" faculty—it thrives by confronting problems, by free and open inquiry, and it produces solutions through a process of self-reflection, praxis, and creative transformation of information.

This leads to a new and radical purpose for business: to transform organizations by affirming the human capacity for self-transcendence—for reflecting and acting with integrity and authenticity, true to one's own spirit, and, in turn, contributing to the growth of the organization, and the larger society.

But honoring and nurturing the self is only a first step. While each of us is undoubtedly a unique individual, our individuality gets its uniqueness precisely from our relationships with all that surrounds us. Self-transformation, then, comes with the realization that who we are is literally a co-creation involving, ultimately, the entire world. At bottom, the self is a note in a symphony, a node in the ever-interdependent universal web of life and being. We are not just individuals; we are *interviduals*.

A New Bottom Line

So, what's driving the digital revolution? Well, we rely on information—from the media, from friends and family, from our churches, from science—to know what to think, what to *believe*. How else would we know how to act in the world?

Blindspot: But being informed is not enough. The human body-mind-spirit thrives on meaning. True progress cannot be measured in bits, bytes, or pixels, or even in dollars. In the end, it comes down to a deepening of meaning—a state of mind that improves the quality of life and our relationships with others.

Imagine, then, a new bottom line for both our personal and professional lives: *transformation*—real honest-to-God progress, humans in harmony with nature. Life beyond the information revolution.

WHAT IS INFORMATION?

Depth Alert: So, just what is *information?* The word is often confused with both *meaning* and *data*. It's neither.

Technically, in science and engineering, *information* refers to a *measurement* of a signal between a sender and receiver, from point A to point B. According to Claude Shannon, a founder of information theory, in this technical sense information has nothing to do with meaning. In digital systems, information is communicated as data organized in bits and bytes (strings of zeros and ones), and in engineering terms, measurement of the flow of bits *is* information.

And just as information does not add up to *meaning,* data are not the same as information. It gets confusing pretty fast. So hold on, here's a simple way to cut through the tangle:

Data: Composed of zeros and ones, digital data represent "off" and "on" states in a system that determine whether and how electrons flow through integrated circuits. In computers, these off and on states are governed by software programs (ultimately based on sequences of zeros and ones). The zeros and ones of data both represent and determine states of physical systems. In short: Data represent or determine *patterns of energy,* most often in the form of electricity. (Note *data* is a plural word; *datum* is singular.)

Information: By themselves, data strings never add up to information. As just noted, *data are patterns of energy.* For data to become *information,* those energy patterns must be *read* or *perceived* by someone. In other words, information has two crucial components—*patterns in energy* (data) and an *observer.* Yes, you got it: Information requires both energy and consciousness. Either one alone never amounts to information.

Blindspot: Therefore, rather than consciousness or energy being a derivative of information, as many people like to think, information is a derivative of consciousness and energy. Without a sentient being (i.e., *consciousness*) to "read," register, or experience changes in *patterns of energy,* no meaningful information exists.

For example, a CD or DVD does not contain information. It contains *data*—objective patterns of energy. Only when those patterns of energy are "read" by a sentient, conscious being do data become information. Until you play your DVD and watch the images on a screen, that silver plastic disc has no information. It just sits in its box as a bunch of data encoded in tiny pits (ones and zeros) on the disc. Information *requires* the presence of a *subjective,* observing, conscious being capable of detecting *objective* changes in patterns of energy.

Information is consciousness perceiving patterns of energy—or, to be more precise, it is consciousness perceiving *changes* in patterns of energy. If nothing changes, no new information is possible.

Meaning: I defined this earlier as *the experienced fit between self and not-self* (see p. 115). Once we read the data and turn it into information, we can see (or feel) how the recorded *patterns of energy* relate to ("fit") the patterns of energy that form *us*. If there's a good fit, we experience *meaning*.

Human Attention
In an information-rich world, the wealth of information means a dearth of something else: a scarcity of whatever it is that information consumes. What information consumes is rather obvious: it consumes the attention of its recipients. Hence a wealth of information creates a poverty of attention and a need to allocate that attention efficiently among the overabundance of information sources that might consume it.

—HERBERT SIMON (NOBEL LAUREATE)*

---

*Simon, "Designing Organizations for an Information-Rich World."

12
Relationship
"Everything Is Connected to Everything Else"

Where do you get your "aha" moments of inspiration? Mine typically come when I'm either in the shower or driving.

A few years ago, as I was preparing for a seminar on the topic of universal interconnection, I had a . . . well, let's call it a *brightspot*. It dawned on me (while taking a shower) that, of course, *everything is interconnected to everything else*—there really is no other option.

Quantum physics confirms it. Logic proves it. Here's what I saw:

Brightspot: If I'm separate from you (or from anyone or anything), that means *something is between us* (it could be other people, concrete, metal, wood, rope, continents, oceans, air . . . or space itself). It makes no difference because . . .

If something is between us, then whatever is *between* us must be *connecting* us. Right? In other words, *whatever separates us connects us!*

On the other hand, if *nothing* is between us, then nothing is separating us, and that means we are together—*connected*. Do you get that?

You see, whether something separates us or not, we are always connected to everything. That's why the idea "everything is interconnected" doesn't interest me very much. It's kind of: "Well, duh! Yes, of course."

Because we have no other option beyond "everything is interconnected to everything else," my next lightbulb moment woke me up: The really interesting question is, *how* are we connected? What matters is not the fact that we are all interconnected; that's a universal given.

What matters most is the *nature and quality of our connections.*

How are we connected? Well, we connect in two fundamental ways: *physically,* indirectly through exchanges of energy and mechanism (e.g., through speaking, phones, e-mail, books, newspapers, and movies), and *nonphysically,* directly through consciousness and shared meaning (e.g., when lovers *experience* each other's presence).

The implications of this are profound for our personal and business relationships, for health and healing, and for how we relate to the rest of the natural world.

Once we realize that everything is necessarily connected to everything else, and that what matters is the *quality* of our connections, we are motivated to pay closer attention to our relationships—with each other, with all sentient beings, and with nature. For health and healing, remember that it's the *intimacy* of connection that makes the difference in the quality of healing (see p. 110).

HOW DO YOU CONNECT?

In these days of global social networking (Facebook, Twitter, LinkedIn, YouTube, Pinterest, etc.), getting connected seems easy. Even expected.

But do we really *connect* online? Yes, we can share and exchange data and information and stay up-to-date on what our friends and colleagues are doing. Mostly, that's probably a good thing.

And yet . . . the more time we spend connecting online, the less time we spend connecting in person with others. We might have thousands of Facebook "friends" around the world, and hundreds of others who "like" us, yet still feel isolated and alone.

The information revolution—almost magical in its ability to turn electrons into limitless digital images (photos and videos), sounds (music and speech), and text—has transformed our lives.

But being connected in meaningful ways is more than just sending each other bits and bytes. Exchanging data and information, though useful, is no substitute for sharing *presence*—connecting together as embodied sentient beings.

Blindspot: We all connect in two fundamental ways: *physically* and *nonphysically*, through energy and through consciousness. As we have seen, physical connections work through exchanges of energy—moving bits of the physical world through space. Nonphysical connections, however, work through shared meaning—through *interbeing*, the inter-subjectivity of consciousness.

We need both modes of connection—because we are both minds and bodies, consciousness and energy. So, let's not forget to connect through the gift of shared presence, not just with texts and tweets.

As I discussed in the previous chapter, we need to move beyond the information revolution to a *wisdom revolution*. Information without wisdom is hardly worth the time and effort.

Bumper sticker: "Shout out *and* show up."

INDIVIDUALITY: ILLUSION OR REALITY?

I'm with the Buddhists on this: In a sense, the individual self is a construct—but not merely a linguistic or cultural one. We are all inter-beings, co-creating each other through relationship (and, just to be clear, by "all" and "each other" I don't mean just human beings—I mean all sentient beings). Here's how I see it . . .

Picture a vast cosmic dynamic web or network of sentient beings, from quanta to queens, atoms to apes, where each node is "constructed" by its relationships with, ultimately, all other nodes in the network. Those nodes, or individual selves, are real, but transitory. The deeper, lasting reality is the web or network of relationships. Nodes come and go; the web remains.

A common image expresses this: Think of individuals as waves on the infinite ocean of transpersonal being—destined to return to the ocean and to participate in the great cosmic "recycling" program.

That's who we are; that's what our individual lives are: waves rising out of the ocean of being, dancing and sparkling in the sunlight for our "four-score and seven" years, before slipping back into the ocean, to be replaced by a new wave.

Having an individual self-identity is directly related to the fact that we have bodies—because, as long as we are embodied, distinct boundaries exist between us and everything else, and as a result, we experience ourselves as individual egos (the ego serves a literally vital evolutionary purpose, protecting and guiding the body as it moves through the world). And, as we all know, our egos are hell-bent on maintaining their individuality—even to the extent of devising philosophies, metaphysics, religions, myths, and cosmologies that preserve individual personality beyond the grave.

Blindspot: Unless integrated with the whole Self, those pesky egos go down kicking and screaming, resisting all the way to the Inevitable Return. The illusion is not that we believe our individuality is real (it is); the illusion is that we believe our individuality is our essential nature (it's not). To paraphrase Chief Seattle: We belong to Nature. Nature does not belong to us.

We are *interbeings, interviduals* momentarily co-creating each other in the vast eternal cosmic network.

ARE YOU REALLY ME?

When you speak of intersubjectivity, do you mean that the first-person perceptions of one subject contribute to, or even constitute, the first-person perceptions of another subject? In other words, does what I believe to be true of me *come to define what you believe to be true of* you—*not because you've had similar experiences, but because you're having* my *experience? I don't see how that could be. It seems extreme to say that two subjects come to share one and the same subjective interiority. Is that what you're saying?*

You ask an interesting and penetrating question, and I'll do my best to give you a clear and sufficient answer.

Essentially, you are asking whether I propose that the experiences of one person or subject could be (at least partly) *constitutive* of some other person or subject. Well, to cut to the chase, yes, that is precisely what I propose. To you, that seems "extreme"—you wonder how two subjects could share the same subjective interiority. And that's a valid question. To answer it, I'll need to summarize an important distinction in metaphysics.

Depth Alert: We need to begin by distinguishing between *substance*-based and *process*-based metaphysics—the topic of my first book, *Radical Nature*. Following the process philosophy of Alfred North Whitehead, I point out why the Cartesian notion of "substance" (inherited from medieval theologians) is incoherent.

In essence, rather than a *"thing*-based" metaphysics, we need an *"event*-based" view of reality (this, by the way, is supported by both relativity and quantum theories—as well as Buddhism). A key consequence of this is that the notion of the independent, isolated Cartesian ego-subject as the paradigm of human consciousness (indeed *any* consciousness) is also deeply problematic.

In a process-based reality, everything is thoroughly *interdependent*. We are, as I like to say, "interviduals," not individuals. Nothing, and no one, exists independently of anything or anyone else. I'm making a case for *strong* (rather than "extreme") intersubjectivity in which *subjects are mutually co-creative and mutually constitutive*. And that claim is what you seem to have difficulty accepting. I can understand that, because what I am proposing involves a radical revisioning of metaphysics—of ontology and epistemology. And I advocate this because, based on a career-long body of research, it seems to me this is the only coherent and adequate option to account for the relationship between embodiment and consciousness.

In my books (particularly *Radical Knowing*), I distinguish between three kinds of intersubjectivity, following a similar analysis of two different kinds of subjectivity. To grasp what I am proposing, you would at the very least need to review those distinctions (see p. 40 in this book).

In *Radical Knowing,* I spend a couple of early chapters making an important distinction between *belief* and *experience.* Beliefs are collections of thoughts, and thoughts are *abstractions,* snapshots of ever-changing, ongoing experience. Thoughts, and the beliefs they form, are frozen fragments of consciousness. So, the intersubjectivity I'm talking about is not a sharing of *beliefs* (or thoughts). Rather it is participatory sharing of *experience.* Part of who I am is literally constituted by part of who you are. While we may (or may not) share some beliefs, that is incidental to our deeply intersubjective nature. What makes us truly intersubjects is that we mutually share experiences and meanings (by *meanings* I don't mean symbolic expressions and exchanges, in words or other symbols; I mean the *"experienced* fit between self and other").

You might wonder, *how* do you and I share experiences? After all, we live thousands of miles apart on different continents. Well, to repeat: Consciousness and experience (all *nonphysical* aspects of reality) do not occur in space—they are *nonlocated*—and are, therefore, unconstrained by distance. So the fact that you are across the ocean makes no difference to the possibility (or fact) that we share meanings and experiences. Yes, we communicate through e-mail, and that accounts for the *physical* transmission of data between us. But such physical exchanges do not account for our ability to *share meaning* (famously, "syntax is not semantics").

Our nonphysical sharing of meaning, our intersubjective participation, is a consequence of our *expressed intentions.* These are nonphysical, even though they accompany our exchanges of physical energy or information.

To be clear: I do not claim that just because we "share" experiences, we therefore have *identical* experiences. Not at all. Each of us remains a unique center or node of subjectivity, albeit within the context of a universal matrix of a more fundamental intersubjectivity. But the "nodes" of embodied consciousness that each of us *is,* while unique, are sustained and mutually constituted by every other nodal subject in the universe. I'm saying that even though each of us is unique (a distinct space-time "node" in the universal matrix), we also mutually co-create each other. So, indeed, you do have your own unique experience, but it is not isolated and totally independent (as Descartes thought); rather, it is to varying degrees constituted by every other "center" of embodied consciousness.

This does not mean that whatever beliefs I may hold somehow become beliefs you also hold. I am saying, however, that the notion of "my" experience (in the independent Cartesian sense) is an illusion. "My" subjectivity simply does not exist independently of "your" subjectivity— even though we retain a unique identity. So I would not say that I have "your" experiences or you have "my" experiences. However, I am saying that we *share* experiences and meanings; otherwise, it would be impossible for us to ever communicate.

Blindspot: First-person subjectivity is inextricably rooted in second-person intersubjectivity. Both are real and true. But intersubjectivity is more fundamental; it has ontological priority. I am saying that the deepest ontological nature of consciousness is *intersubjective* and that individual subjects are finite and temporary events ("blips," "eruptions," "coagulations") in the ultimately eternal universal flux of intersubjectivity that I call the Creative Ultimate and others call God.

WE ARE NOT ALONE

Let me emphasize this again: We are not isolated individuals who happen to come together to form relationships. No, *our deepest nature is relationship.* We are not individuals—we are *interviduals.*

Relationship comes first. Individuality is secondary. Like waves rising out of the ocean, each of us emerges from the universal matrix that connects us all.

You might want to point out the obvious: Our bodies do exist individually, autonomously, and separately from other bodies. And of course that is true—up to a point.

We don't get confused about whose mouth to feed when either of us feels hungry. I am aware that my experience of hunger belongs to my body, so when *I'm* hungry, I don't feed you, and when you feel hungry, you feed *your* body, not mine! Through our senses, our bodies constantly feed information to our minds, which is why "your" consciousness is not the same as "my" (or anyone else's) consciousness. Your ego is associated and correlated with *your* individual body, and mine with mine.

Yes, our bodies have a great deal of autonomy, and we all do appear to be separate. But even that's an illusion or misperception.

Blindspot: Every "individual" necessarily exists in an *environment* with other bodies (other people, other animals, and plants)—as well as within an inorganic substrate of minerals, air, water, sunlight, and so on. Whether we are aware of it or not, whether we like it or not, we all *share* these elements. The oxygen you are breathing now was once part of a tree and has passed through the lungs of countless other animals. Same with carbon dioxide, except in reverse—while we inhale oxygen given off by trees and plants, they absorb the carbon dioxide we and other animals exhale. Furthermore, not only are we all connected across space through a shared environment, we are also connected across time. Carbon molecules in your body (maybe even the carbon dioxide molecules you just expelled from your lungs) were possibly once part of a dinosaur, sixty-five million years ago.

Nevertheless, as mobile animals within this deeply interconnected and interdependent system, we can move our bodies around with remarkable degrees of freedom.

Consciousness is a different matter. It has no location in space and, therefore, it cannot be confined to any "individual" body. Because consciousness is *nonlocated,* it is essentially *intersubjective.*

However, consciousness is also always embodied. Because of this intimate and inseparable unity of body-mind, our consciousness strongly *identifies* with its "host," and so, it assumes a similar degree of autonomy—giving rise to our sense of separate "egos."

The illusion of individuality, therefore, is twofold: First, we believe our *bodies* are independent and separate (which they're not), and second, we believe our consciousness—condensed into individualized ego-minds—exists apart from other egos (which it doesn't).

This, then, is the source of the illusion of individuality, and it lies at the root of so many of our modern ills—personal, social, economic, political, and environmental.

The remedy to these "ills of illusion" lies in cultivating integrated body-mind practices that raise awareness of our fundamental nature as deeply interconnected and interdependent *interviduals*.

Embodiment and interviduality play an essential role in health and life. The body is an object, and any two bodies are distinct from each other—in the sense that they occupy different locations in space. Experience, by contrast, is subjective and is not located in space, yet it is always embodied. That means you can't have an experience without your body. However, because your experience is not located in space, it is never separate from anyone else's experience. But, inevitably, our ego's mental chatter kicks in and convinces us that we are, after all, separate individuals—because we have individual bodies.

We spend most of our lives identified with our bodies, thinking we are separate "atomized" egos, as though our egos exist as independent "atoms of consciousness." We rarely notice that consciousness is much more than our little ego-minds. We think our thinking mind is all that consciousness is. This atomized consciousness allows us to think our own private thoughts, safe in the illusion of isolated subjectivity. We don't usually know what others think, unless they tell us. Our thoughts, beliefs, and emotions are expressions of our sense of individual identity.

Of course, consciousness is much more than egoic thoughts or beliefs. It also expresses itself through other ways of knowing, such as feeling and intuition—liberating us from the illusion of separateness. When we feel our embodied sensations, we not only tap in to personal experience, we open to the intersubjective presence of others. And when we tune in to intuition, we tap into shared collective consciousness.

That's why it is important to wake up to our internal felt sense and embodied sensations. When we do so, we connect with our interconnected and embedded-embodied self and shift from an individual to an *intervidual* mode of living. We are *intersubjects,* not just subjects.

As I point out in *Radical Knowing,* the deepest nature of consciousness is intersubjective (formed by relationships between all sentient beings). However, this does not eliminate the reality or significance of individual subjects. We are both *intersubjective* and *subjective* (in the Cartesian sense of individualized egos). However, although intersubjectivity—the cosmic "network" of relationships that gives rise to us all—is the essential nature of reality, each individual "node" in the network is, nevertheless, also real. It is just not *primary.*

The intersubjective network is the fundamental and eternal reality, within which individualized nodes or egos arise for a time and eventually die, folding back into the great transpersonal matrix. Yes, intersubjectivity is an ontological fact, but so is subjectivity. It's just that intersubjectivity is more fundamental and enduring.

Ego or Soul Projection?

First, mutual interdependence is the fundamental nature of existence. Period. We are fundamentally intersubjective beings—our very sense of individuality arises out of the quality of our relationships.

This means that in order to develop a sense of "me," each of us needs another "I" (a "you," another subject) who can mirror back to us our projections. By the way, that's part of the reason why projection is not "bad"— it is a natural and necessary component of being in relationship. If we don't project ourselves out into the world, how can we ever connect with others?

Blindspot: When we project ourselves, we contribute to the being of others, just as their projections contribute to our being. Through this back-and-forth play of projections, we develop a sense of "me." However, be careful not to confuse projecting self (or soul) and projecting ego.

Soul-projection is authentic self-expression—it literally co-creates and develops our sense of self when it is accurately reflected back to us. Ego projection, by contrast, is inauthentic to the extent that it involves disowning a part of ourselves (the part we overlay on the other). Mostly, we project ego "stuff" (our repressed psychic "shadow," our deep-rooted fears, anxieties, shame, guilt, anger, etc.) because we don't want that as part of ourselves, and, therefore, we don't want it reflected back to us.

THE LONG BODY

Depth Alert: The main point I want to emphasize here is this: At every moment, each of us is an individualization of the universe. It takes the whole past universe to make us what we are right now. As a physical object, the body is the growing tip of the entire past history of the universe. It takes data from the physical world and processes those data into information we can work with. In some implicit way, we feel all of that.

And not only that: Given the intimate relationship between body and mind, the personality is also formed by the entire past history of universal experience. What we receive from the world is not information about a dead, abstract situation, but the feeling of every feeling that has ever happened before. All past experiences flood in on us at every moment. And even though each body is fundamentally the whole world, each of us has a unique physical location and point of view within that world. Each unique node in the universal matrix, then, filters the information coming from the rest of the world into forms that our quasi-individual minds can work with.

In short, each body is a unique point of convergence of the entire prior universe. And because it's a point of convergence, it has a unique perspective that serves as a filter, selecting parts of the world most relevant to our needs at any particular time. The body, then, delivers a subset of reality, an *appearance* and interpretation, which Whitehead called "presentational immediacy."

Furthermore, the appearance our body makes of the world and itself is conditioned by our aims. Therefore, if we shift to a more universal aim, we can begin to penetrate more deeply and directly into the reality outside our body. In effect, we expand our body to include the environment around us, and so, in that way, we can tune in to the situation and feel its inherent dynamics. By flowing with that, we can do the right thing.

Once we realize we are individualizations of the universe, we can aim to experience the universe as directly and as fully as possible—expanding our definition and experience of the body to include the whole situation in which we find ourselves. In principle, this extends to the entire process of cosmic evolution.

When we realize this, our psychospiritual project becomes less about *expanded awareness* and more about *expanded embodiment*. My colleague Eric Weiss calls this "the long trajectory."*

Blindspot: The whole situation in which we find ourselves at any given moment becomes internal to our body. Over time, if we focus our subjective aim, we can expand our body so *it is the situation,* and then we can feel our environment as intimately as we feel the inside of our own body. Given the environmental crisis created by modern civilization, this is an important skill for us to cultivate—a skill possessed by indigenous shamans for millennia.

Intuitions of the larger universe come to us sometimes in the form of inner pictures, words, or proprioception, which we can interpret as part of our expanded body. When that happens, our feelings become the feelings of the environment.

Our bodies are not limited by the boundary of our skin. They are fluid and flexible, and they can extend to *feel* and *be* the entire situation we happen to find ourselves in at any moment. In a phrase: *We are the universe.*

---

*Weiss, *The Long Trajectory*.

13

Humans

"Humans Are Special"

It amazes me that often when people talk about consciousness, they mean just *human* consciousness—as if the ability to be aware and feel didn't exist until our species evolved. (How absurdly self-centered!)

In my books and talks, I do my best to show how pervasive consciousness is in nature. I want people to stop assuming that "humans are special" just because we have consciousness.

It started with Descartes four hundred years ago when he claimed that only humans have "souls," and that other animals can't feel pain or pleasure. That way of thinking is a major part of the problem facing the world today, as we obliterate countless other species. The self-serving myth of "human specialness" actually doesn't serve us at all. For instance, we need other species for our own survival, and, furthermore, human consciousness did not evolve in a vacuum.

Instead of privileging humans (or human consciousness), I'd like us all to realize that what is "special" about consciousness in our universe is by no means unique to humans. All species feel, possess awareness, and experience subjectivity, meaning, and purpose. At least, we have no good reasons to assume otherwise.

HUMAN MATTER?

Imagine for a moment that scientists tell us they study "human matter"—implying that the stuff of our bodies is somehow special or different from all other matter in the universe. Of course it's not; that would be silly. We are made up of the same elements found throughout nature. No special human element ("Hu") exists in the periodic table. Matter is matter wherever it is found. Likewise, mind is mind whenever it occurs. Human consciousness is essentially no different from the consciousness of other sentient beings.

Yes, matter takes on specific animal forms (that's what distinguishes different species)—including specific human forms. The Human Genome Project focused specifically on human genetics. But that was possible only after hundreds of years investigating universal characteristics of matter through physics, chemistry, and molecular biology. Geneticists never claimed they were researching "human matter."

Similarly, in studying consciousness, we aim to identify and explore its universal characteristics (such as feeling, experience, subjectivity, self-agency).

Human consciousness is just one form among countless others. Why limit ourselves to merely human manifestations of a universal reality?

STEWARDS OF THE EARTH?

One way the myth of human specialness shows up is the claim that we are "stewards of the Earth." Well, who said so? Who on Earth (literally) appointed humans as stewards for the rest of nature? Well, surprise, surprise . . . it was humans! I don't recall any "conference of all species" deciding to elect us to that role. The very idea of human "stewardship" is code for "covert domination."

Are we really stewards or should we be? I'd say a resounding "no" on both counts. Here's why: Nature, with all its countless species, got along just fine for billions of years before our species came on the scene. Nature doesn't need our "stewardship." It just needs us to stop thinking and acting as though we are "special" (including being special enough to be "stewards").

Blindspot: It's way past time for us to recognize, as our indigenous ancestors did, that the human species is just one "nation" among all other species (and inorganic elements). We are one strand in the complex web of life we call the *ecosystem.*

All species are special—each one has something unique (that's what distinguishes one species from another). And there's simply nothing "especially special" about human specialness. Let's stop pretending otherwise and just "learn to get along." It's way past time to let go of the self-serving, self-important myth of human specialness and give up our self-appointed role as Earth stewards.

The rest of nature will thank us for it. And, in time, we will, too . . .

ARE HUMANS SPECIAL?

You challenge the idea that humans are special—yet isn't it true that we are unique? No other species has developed civilization, constructed cities, created art, invented technologies, sent men to the Moon, built the Internet, engaged in philosophical conversations, or written books. That makes us special, don't you think? Besides, isn't the human species responsible for the vast ecological crisis that challenges us today? It seems clear to me that humans are special, and to deny that fact is to deny the obvious.

This is a big and complicated topic. It's big because our species is responsible for bringing the world to the brink of eco-collapse. And if we don't deal with that *right now* and in a *big way* we are not likely to survive beyond the next century.

It's complicated because in order to create a solution, we will have to confront both our greatest glories and our greatest shame.

Yes, of course, there is something quite unique—even special— about the human species. We just need to look at anatomical design to see how we stand out. Anatomy has contributed to our emergence as a dominant species on the planet (I say "a" dominant species because, from a different perspective, we could make a case that the truly dominant species in terms of sheer numbers, mass, pervasiveness, and longevity are the various species of *bacteria* and other single-celled organisms).

Here are some of our special anatomical features:

Opposable thumbs. We are not the only species with this ability; other primates share this evolutionary gift. However, combined with our highly developed intelligence, we have used our opposable thumbs to manipulate the environment in exceptional ways.

Upright posture. While other species do stand upright, we are the only species to maintain a fully upright posture when walking and running. We are the only mammal species to completely expose the front of our body (including our genitals), making us highly vulnerable.

Fully extended spine. We achieved our upright posture by developing a fully extended spine that enhances flexibility and strength. Plus we have . . .

Arched feet. Planting our whole feet, toes, and heels flat and firmly on the ground (plantigrade motion) enables us to stand and walk upright. We are not the only species with plantigrade feet, but humans alone combine plantigrade locomotion with an arched foot. This gives us greater stability when walking and running upright.

Liberated arms and hands. Through the course of evolution, we have shifted the use of our front limbs from locomotive aids (gravipodal function), liberating them for greater manipulative ability, increasing our options for interacting with and changing our environment.

Highly developed neocortex. Human brains have evolved a highly complex neocortex, giving us capacities for great intelligence and sophisticated symbolic language.

Speech and abstract language. Humans have a rare combination of larynx, tongue, and teeth suitable for vocalizing complex speech patterns. Human languages have evolved to express complex and abstract ideas that enable us to strategize and to communicate plans to fellow humans.

Prolonged childhood. As much as 75 percent of our brains' development occurs after birth. This involves a prolonged childhood that requires a stable family structure to support and protect the infant, which, in turn, adds to social cohesion and cooperation.

Blindspot: While these, and other, characteristics have undoubtedly contributed to our survival as a species and have enabled us to create vast and complex civilizations, none of these attributes alone is unique to humans.

Other primates have opposable thumbs and have liberated their front limbs from gravipodal to manipulative functions. Penguins walk upright and have extended spines. Bears, kangaroos, mice, rats, hedgehogs, raccoons, and skunks also walk with their whole foot flat on the ground. Whales, dolphins, elephants, crows, parrots, and octopuses are species with highly developed brains, possessing a complex neocortex. Many other species have complex languages and can communicate information about abstract and distant realities—cetaceans, birds, and bees, for example.

What is unique is the *combination* of these characteristics in a single species. And perhaps the long childhood of humans is a decisive factor in the social cohesion necessary for developing advanced civilizations— along with the industrial technologies that have drastically disrupted the ecosphere.

Given all this, we can make a good case that humans *are* special— indeed, unique.

But so is every other species. Possession of unique characteristics *defines* a species *as a species.* Some form of uniqueness is what distinguishes one species from another. Yes, humans are special—but we are not *especially special.* Every species is special—that's what makes it a distinct species.

BEYOND THE MYTH

In *Radical Nature* and elsewhere in my work, I point to the myth of human specialness as the root cause of the crises we find ourselves in today. Both modern science and mainstream monotheistic religions support this myth.

Science, claiming that only animals with highly developed brains can possess consciousness, denies the possibility of widespread intelligence in nature. Because humans are assumed to have a uniquely developed neocortex responsible for higher forms of cognition, we are led to believe that only humans possess intelligence.

Religion, when it draws on biblical scripture, reinforces the myth that only humans have souls, or consciousness, and likewise conspires in the conceit that "humans are special."

When we tell ourselves this story, and go to great lengths to defend it with science and religion, we set the human species against the rest of the natural world. This myth has its roots in philosophy, in metaphysics. The bottom-line metaphysical assumption of modern science is *materialism*—that matter, nature's essence, is "dead" and insentient, without any intrinsic value, purpose, or meaning. How could it have these qualities? Only creatures with consciousness have intrinsic value.

The logic is stark and final: Only creatures with brains have minds or consciousness. Nature doesn't have a brain of its own; therefore, it couldn't have a mind of its own. Therefore, it couldn't have any intrinsic value or meaning. Therefore, nature is available for humans to do with as we please. We are free and entitled to take whatever we desire, serving our own human-centered needs and wishes.

The results of living out this self-serving story—of believing and enacting the myth of human specialness—are equally stark and final.

Very likely, within a generation or two—*if we don't radically change our relationship to nature*—the world will no longer be able to sustain the survival of our and countless other species.* We are victims of our own self-centered myth.

Blindspot: And here's the clincher: We will not change our behavior or lifestyles—we will not change our relationship to the natural world—*unless we change our fundamental guiding myth.*

Unless we give up the myth of human specialness, nothing significant will change. Without that fundamental shift in our story, anything else we do to "save" the environment—no matter how ingenious or well intentioned—will amount to nothing more than ineffective band-aids.

At the core of the ecological crisis is a psychological attitude rooted in a profoundly incoherent and dangerous metaphysical belief: that matter, nature itself, is essentially "dead." *That's* the fundamental story we have to give up.

CONSCIOUSNESS ALL THE WAY DOWN

Blindspot: Humans are not special because we have special brains with special or unique consciousness. How can we be that special when nature itself teems with consciousness—*all the way down?* Every cell in every living creature, every molecule in every cell, every atom in every molecule, and every subatomic particle, quark, quantum, or superstring—or whatever lies at the deepest level of physical reality—"tingles with the spark of spirit." *Matter is sentient to its deepest roots.*

When we accept this, when we open to the essential sacredness of nature, we will radically alter our relationship with every other living creature and with the wider inorganic environment of rivers and oceans, wind and rain, mountains and deserts—with the underlying geology of the planet itself—and we will begin to move through and live in the world with deeper respect.

---

*For an extreme and alarming scenario of what might lie in our future, see the epilogue in this book.

We will, like indigenous peoples across the world and throughout time—like our ancestors for millions of years—experience ourselves as integral elements in a vast and eternal natural cycle of life and death. We will live with the knowledge that whatever we take is always returned, viable for future life. We will be sustained.

IS HUMAN SELF-REFLECTION UNIQUE?

Human consciousness is highly evolved because of our greater capacity for self-reflection. I have heard that dolphins are highly intelligent, too. But if they possessed this ability, wouldn't they be creative—not in the sense of survival (like birds building nests) but in the sense of creating symbolic forms to express aspects of reality they reflect upon? Isn't this what separates humans from the rest of the animal kingdom?

I think it might be useful to distinguish between *self-reflection* and *self-awareness*. If we understand self-reflection as a process that involves conceptual and linguistic thought (i.e., having *thoughts* about ourselves), then I would be inclined to agree that humans probably have more of that going on than dolphins do. Because of our capacity for symbolic communication, either with other humans or privately with ourselves, we have a greater ability for abstraction and, therefore, for spinning out fantasies that may have little or no relation to actual reality. Abstract thinking can be a liability when it comes to holistic living.

On the other hand, if by *self-reflection* we mean a capacity for *self-awareness* (i.e., an ability to be *aware of our own awareness* and to wordlessly inquire into our own sense of self), then I think it is possible, even quite likely, that dolphins and whales surpass humans on this—mainly because they are unlikely to be distracted and led astray by abstract thinking. What we humans can achieve through the practice of meditation, I think dolphins and other animals naturally experience as their "default" state of consciousness. Unlike us, they don't need to "still the mind" of thoughts, judgments, plans, and so forth. They are already deeply immersed in *embodied feeling* as their dominant mode of connecting and communicating with themselves, with other dolphins, and with their environment.

I also think it quite likely that dolphins are just as creative as humans, though, of course, they express this creativity in very different ways. Human creativity is, for the most part, expressed through our opposable thumbs. We, literally, *manipulate* our environment to suit our needs (often considered the distinguishing mark of civilization). However, dolphins and other cetaceans have evolved a very different strategy for relating to their environment: Without an opposable thumb to manipulate the world around them, they have adapted and streamlined their own bodies through the long process of evolution to fit almost perfectly into their environment. Consequently, they don't need to build cities, freeways, the Internet, or any of the other trappings of modern technology that many humans see as the crowning glory of intelligence on Earth.

I take a different view. Given the long term, I see civilizations built on a combination of high intelligence and opposable thumb, leading to the creation of industrial technology, as a potentially self-destructive evolutionary strategy. As we all know only too well by now, we are poisoning and destroying the very ecosystem we rely on for survival. Dolphins, whales, and other species apply their creative potentials in very different ways—for example, in developing their "songs" that enable them to build communities that remain in balance with their environment. A friend of mine, writer Peter Russell, once made the case that the combination of high intelligence plus symbolic language plus opposable thumb is destined to destroy its own environment because it gives us the ability to change our environment to suit our needs, rather than adapt as a species to fit the requirements of our environment.

Unless, and until, we give up the myth of human specialness—that we have some god-given right to exploit or even just change the environment to suit the needs and desires of our species without due regard for the well-being of other species, on whom we depend—we don't stand a chance of surviving much beyond the next few generations.

If, however, we continue to insist that humans are special, then we need to acknowledge that every species is in its own way "special" and that there is *nothing especially special about human specialness.*

THUMB VS. FLIPPER CONSCIOUSNESS

Consciousness shows up differently in different species. For example, humans have what I call *thumb consciousness,* while cetaceans (whales and dolphins) have *flipper consciousness.* (I write about this in *Radical Knowing.*)

By thumb consciousness, I mean the ability to manipulate the world around us using our opposable thumbs. Few other species have that ability. Coupled with our specific form of intelligence, along with our ability to record and communicate ideas to others, our species has used the precision and dexterity of thumbs and fingers to build ingenious technologies that have radically altered our environment.

We have used thumb consciousness to adapt the environment to suit our needs. For cetaceans, it's different. Although they, too, have high intelligence and communications abilities, they lack an opposable thumb. We change the world when it doesn't suit us. Whales and dolphins change themselves to suit their world.

Thumb consciousness, then, refers to what we as a species have collectively done to the rest of nature. Of course, there are exceptions— for example, indigenous cultures tend to adapt to their environments. They, too, have thumbs, but they did not, and in most cases still do not, plunder and pillage the natural world.

It all comes down to the *guiding story,* or paradigm, that each culture or civilization lives and enacts. The guiding story of scientific materialism has dominated most human societies for the past four centuries. As previously noted, it is based on the metaphysical belief that matter is essentially "dead" stuff, which led to the development of industrial technologies that devastate ecosystems and that now threaten all life on our planet.

What happens when such a metaphysical story guides the thinking and actions of a species that is equipped with opposable thumbs (for precise manipulation of the physical world) and possesses sufficient intelligence to use those thumbs to create industrial-scale machines and the linguistic ability to share information?

Well, as Peter Russell suggests, it looks like the combination of thumbs, intelligence, and language could be intrinsically pathological—particularly when it leads to a species that manipulates its environment to its own ends, at the expense of the rest of the biosphere. Keep in mind that every technological invention, including modern industrial machines, came from a society that was once an indigenous culture. The shift came when our forebears changed their guiding story about the nature of the world to scientific materialism and changed their relationship to the world with the idea that humans are special. That's when the shift began to hit the fan.

The point is that even if whales and dolphins, with high intelligence and language (like us), had a metaphysical story of "dead" matter (like us), they would still not destroy their habitat (like us). Why? Because they lack opposable thumbs to manipulate the environment for self-serving ends.

Cetaceans have adapted to their environment through millions of years of evolution; they don't adapt it to meet their needs, as humans have done and still do. That's why the distinction between "thumb consciousness" and "flipper consciousness" is important.

Do Animals Have Egos?

Do other animals have egos? I'd say "yes"—egos occur on a spectrum from dim self-awareness to enlightened recognition and integration of the ego. I guess the central question is: *What do we mean by "ego"?* I take it to mean a felt sense of an *individual self.* Many other species (and some human groups) identify with their *community* or *pod.* Humans and other animals with egos identify with their perceived *separate identity.* But, as we learn from spiritual traditions, that sense of separateness is an illusion. Essentially, we are constituted by our *relationships.*

The problem with humans is not our egos per se—it's identifying with the ego as the core of who we are. That's the illusion. The trick (or practice) is to *have* an ego, and not to *be* our ego. Creatures, like us, who have an advanced cognitive capacity are both blessed and cursed with highly *self-reflective* egos, and that ability to be aware that we are aware of ourselves as individuals intensifies the coagulation of consciousness into the illusion of separate, individual selves (enhanced, of course, by the fact that our bodies have independent motion).

I do not think the goal or value of spiritual practice is to get rid of, or transcend, the ego, though some doctrines hold this view. Rather, the point is to cultivate the ego, moving along the path of individuation—to be as fully aware as possible of the autonomy of our own monad of consciousness (we can and do make choices), while recognizing and realizing that each monad is inextricably interdependent with every other monad, or self. We are simultaneously both individuals and *inter*viduals.

Do Other Species Experience Alienation?

I know you don't agree that we are the only species to be self-reflective, but will you say more about that? Do you believe any other species experiences alienation from self or source and, therefore, lacks a sense of meaning or purpose? Maybe the need to see ourselves as "special" and our resulting environmental actions are psychological overcompensations for human arrogance and narcissism, leading us deeper and deeper into alienation?

First, I don't think any other species on this planet has a sense of alienation from nature (self or source) or lacks a sense of meaning as many humans do. As you suggest, that sense of alienation is a symptom or consequence of both our self-reflexive consciousness and how we *apply* our consciousness to *impact* the rest of nature in negative ways.

My point is that our *impact* is a direct result of the story we tell ourselves that we are "special" in some morally superior way. If we didn't tell and *enact* that story, we would not have that sense of alienation. Indigenous peoples don't suffer from that form of existential anguish.

So, yes, the alienation is probably unique to humans—but it is a condition we ourselves have created. We can change that by changing our fundamental story.

Should we have compassion for humanity's unique sense of alienation? Possibly—but in the same way we'd have compassion for an alcoholic. We are addicted to our beliefs about human specialness— "specialaholics." And just as compassion for an alcoholic is insufficient to bring about change of behavior, we also need to *intervene,* to hold up a mirror, so that we humans see the consequences of clinging to our belief in "specialness." The key question, of course, is what *kind* of intervention is most likely to be effective.

"Psychological overcompensations for human arrogance and narcissism, leading us deeper and deeper into alienation." Good insight. I think you have named the spiraling dynamic at work here. And, because of that, we have an urgent need to *intervene* before it's too late. The clock is ticking; time is running out for us if we keep going the way we are. Something needs to change, and fast.

A CALL FOR COMPASSION

In order to bring about change, one must find a delicate way to expose flaws without raising defenses. I worry that perhaps you are evoking contempt for human arrogance—understandable, but not necessarily the most helpful approach to healing it. Might it be more effective if we embrace the shadow of human narcissism and recognize that it exists as a protection for the pain and fear that surely lie beneath it? Might we do better to approach it as a response to some deep psychological wounding and hold it with compassion and reverence rather than disdain and ridicule? Your message might be more palatable that way.

Interesting feedback, and I appreciate it. I do understand your point. Tolerance and compassion certainly would be one way to approach the notion that "we are special."

Right now, though, it's not an approach I wish to take, and I'm not sure it would be the most effective. Times have changed. I'm sure you have noticed. Now that we are in the post-9/11 era, with the U.S. administration forging ahead on its dominator agenda, it seems to me the time has come for strong voices to speak up and counter the lies and deceit foisted on us by a highly cunning and dangerous group of politicians—and their corporate backers.

Too much is at stake. Hundreds of thousands, perhaps millions, of people are dying as a result of their globalization policies—including the disgusting wars in the Middle East, part of a larger fundamentalist Christian "War on Islam" that's triggering an almost inevitable Islamic fundamentalist reaction.

Our environment is being destroyed at an alarming rate. Of course, not all is attributable to U.S. government policies—but their lack of any significant legislation to reduce carbon pollution and other environmental contamination is a significant factor. Millions of indigenous people, too, are in danger of losing their livelihoods and lives as this march toward eco-insanity stampedes relentlessly onward.

No Tolerance for Intolerance

We no longer have time to be "nice" to the people who are systematically destroying our planet. That's exactly what they want. It's what they expect from the "softies" on the "liberal left." We need to respond to their atrocities with comparable strength of will, creativity, and intolerance. I have compassion for the countless species endangered by human ignorance, selfishness, and blatant greed. I no longer have compassion for those who abuse compassion and manipulate goodwill. My heart pours out for this beautiful planet, but not for those who plunder and rape it.

The U.S. administration (by the way, this applies to most other national governments, too) is merely a symptom of a much larger

malaise—a pathology rooted in the dominant worldview that hypno-
tizes the vast majority of "civilized" human beings into believing "we
are special." My books, blogs, DVDs, lectures, and courses are all aimed
at showing how that story is the root cause of the rapid decline of our
biosphere and noosphere. I'm lending my voice to the growing minor-
ity of concerned citizens of Earth who declare: "Not in my name" and
"Stop before it's too late."

Yes, I do have contempt for puppet politicians who serve the agen-
das of their rich and powerful corporate backers, rather than serving
the people who voted them into power—and I have very good reasons
for expressing it.

I'm not sure how else you would like to see my message packaged
and delivered. How effective (not to mention authentic) do you think it
would be to approach, for example, the U.S. "drone wars" from a compassionate perspective?

INTERSPECIES WOUNDING?

On the larger scale, I don't see the arrogance explicit in the myth of human
specialness as a consequence of some traumatic interspecies "wounding."
The drive to believe in and act out the myth of human specialness did
not arise because we needed to protect ourselves by eradicating other species who were threatening to wipe us out. If that were the case, then the
indigenous people who survive today and who are far more exposed to the
vagaries of the "wild" than us cozy citizens of urban civilization would be
on the frontline of humans trying to decimate other species in the name
of "self-defense." That's simply not the case.

Blindspot: No, belief in human specialness arose because of an
impulse for unrestricted greed and power—beginning some thirteen
thousand years ago when a subgroup of our species decided that the
Earth belonged to us. And then, throughout the millennia, this dangerous absurdity was established and enshrined in the dominant myths

(worldviews, philosophies, cosmologies, and paradigms) that became the guiding visions for mainstream monotheistic religions and modern science. The rest, as they say, is history . . . literally.

I know that some—perhaps even many—people find it difficult to hear my message, to let in the possibility that "humans are not so special." But there are also many who do resonate and respond. And, right now, those are the people I'm writing for and talking to. I want to inspire others to stand up and speak their minds—especially on behalf of those voiceless other species who cannot argue their case in the courts of justice or common decency.

If you are among the people who, for whatever reasons, wish to continue to believe and to live as though the myth of human specialness is ordained as some god-given right, then, I'm afraid, I would have to consider your views and beliefs as part of the problem, blocking the way toward a solution we so desperately need. However, if you happen to agree with my message but just don't like the way I deliver it, then I urge you to go out and make *your* voice heard in whatever ways work for you and your audience. I promise: You have my heartfelt support.

Is Human Consciousness Unique?

> *I commend the spirit of your position, but I feel strongly nonetheless that it is simply wrong! To say "consciousness is not unique to humans" (I totally agree) is not the same as saying there is nothing unique or special about human consciousness. Even Whitehead, the main source of your views on panpsychism, would take you to task for this kind of flattening of the cosmopsychic landscape. It is this uniqueness, after all, that has gotten us and the planet into this pickle!*

Yes, of course, I'm aware there is something different about being human—that, after all, is what makes us a distinct *species*! My point is that consciousness is not by any means unique to humans. So we are *not* special on that count. You agree with this.

Depth Alert: But then you go on to express a "strong" objection to what you assume (incorrectly) to be my position that would equate (1) "consciousness is not unique to humans" with (2) "there is nothing unique or special about human consciousness." I have never said anything to that effect, so you are misreading something into my position I haven't expressed.

I *do* maintain there is nothing *especially* special about the fact that humans have consciousness, or indeed about our particular form of consciousness. This is an important distinction. Of course, there is something "unique" about human consciousness—just as there is about cetacean consciousness, or canine consciousness, or bat consciousness, or mouse consciousness, or bacterial consciousness, or molecular consciousness, or atomic consciousness, or quantum consciousness.

Yes, humans have mental capacities apparently not present in other species. But the reverse is also true: Other species have mental capacities we do not possess. The world shows up for us to a great extent according to our particular set of senses. The way we experience the world is filtered through our senses, in our case predominantly through vision, hearing, and touch. But bats, cetaceans, and other species have senses we don't possess, and so *their* world is "unique" to them. I wouldn't assume (as you might) that "our" world is somehow a more accurate or better representation or experience of the "real" world.

Further, if you are assuming that human consciousness is "special" because we have language, self-reflexivity, or any other mental capacity, then I would say, strongly, that your position is "simply wrong!" If you study the ethology literature, you will find evidence of language, reasoning, and self-reflexivity in nonhuman animals. So, my question to you is: What specific human mental capacities do you believe are *completely* unique to humans? And, further, in what ways would such capacities (if they existed) bestow on humans the notion that "we are special"—meaning that we have some morally or even biologically privileged place in the evolutionary web?

My point is that human mental capacities are on a *continuum* with similar capacities in other species. In *that* sense, there is nothing special about human consciousness. To believe otherwise, I'm saying, is to be part of the *world problematique*—issuing from the dogmas of monotheistic religions and a science based on the metaphysics of materialism. Yes, I am pretty vocal about the need to get beyond the biblically inspired myth that humans are special because that myth is doing unspeakable harm to our environment and to other species.

Your "strong" objection suggests to me that you haven't read and understood *Radical Nature.* I do not "flatten the cosmo-psychic landscape," as you say. Far from it. I celebrate the rich *hierarchical* diversity of species' biological, psychological, and spiritual evolution. But what I do hope to "flatten" is the accusation or implication that the position of radical naturalism or panpsychism in saying that consciousness goes all the way down is some form of naive anthropomorphism. My response: When people dismiss the idea that consciousness goes all the way down as anthropomorphic—projecting human qualities onto other species—they reveal their own (often unquestioned) *anthropocentric* assumption, the idea that humans lie at the center or at the apex of the evolutionary web or tree of life. In short: Accusations of anthropomorphism are often disguised (or unconscious) forms of *anthropocentrism. That's* the problem.

To my mind, it is not surprising that some human beings will go out of their way to create stories (philosophies, metaphysics, religions, even science) based on the assumption of human specialness. But notice that *every* claim and defense of human specialness is made by a *human.* Interesting, huh? Probably not a coincidence!

Side note: It has always puzzled me why scholars who get excited by the anthropic cosmological principle (the idea that the universe is structured in such a way that it *had to* produce the human species) don't see that this notion harbors a self-serving *tautology*. If a bat or a worm were to develop and communicate its cosmology, it would conclude that the universe came into being so that bats or worms would be able to spin out cosmologies depicting a universe that was destined to produce thinking bats or feeling worms. For all I know, we would more fruitfully spend our time and ingenuity elucidating a *bat-centered* cosmological principle. Now *there's* an idea to get excited about!

Are Humans Uniquely Unique?

The debate about whether humans are a "special" species has generated strong views on both sides—most commentators taking the view that, yes, there is something unique or special about humans. I have argued forcefully against that view.

As I watched the debate unfold and paid close attention to the views expressed, something didn't feel right, something wasn't connecting, something seemed to be missing. At first I couldn't pin it down, but one night I had an insightful dialogue with a friend who helped me untangle a few knots. As a result, I spent a few days contemplating the issue and now would like to clarify, even qualify, my position.

Part of what didn't "feel right" was the fact that so many people seem deeply committed to the notion of human specialness—which, I have argued, is the root cause of the ecological, psychological, and spiritual crises we face today. Yet many of the people who challenge me on this issue are, like me, also strong proponents of the need to respect the sentience (and perhaps even the "rights") of other species. I see that as common ground where we stand together.

So why the disconnect? As is so often the case in debates like this, I think the problem is essentially semantic, hinging on our differing interpretations of the word *special*. Because I introduced the issue using that term, I take responsibility for not adequately clarifying an important distinction. So, I will now do my best to make that clarification.

SPECIAL IMPACT

Depth Alert: It seems clear to me now that a common theme in the opposing views is that obviously humans are having a huge and unique impact on this planet. After all, isn't that why I raised the issue in the first place? That's a fair point, and I need to address it by offering a revised or more nuanced position:

1. Our species (at least our dominant planetary civilization) urgently needs to change our mode of being on the planet to cease the massive and widespread destructive effects we're having on the rest of the environment. I don't anticipate any basic disagreement from my colleagues on this—though some may have a different or better way to express it.

2. At the very least, the uniqueness of this destructive impact suggests there's something unique or special about our species—our "special" ability to wreak such global devastation. I agree with this.

3. What is the root cause of this global crisis? I have suggested that it is our story (worldview, metaphysics, cosmology) that elevates humans to a position above the rest of nature—somewhere between animals and gods. In short, the root of the problem is the story "we are special."

4. This "special" human status, I have argued, is often supported by appealing to scientific evidence for the advanced complexity and development of the human brain, notably our neocortex. This is, equally often, followed by the assumption that the human brain has produced a special form of sentience, consciousness, or intelligence, and that only humans possess this intelligence to such an advanced degree that we can use it to manipulate the natural world as we see fit, far beyond what any other species can achieve.

     So, we are "special" in the sense that we have a special brain, with special consciousness, including, for example, abstract reasoning, imagination, and analytical foresight, that enables us to manipulate nature in ways and to an extent far surpassing any other species.

While I challenge some of the assumptions in this view (e.g., that human brains produce human consciousness), I agree in essence with this perspective. I would add, of course, that our particular form of consciousness is necessary but not sufficient to account for our unprecedented manipulative ability. Most notably, our intelligence is applied so dramatically and with such effect because of our opposable thumbs and bipedalism. I agree, therefore, with those who insist there *is* something special about us humans.

Until now, I have countered by insisting on the distinction that we are not "especially special." I argued that our particular form of consciousness (and embodiment) is part of what distinguishes us from other animals, but that other animals have "special" characteristics too, including other mental capacities, that distinguish them from us. In that sense, every species is special, and there is nothing particularly special about our specialness.

But, some people object, there *is* something "especially special" about us: No other species has such a global impact on the rest of the environment. Of course, I acknowledge this. There is something remarkable, even unique, about the impact humans have on the rest of nature and perhaps on the course of evolution—though that's really a different issue, and one I'd like to come back to another time.

Might Is Not Right

Two questions arise:

1. Does this "uniqueness" imply any kind of moral superiority? Do we have any "special" rights or privileges in our dealings with the rest of the natural world?

2. Does our ability to tell the story of our own uniqueness reinforce in any way a positive answer to question 1?

My response to question 1 is, unreservedly, "no." Our "special" status as an intelligent manipulative species does not bestow on us any moral superiority (even if we are the only species with the ability to make moral judgments). Possessing a moral sense does not give us moral superiority, though it might mean we have a greater, or unique, moral responsibility.

My response to question 2 is "let's be vigilant." I think we need to be very careful: Even if humans happen to have a degree of manipulative intelligence much greater than that of other species, this doesn't mean we have unique or special rights vis-à-vis the rest of nature.

We may be different, but we're not special. We are not special in the sense that we have any moral superiority or claimants' rights over the rest of nature. Special might does not bestow special right.

There is no scientific support for the notion of human moral superiority. And even if the notion of "superior" manipulative intelligence were confirmed by science (which it is not), that would not mean we are morally privileged. This is where the influence of biblically based monotheistic religions can be a danger. The notion that only humans have "souls" or that we are "created in the image of God" implies a divine imprimatur for human license to exploit the natural world—a version of the myth of manifest destiny.

And even if we succeed in bracketing out this biblical influence, the danger remains that some people assume, and act out, the dictum that "might is right." Just because we have superior manipulative intelligence (the "might") does not give us the moral latitude (the "right") to apply it willy-nilly without due regard for the welfare and well-being of other species.

Better Off without Us?

My thinking opened up more when a friend posed a couple of really intriguing questions:

"If you were to ask any other species whether there is something uniquely unique about humans, and if they could answer, what do you think they would say?"

I thought for a moment and realized they would probably say, yes, humans are unique as a species in their ability to impact the environment. No other species comes close. And it is this unique ability of humans that is such a problem for the rest of us.

The second question: "If humans are so unique in their destructive impact on nature, should the human species be eliminated?"

My response to that was more immediate, and also more nuanced: No, I don't for one moment advocate wiping out the human species— for a number of reasons.

First, it is not the human species that is the problem; it is a now-dominant subset of our species, the subset we call *modern civilization.* It is the group of humans who assume, whether as a result of divine fiat or evolutionary accident, that our species has the right, backed up by the might, to manipulate the rest of nature to meet our needs and desires—whatever the cost to the rest of the environment. The problem is the dominant subgroup, which tells and lives the story "we are especially special." Not all humans by any means buy into that story—most notably indigenous peoples and Buddhists.

Second, if we keep on our current globally destructive path, sooner or later nature itself will eliminate us, or a great portion of us— unfortunately taking down countless other species along the way (see the epilogue for more on this). The "good news" in this apocalyptic scenario is that the humans most likely to survive the collapse of our social and economic systems, along with the massive disruption of our ecosystems, are those of us whose ways of life have remained closer to and more in harmony with nature's ways—specifically, indigenous and other marginalized subsistence-living peoples. The mythopoetic justice in that scenario appeals to me.

Third, I and most of my friends belong to this species!

Change of Story

So, where does all of this leave us? For me, it comes down to this:

1. Humans are unique in our capacity for manipulative intelligence. However, when not guided by wisdom, this can seriously backfire (see the epilogue).
2. Humans are not special in any sense that gives us moral superiority. Quite simply: *Might is not right.*
3. Our unique capacity for manipulative intelligence per se is not the problem because indigenous cultures also possess that capacity.
4. The problem is coupling manipulative intelligence with one of its products: our ability to spin out stories—in particular, the story that says *because we have the intellectual might, we therefore have the moral right to use it to our species' advantage at the expense of any or all other species.*

That's what needs to change—not our manipulative intelligence as such, but the guiding story we act out.

Specifically, we need to give up the self-serving myth that puts humans at the forefront of biological (or even cosmic!) evolution. I question both the accuracy and implications of a story, told by humans, of course, that places *humans* in an evolutionarily privileged position. But as I said, that's another story for another day.

A PERVASIVE MALAISE

I see us facing a double-headed "pervasive malaise"—with two distinct, but interrelated, components. One I have already referred to, variously, as the biblically inspired or monotheistic myth that humans are "special" because we are God's "chosen" species. The other is the myth of scientific materialism, which supports the story of human specialness by assuming that consciousness (or intelligence) is produced by complex electrochemical events in neurons and brains, and that we humans possess the most advanced version of this, and extrahuman nature itself has none.

Fundamentally, the malaise is metaphysical. It stems from our understanding of the nature and origins of consciousness, and the ontological relationship between matter and mind. It is a problem of worldview.

We are all pawns in the paradigm, born into the spirit of our times. Of course, the problem is deeper than any particular science, philosophy, politician, or political group—it is systemic. However, because of their privileged positions of power in the global system, the people in government are particularly dangerous exponents of this "metaphysical malaise."

Like many people, I would like to see a "regime change" in the United States. But even more, I long for a shift in the fundamental worldview that informs how we relate to the rest of the natural world.

Who Would You Save?

I have wondered: If I saw a young boy or girl drowning alongside a little puppy, whom would I save first? I thought this might be a measure of whether I do value humans over other species. Well, I gotta tell ya, I'd go for the human. But why? If I honestly don't see humans as superior, why would I save the human first? I think it's the potential impact this human being could have on the world.

This is an excellent question, and it really does highlight a dilemma. I will give my answer in a moment. But first, let me ask you: What would you do if you saw *two humans* drowning but could save only one? Or what if one of the drowning people was a member of your immediate family and the other was a stranger? What then?

In the scenario you describe, I would probably try to save both human and dog. But, and I think your point is, what if I could save only *one*? Quite honestly, I don't know. If it were my dog, Oblio, versus a human stranger, I think I'd probably save Oblio first. However, that's because I consider Oblio part of my *family.*

And so, to get more theoretical about this hypothetical situation, I think the drive you have (and it's possibly one I share) to instinctively save humans could well be biologically based. We are probably *evolved* to care for our own species first (part of "survival of the fittest"). It may be a drive rooted in our genetic dispositions—"save the gene pool"!

Now, of course, in Oblio's case saving him would not be saving my gene pool. So some other motivation would be at work—for example, the deep bond of caring and relationship I have with him.

Almost certainly, I would not be standing on the riverbank thinking about which being, dog or human, is most likely to make the most beneficial contribution to the future of our planet. I would act out of my sense of *what matters most to me at that moment.*

Healing Our Eco-footprint

Even though we have the ability to be far more destructive than other creatures, we also have the ability, responsibility even, to impact the environment in a positive healing way.

I agree; we should look for ways to enhance healing the planet. But I think we need to be careful here. We may be able to reduce our negative impact on the planet by changing our story about human specialness and how we act it out. That would involve cultivating and applying our consciousness in different ways. But the *absence* of negative impact is not *intrinsically* a *positive* impact; the positive impact comes from allowing nature to heal itself.

I take a Taoist-like position that humans, as integral parts of the natural system, cannot—and should not attempt to—"save" nature. Nature was doing just fine for billions of years before we came along, and will probably do so for billions of years after we're gone.

So, I'm calling for us to reduce the impact of our eco-footprint, and by doing so bring about healing. But as I've said, I do not support the idea that we should be "stewards" of the planet who "know best" how to "save" or "heal" nature. Let's leave that up to the Tao, to natural processes. Our job, as I've said elsewhere, is not to get in the way, but to *listen* and respond to nature's innate wisdom.

WAKING UP TO CONSCIOUSNESS

Just in case you missed the news: Scientists now agree that other animals have consciousness—just like humans. In the summer of 2012, a group of scientists signed the Cambridge Declaration on Consciousness, finally acknowledging this "breakthrough" realization.

Of course, *you* already knew this, right? But it is encouraging to see the mainstream world of science and philosophy finally step up to the mark. The Cambridge conference and declaration included some of the world's leading neuroscientists and behavioral researchers, who signed the declaration in the presence of the most famous scientist in the world today: physicist Stephen Hawking.

Cambridge Declaration on Consciousness

We declare the following: "The absence of a neocortex does not appear to preclude an organism from experiencing affective states. Convergent evidence indicates that non-human animals have the neuroanatomical, neurochemical, and neurophysiological substrates of conscious states along with the capacity to exhibit intentional behaviors. Consequently, the weight of evidence indicates that humans are not unique in possessing the neurological substrates that generate consciousness. Non-human animals, including all mammals and birds, and many other creatures, including octopuses, also possess these neurological substrates."*

---

*http://fcmconference.org/img/CambridgeDeclarationOnConsciousness.pdf

One thing particularly struck me: the list includes *octopuses.* For many years, I have regarded octopuses as invertebrates with high intelligence. It's great to see they have now made it to the "mainstream."*

The fact that the scientific "consensus" includes insects is an encouraging sign. It means they recognize the existence of group or collective intelligence, too.

Although the Cambridge declaration got a lot of press (deservedly so), no doubt you would still search in vain for the *really big news.* It should be splashed all over the front pages of major newspapers and blogs and headline the evening news: MINDS DON'T NEED BRAINS.

Berkeley philosopher John Searle famously insisted: "It's just obvious that brains 'squirt' out consciousness." That was never obvious to me.

Until now, like Searle, most philosophers and neuroscientists believed that in order to be conscious you not only needed a brain, but your brain also had to have a *neocortex,* the thin outer layer of brain tissue in humans and other higher mammals. But octopuses and birds, for example, don't have a neocortex. And while individual bees have a tiny clump of neurons in their heads, they can hardly be said to have brains. Certainly hives of bees don't have brains. Conclusion: *You don't need a brain to be conscious.*

Where, then, does consciousness come from? Short answer: It doesn't come from *anywhere.* Matter comes with mind already built in. Consciousness is intrinsic to matter/energy—part of its very essence. Those of you familiar with my work (see *Radical Nature*) know I'm

---

*Let's see if the mainstream wakes up to other species, or rather groups of species, that I also consider to have high intelligence—for example, *corals.* Although obviously very different from mammalian consciousness (they don't have brains, for one thing), corals "hum" with awareness of their environment. They have been taking care of ocean habitats for millions of years. I suspect that many other species, such as groves of redwoods, oaks, and likely mushrooms, too, also rise to this level of group intelligence. Because consciousness goes all the way down to cells, molecules, atoms, and beyond, and because corals, like all other organisms, are made of atoms, molecules, and cells, logic tells us that corals "hum" with awareness. (Hell, some of them even look like gigantic underwater brains!)

fond of the slogan, "Consciousness all the way down." Cells, molecules, atoms, subatomic particles, quarks, and quanta . . . all "tingle with the spark of spirit."

That's the only way to make sense of the fact that we are all made of that stuff, and we tingle with consciousness. If we have a capacity for awareness and feeling, then *whatever we are made of* must likewise have that capacity to some degree (*you can't get something from nothing*). And if our cells, molecules, and atoms tingle with sentience, it must be true of all other cells, molecules, and atoms, too. Last time I checked, there's no special human element "Hu" in the periodic table.

The Cambridge declaration is a start—a good start. It should be good news for our fellow nonhuman species. Let's hope the Cambridge declaration soon translates to more humane treatment of all sentient beings. Next step, we need a Declaration of Nonhuman Rights—better still, let's get international endorsement of the Declaration of the Rights of Nature, signed at the World People's Conference on Climate Change in Bolivia in 2010.

14
Evolution by Design?
"Life Is Either Divine Creation or Random Evolution"

What if both science and religion are wrong about evolution? What if both are right?

Let's get right down to the heart of the matter: What fuels the hot debate on intelligent design versus evolution? Why do so many in the media, in our schools, and in government show so much interest in this issue?

Here's my take: Many common folk seem to find the idea that humans evolved from other animals (or worse, from single-celled organisms, or worse still, from *inanimate* molecules) simply preposterous. But why? Why is it so preposterous to see humans on a continuum with the rest of the natural world, including the larger cosmos?

Undoubtedly, an unfortunate time lag exists between scientific discovery and when that knowledge filters through to the common imagination. But that is only part of the problem. The deeper problem, it seems to me, is that the "common folk" simply aren't interested in finding out about scientific details that would upset their beliefs about who we are as human beings.

Their religions (I'm talking mostly about monotheistic doctrines here) have told them that as humans *we are special.* And that myth seems to be *very* important to a great many people. As we've seen, the story that we are "special" is a direct consequence of the dualistic belief that we have "souls" inserted into our otherwise soulless bodies by a supernatural divine creator. We are "special" because we alone are made in "God's image."

Any scientific evidence or theory that might challenge this myth is resisted *at all costs*. The issue gets more complicated because science, too, tends to support this notion of human specialness—often supported by the very stories of *evolution* the science community wants the "common folk" to hear.

The standard story in modern mainstream science (in physics, chemistry, biology, even cosmology) is that only creatures with brains or nervous systems can possibly possess minds or consciousness. Mind, we are told, "emerges" from the complexity of the brain's nervous tissue, and, as is often pointed out, *human* nervous tissue is "special" because we have this highly complex and evolved neocortex.

Want to know where consciousness or mind comes from? Squeeze a brain and watch mind come squirting out! Well, the standard story is not quite so blatantly absurd as that. But scratch the surface of this "mind-from-brain" assumption, and you'll find it is equally absurd.

As I have discussed elsewhere (in this and other books), the notion that mind (a *nonphysical, subjective* reality) could possibly evolve or emerge from *wholly* mindless (*physical, objective*) matter in brain cells or their constituents is both logically and ontologically incoherent. It would take a miracle, a supernatural intervention, to be true. There is *no explanation* for how this "miracle" could occur.

Blindspot: What we're all dealing with here is a crisis of *story*. By "story," I mean our metaphysical worldview or cosmology from which we draw our beliefs about the nature of reality, about the nature of mind and matter, and about how they are related. As long as we believe in a story that either separates mind and matter or assumes one emerges from the other, the crisis won't go away.

That's why I'm passionate about this issue—about generating interest in the debate on how consciousness fits into the physical world. *That's* what lies at the heart of the Great Story debate. As long as this issue is left unaddressed, the Great Story is not only left unfinished, it really hasn't even begun.

To get to the starting line, to ground the Great Story in a "plot" that makes sense, we (scholars and lay folk alike) need to discipline our thinking to go deeper than we may be accustomed to, so we can understand the subtle metaphysical assumptions and distinctions lurking in the heart of both science and religion.

The idea of *sentient matter* (that consciousness or spirit *goes all the way down,* so that mind is present in all matter at every level) is not at all "preposterous" to indigenous peoples. They are not attached to the myth of human specialness. They recognize the sacredness of *all* nature because *their* story acknowledges that matter itself "tingles with the spark of spirit." Curiously enough, they don't need *science* (or philosophy) to validate their story. Of course, the Great Story is a modern scientific version of their story—*as long as our science assumes the essential sentience and sacredness of matter.*

Do ordinary people have difficulty grasping the slogan "spirit matters"? Probably not. And it may not be such a long shot for them to also accept that "matter spirits." As I will outline in a moment, this idea—that matter quivers with spirit and intelligence—offers a way out of the seemingly endless and pointless debate between creationists and evolutionists, between religion and science.

DARWIN OR JESUS?

We've all seen them: bumper stickers and decals of a fish with legs symbolizing Darwin's theory of evolution. And then, from religious creationists, the "counter-decals" of a fish with a cross swallowing Darwin's amphibious fish. The battle of the decals is just one way the debate between creationists and evolutionists overflows onto our streets.

But there's an alternative: a philosophy that shows why both religion and science have got it wrong—and right.

To move beyond the ideological clashes and wars in these troubled times—between fundamentalists in both religion and science—we need a wiser, more coherent account of who we are and how we came to be. We need a revised and renewed vision of creation and evolution. We need a deeper and broader understanding of both religion and science.

Both Wrong and Right

Religion is wrong to place the "Creator" beyond nature, in the realm of the supernatural. Science is wrong to deny intelligence—consciousness or spirit—at work in evolution.

Religion is right to hold the view that there is *creation* and that creation possesses intelligence. And religion is right to deny that the birth and evolution of our world happened by chance.

Science is right to hold the view that evolution produces different species, including humans. And science is right to deny that some supernatural intelligent designer is responsible for the wondrous diversity and interconnectedness of living and nonliving forms.

Best of Both

In the new view I'm proposing, creation is not the result of some supernatural Creator—nor is creation a one-time event. Instead, creation is *continuous* and *natural,* as I will explain shortly. Evolution is not random and does not unfold without the guidance of a deep intelligence. Instead, we need to appreciate that nature itself is naturally intelligent and creative—and *that's* how evolution occurs.

Instead of a "higher" intelligence, I say let's be open to a *deeper* intelligence. Instead of "dead" and "dumb" matter, let's be open to *sentient* and *intelligent* matter. Then we can have the best of both worlds—integrating the great insights of both religion and science.

The "missing link," of course, is *consciousness.* The ability to have experience, to feel, to be aware is a complete mystery to science. Evolution cannot explain it. Religions take for granted that consciousness or soul is unique to humans. But when we look more deeply at the issue, and with unbiased eyes, the very *fact* that consciousness exists at all highlights the shortcomings of both science and religion.

New Worldview

We need a new worldview in which religion recognizes that consciousness—intelligence or spirit—is not supernatural but is part of the natural fabric of the cosmos, Earth, and life, and one in which science recognizes that matter itself "tingles with the spark of spirit," that evolution is guided from within. This "new" worldview is called *panpsychism* or *radical naturalism*. (Actually, it's a very ancient philosophy, shared by indigenous cultures throughout the world.) We could also call it *intelligent evolution*.

If we shift to such a view, then we can begin to transcend the squabbles between those who believe in supernatural intelligent design and those who believe in random evolution.

The biggest challenge facing modern science is to explain the mystery of consciousness. Science based on the assumption of "dead" insentient matter exploding from a random big bang cannot account for mind. Yet, as we have seen, consciousness is one reality we can be absolutely certain exists. The biggest challenge facing mainstream religion is to remain relevant in a world increasingly dominated by scientific knowledge. The philosophy of *intelligent evolution* can help science and religion meet these challenges—by taking us beyond the dogmas of both.

Blindspots:

Beyond Religion: The world was not created by a supernatural transcendent God in seven days or in 13.7 billion years.

Beyond Science: The world did not come into being from a random big bang followed by billions of years of random cosmic, chemical, and biological evolution. Instead, the most coherent story about how the world came to be (a world where both matter and mind are real) recognizes that:

1. Spirit is not supernatural (above and beyond nature), and
2. Evolution is not without purpose or intelligence.

Intelligent Design: Yes, there *is* an "intelligent designer" at work in evolution. But the intelligence (call it God or Spirit) is *intrinsic* to nature. Nature itself is intelligent (has sentience and consciousness, purpose and meaning) all the way down to single cells, molecules, atoms, and subatomic particles.

Evolution: In this new view of nature and evolution, matter itself is intelligent and adventurous. When we understand this, we can see that *evolution is the adventure of matter exploring its own creative potentials.* As matter evolves, its native intelligence or consciousness evolves, too. So by the time human and other advanced brains come on the scene, matter, or nature, has achieved the remarkable ability to be self-reflective— to know that it knows—and to ponder the eternal questions in religion, philosophy, and science: Where did we come from? Who are we? Where are we going? Why is there anything at all?

Intelligent Evolution: How about a sacred fish with legs? Instead of the amusing (and silly) bumper stickers pitching Darwin against Jesus, evolution versus religion, we can come up with a new set of symbols and sound bytes. Picture a decal that shows a fish with legs and a halo, indicating that evolution is a sacred process because spirit is active in the development of species. Evolution is *natural* and *creative*. We could say "spirit matters" or, just as meaningful, "matter spirits."

Figure 14.1. Evolution is natural and creative.

Scientific Evidence for Intelligence?

> *You talk and write a lot about intelligence in evolution, and although I'm sympathetic to this view, I wonder: What scientific evidence exists for any kind of intelligence?*

Short answer: *None. Zero. Zilch.* Given that scientific methodology relies exclusively on *sensory* empiricism, there just isn't any way that science could confirm or refute the presence or absence of intelligence or consciousness—in *anything*, including humans.

The most we can conclude from physics, cosmology, and evolutionary sciences is that *it seems* plausible to *infer* that there is (or at least could be) some intelligence at work in the evolution of the cosmos and life on our planet. This lies at the heart of the debate between intelligent design versus random evolution. Religious creationists propose that God's hand is guiding the evolution of species, while modern scientists reject the possibility of any intelligence directing evolution and claim that life evolves merely through natural selection of random genetic mutations.

Blindspot: Creationists try to argue that intelligent design amounts to scientific evidence for God, but the intricate complexities found in evolution provide no such evidence. Here's the problem: Consciousness (and all its attributes, such as intelligence) is *nonphysical*. That means *it cannot be measured* and, therefore, is not amenable to scientific investigation. As I've noted before, we have no "consciousness meter" or "mindalyzer" to detect consciousness or intelligence. Philosophically or theologically, we may *infer* that some intelligence must be at work in evolution, but that does not amount to *scientific* evidence.

Science cannot provide evidence to either support or reject the notion of intelligence at work in evolution. We need to turn to philosophy to make the case, and, according to panpsychism, the most coherent account of how conscious living systems came to be is that some kind of intelligence is intrinsic to matter itself. Matter is *adventurous,* and what we call *evolution* is matter creatively exploring its own vast potentials.

Survival of the Fittest?

> Science has revealed a multitude of complex life forms, all closely entwined in a global self-sustaining ecosystem. Doesn't a self-organizing biosphere support the idea of intelligence in evolution? Why, then, does science try to explain evolution in terms of survival of the fittest through natural selection and random mutations—avoiding any reference to intelligence or consciousness?

That is exactly what science tells us about evolution—it's all a product of natural selection acting on spontaneous genetic mutations. However, this story clearly misses something obvious and important: *Consciousness is an undeniable evolutionary fact.* Here we are . . . conscious, sentient beings, products of the grand sweep of evolution from the Big Bang to the appearance of big-brained humans and other mammals. How could that happen merely through the evolution of "dead" insentient matter? Impossible.

Let's first deal with the idea of "survival of the fittest."

Blindspot: For scientific materialists, evolution progresses solely through a series of random physical processes—genetic mutations and natural selection. Neither of these requires or implies consciousness or mind. For them, a mutation is a random event at the level of DNA molecules, brought about by random quantum events (e.g., being struck by cosmic rays from deep space or the inevitable "jiggle" of quantum uncertainty spontaneously disrupting links between atoms). Once these mutations happen, most of them produce dysfunctions that kill off the mutated organism. However, from time to time, a few mutations actually enhance an organism's ability to feed itself and to find a mate and reproduce, thereby allowing it to pass on its genetic profile to the next generation. This process is called *natural selection.* It can even be sim-ulated in a computer program called Artificial Life—in which shapes and patterns on the screen follow evolutionary principles guided by algorithms designed to mimic natural selection. None of this involves or requires consciousness (except, of course, in the people who designed the computer systems).

But what does "survival of the fittest" actually mean? Well, it sim-ply means those organisms that live long enough to pass on their genes are more "fit" than those that do not. "Fit for what?" you might ask. Well, they are "fit" to pass on their genes. It's a tautology: It means, really, nothing more than "those species that survive to pass on their genes, survive." Or, more starkly: "Those that survive, survive." Well, great. Which logical genius figured *that* out? Like all tautologies, it tells us nothing new. It is simply true by definition.

When materialists say something like "survival is key," they mean nothing more than the simple fact that for a species to survive, some of its members must live long enough to reproduce and pass on their genes to the next generation.

Now to your point about the mind-boggling complexity of the eco-system and the finely tuned interconnections between the life forms that make up the biosphere. How could all of this have come about without the guidance of some kind of intelligence? That's your question.

Well, yes, it's true that biology, chemistry, and physics have revealed systems of truly amazing and puzzling complexity in nature—and to open minds this suggests that some intelligent "hand" could be at work, guiding the unfolding of evolution.

However, it is prima facie *plausible* that all this came about without any intelligence guiding it—at least that is the mainstream scientific position. Evolutionary complexity per se does not suggest (never mind compel us to believe) that intelligence is afoot in nature. Thirteen-plus billion years is a *lot of time* for unimaginable complexity to arise, and for a great variety of complex living systems to emerge from far simpler systems of matter and energy.

However, the real conundrum for science is not "life" or how it evolves—it is *consciousness*. We know for certain that consciousness exists—we are conscious embodied beings. How did *that* come about? How has it been possible for material beings (e.g., humans) to "tingle with the spark of consciousness or experience"? *That's* where science (and materialist metaphysics) quickly runs off the rails.

In other words, because we know consciousness exists in our own case, the most likely story to account for that fact (along with the fact that we are embodied beings) is to start with the assumption that consciousness *in some form* existed from the beginning of the physical universe.

If we define *intelligence* as "having a purpose and the means to creatively move toward fulfilling that purpose" (see below), then it makes sense to posit some intelligence right at the start of the process. We can call this "God," but it is not a god supported by scientific evidence. It is a god made inevitable (or at least very likely) by rational *extrapolations* from our own direct experience. The idea of intelligence at work in evolution has got very little, if anything, to do with science. It's a *philosophical* conclusion based on experience and logic.

The idea of a primordial intelligence has nothing to do with the religious myth of an almighty god, either—of some supernatural father figure watching over us and judging us from the heavens. The "god" of intelligent evolution is the innate consciousness in all matter/energy throughout the cosmos and throughout time.

Defining Intelligence

How do you define intelligence? *Isn't it simply the ability to solve problems? In which case, computers would be intelligent. But I wouldn't say they are conscious. Also, I think it is possible to measure intelligence—that's what IQ tests do.*

I define *intelligence* in two ways: "having a purpose and the means to creatively move toward fulfilling that purpose" or "having a purpose, perceiving possibilities, and choosing actions that realize a goal."

In short, intelligence is a characteristic of consciousness. You simply cannot have intelligence if you don't have consciousness. Anyone who attempts to define intelligence as a problem-solving ability, and tries to avoid implying consciousness, is likely to produce something far removed from anything the word *intelligence* typically means.

Blindspot: The very words *problem* and *solving* already imply consciousness. Nonexperiencing entities (such as rocks, forks, beer cans, hammers) never experience problems and never discover solutions. A problem arises only when some experiencing entity has a goal or purpose in mind that is thwarted or is perceived to be thwarted. And only creatures with consciousness can have goals or purposes or perceptions. Nothing purely physical can have a goal or purpose.

Using their own human intelligence, scientists and engineers design artificial intelligence (AI) machines that produce behaviors that they (the investigators) interpret as "intelligent." However, the best AI can do is *simulate* intelligence. If the parts used to construct the machine, including software, don't already possess consciousness, then no matter how ingeniously the machines are constructed, *they will never be intelligent.*

To understand why, it is important not to confuse "intelligence," which is a *subjective* phenomenon, with "intelligent behavior," which is based on evaluations of *objective* behaviors. Intelligent *behavior* is not the same as *intelligence.*

Bottom line: Intelligent behavior is in the eye of the beholder—where the intelligence exists—not in the impressive behavior of a well-programmed machine.

Likewise, IQ tests don't measure intelligence—they measure *behaviors.* And the interpreter of the behavior then infers (or not) that some intelligence is guiding the behaviors. Being subjective, intelligence is not observable or measurable. There's no getting around that. We have no technology to detect or measure mental events—*only consciousness can observe consciousness.*

DOES IT REALLY MATTER?

Isn't this whole debate about evolution versus intelligent design a waste of time and energy? Isn't it an error to insist, or even assume, that differing views of science and religion should find convergent solutions? Even though they inspect the same phenomenon, science and religion have different ways of knowing and therefore generate different stories. Shouldn't you leave science and religion to teach their own creation myths, rather than try to build bridges between them, forge a meeting of minds, or turn one into the other? Isn't it better to focus on things that really matter?

Keeping science and religion apart is an interesting perspective, though not new. It's one shared by the great philosopher of religion Huston Smith. Just to be clear, I don't advocate turning science into religion or religion into science. Yes, of course, each discipline has its own epistemology and will, therefore, arrive at its own different mythos.

I don't think science and religion "inspect the same phenomenon," not at all. Science investigates the *objective physical* world; religion and spirituality investigate the *subjective nonphysical* world.

By all means, let's be mindful of their epistemological and methodological differences, and not try to smooth them over. Nevertheless, that does not mean we should abandon engaging in dialogue or looking for areas of commonality between the "two cultures." When I suggest that we look for ways to build bridges between science and spirituality, I'm honoring their intrinsic differences while recognizing common ground—a bridge scientists and sages can walk across to shake hands.

A meeting of minds is not unattainable. After all, we do live in the same *uni*verse. The unavoidable reality common to both science and religion is *consciousness*. By focusing on understanding how consciousness relates to the physical world (whether through science, philosophy, or religion) we will, for the first time since the establishment of modern science, have a common "phenomenon" to investigate. And when we do, science will have to radically change its methodology to include subjective data, paying attention to the wealth of knowledge and wisdom about the "inner realms" accumulated over millennia through spiritual practices and traditions.

To keep the two disciplines, science and spirituality, separate—one exclusively in the objective physical domain, the other in the subjective nonphysical domain—is to remain entranced by Descartes's mind-matter dualism. Besides being philosophically catastrophic, Cartesian dualism has had profound and drastic consequences for countless individuals and species ever since both science and religion agreed to go their separate ways. It seems to me that what is happening to other species, to the environment, to the health and livelihoods of millions of indigenous peoples *is* something that "really matters."

A rapprochement between science and spirituality, through the alternative view of "intelligent evolution" that I propose, in which mind is native to matter, would go a long way toward healing that unfortunate and pathological split.

Who's Leading the Evolutionary Race?

I would say that at this point in time, humanity's place is special—because we are riding the crest of the wave of evolution. Humans are the only animals that self-reflect and think about evolution and the role of human consciousness in the entire spiritual process. But I agree with you that that does not make us more important. To humankind, I say: "Do not separate yourself from the wave of the world."

Be very careful here. Ask yourself who (which species) decides on the criteria for evaluating evolutionary "development" and "progress." And is it just a coincidence that the criteria humans come up with happen to place *us* at the pinnacle of progress? We need to be extra attentive to unconscious self-serving anthropocentrism that leads to the myth of human specialness.

Yes, it seems to be the case that humans are the only species that can reflect on evolution and spiritual progress. And until we develop better means for interspecies communication, it is likely to continue to appear this way.

However, from the perspective and experience of shamans and other indigenous peoples, this view—that only humans engage in spiritual development—is rejected as a self-congratulatory illusion.

By all means, "do not separate yourself from the rest of the world." And I would add: Do not engage in the inflation story that places humans in some special or privileged place in evolution—at least not before consulting other species to discover how they view things. I would hold off from privileging humans until we get consensus from other species that they agree with our own self-assessment.

Part of the difficulty, as I see it, is that as long as we engage in the "humans are special" story (because we have "special consciousness"), then very likely we are closing off channels of communication with other species. I notice that indigenous peoples who do not hold this "humans are special" view report quite profound "conversations" with the animal and plant worlds. So far, they have not reported anything close to an interspecies consensus that humans have the privileged place in nature that many humans like to think we have.

FREE-RANGE HUMANS

I would love to be able to travel back in time to when humans first split from nature, with the invention of agriculture. I'd tell the people to grow food in harmony with each other and nature. If only our ancestors had realized the devastation farming and industry would eventually have on the rest of the world.

If only it were so easy. Even if you could hop into your time machine and plead with your ancestors, it would not have made any difference. You first need to understand *why* early humans turned from a nomadic hunter-gatherer way of life—in close-to-perfect harmony with the rest of nature, one wild animal species among all the others—to a sedentary agricultural way of life.

The hunter-gatherer lifestyle was far less labor intensive and much more healthy. Why, then, did our ancestors give all that up and opt for the drudgery of farming? Short answer: *climate change.*

At the end of the last great ice age, the world's forests sprouted up in vast and thick profusion. In time, the nomadic peoples could no longer range freely in search of food. They were trapped in relatively small clearings in impenetrable forests (usually near rivers or lakes). As a result, *they had to start growing their own food in order to survive.* It was not by choice. They were *forced* into farming by the encroaching trees. As British scholar Peter Prew puts it in his remarkable book *The Human Reality,* our farming ancestors became "de-ranged" when they could no longer range free and wide across the land. We stopped being "free-range" humans and, with the advent of farming, became "deranged" animals. If this topic interests you, I highly recommend Prew's book.

We face a similar crisis today.

CONSCIOUS EVOLUTION

What drives evolution of consciousness and culture, I wonder, and how do we consciously, creatively participate in it? Some of us believe that humans are *the living face of evolution today—that we are, in fact, evolution becoming conscious of itself. Do you agree that through us evolution is coming to understand its own dynamics and is now poised to direct the future of evolution with intentionality, purpose, and intelligent design?*

I think the phrase "intelligent design" is deliciously appropriate in this context. A deeper understanding of consciousness in evolution can help us in two ways: First, by showing how consciousness shapes the development of societies and cultures; and second, and much more important, by accepting that consciousness is a decisive and directive influence on the trajectory of species evolution itself.

In my work—especially in *Radical Nature* and my novel *Deep Spirit*—I make a strong case that consciousness has *always* been a factor directing the "adventure of matter" we call evolution. And I do think that self-reflexive consciousness is, as you say, "evolution becoming conscious of itself." While I don't think this is unique to humans, I agree that we do (or, at least, *can*) have a significant role to play in the future of evolution on Earth, and perhaps beyond.

Because humans are natural products of evolution, whatever attributes we have, including self-reflexive consciousness, are natural expressions of evolution, too. Yes, we are *a* "living face" of evolution today—but we are not alone. We have very good reasons to believe other species, such as cetaceans and some of the other great apes, also possess forms of self-reflexive consciousness.

The newfound human ability to tinker with genetics, of course, gives us a way to interfere with the process of natural selection that other species don't possess. However, I think conscious *intention*—much more than any DNA "fix"—will guide the future unfolding of evolution. In that case, human genetic manipulation pales in comparison to the collective intention at work in *all* species—not just humans.

As always, I'm interested in shifting attention (or expanding attention) from a self-serving, self-absorbed focus on *human* consciousness or evolution. We share this ecosystem, and consciousness, with a host of other sentient beings, without whom we would not be who we are or be able to survive. The evolution of human culture and society will always take place within a larger context and network of other sentient beings who are also evolving. Like most indigenous cultures, we need to see our species as just one "nation" sharing this beautiful planet and awesome cosmos with a more-than-human world.

As I discussed earlier in this chapter, the "intelligent design" at work in evolution is not something new that came on the scene with human consciousness. It has always been there—in all species, in all matter—as a *natural* ingredient of the sentient energy that pervades the cosmos and underlies all of reality.

Creation is at work in evolution—the natural creative capacity that matter/energy itself possesses. Creation is ongoing, not a one-time event. That's why I speak of "intelligent evolution" as an alternative to the rather strange debate between proponents of intelligent design and neo-Darwinian evolution. Evolution is, literally, the Great Story that intelligent, sentient matter/energy expresses for itself.

I delight in the fact that you and I—and all our sentient colleagues—are part of this wondrous cosmic evolutionary tale.

15

Fate or Free Will?

"Everything Is Determined by Fate or Physics"

It's an age-old question: Do we have free will or is everything we do determined by physics, genetics, environment, or God?

Well, most of the time it really does *seem* as though we can make choices. You wake up in the morning, lie in bed enjoying the comfort and warmth ("just a few minutes more"), and next thing you know you're out of bed. *You made a choice.*

Or did you?

What if, behind the scenes, your nervous system was shooting messages back and forth between synapses in your brain—all unconsciously—and then, when this activity reached a certain threshold, it triggered you into action? It might have *felt* like you made a choice, but in actual fact it was all determined by electrochemical firing in your brain and nervous system.

That's the standard explanation in mainstream science and philosophy. According to this materialist view, everything we do either is determined by physics and biology or happens randomly. When random events occur or when synaptic firing hits a critical threshold, we act and we *think* we made a choice.

From a spiritual perspective, it's much the same—except in this case God, Spirit, the Creative Ultimate is the source of everything we do. "Let thy will be done" and all that. As if we had a choice.

For most of us, it really matters whether we have free will. We don't want to believe we are just machines, determined by the laws of physics and biology, or by the unpredictability of random events. Most of us don't like the idea that everything we do is determined by God or karma, either. We cherish our free will and creativity.

But what if, as science and many spiritual traditions teach, the experience of choice is just an illusion? What if choice is nothing more than our egos claiming a power and agency they don't really have?

WHO CHOOSES?

Many spiritual traditions encourage "letting go" and surrendering to some "higher power" or simply to *what is.*

Blindspot: If we are not in control in the first place (i.e., if we don't have the power of choice), how then could we ever "let go" and surrender? The paradox is stark: In order to let go of choice and control we have to be able to exercise choice and control. *We have to choose to not choose!*

It gets more complicated. Even if each of us does possess an inner "divine spark" with freedom to choose, and if every sentient being is making choices at every moment, then the sum total of all those choices shapes the unfolding of reality from moment to moment.

The outcome at any time is decided by the Great Cosmic Democracy. We might be able to contribute our own individual "vote," but what happens is governed by the Cosmic Collective. In other words, *we get to choose, but we don't get to decide.*

So, do we have free will or are our actions determined? I think the answer to that question is "yes." (See "The Paradox of Free Will" on p. 206 for a more in-depth discussion.)

Most of what we do is determined—by the past, by physics, by biology, by genetics, and these in turn are the result of gazillions of choices made at every moment by all sentient beings.

For the most part, as the spiritual teacher Gurdjieff said, we are sleepwalking machines going through life declaring, "I am not a machine. I am not asleep." And then, through spiritual practice, serendipity, or grace, we momentarily wake up and realize, "Oh, I am a machine. I am determined by . . . (fill in the blank: habit, ego, physics, genetics, God, etc.)."

But the moment you wake up to the fact that you are a machine, you stop being merely a machine. *Machines never wake up!* The problem is that most of us promptly fall back asleep again.

Enlightenment takes work.

Free Will or Free Won't?

Try a little experiment of your own: Choose to close the covers of this book (or, if you are reading on an iPad or Kindle, switch to another page)—then immediately open the book up again to this page. Easy enough, right?

You've just demonstrated the power of choice—that consciousness can make things happen. But hold on, maybe not . . . Some years ago, a U.S. scientist published a paper that, to many people, seemed to blow the idea of choice and free will out of the water.

In 1985, Benjamin Libet, a neuroscientist at the University of California, published a controversial paper, "Unconscious Cerebral Initiative and the Role of Conscious Will in Voluntary Action." It shook the community of consciousness researchers.

In brief, Libet discovered that *unconscious* events in the nervous system happen *before* we make a choice to do something. In fact, the neurological events occur about half a second before we are even aware we made a choice. Logically, it makes sense to assume that the decision to act would come *before* the action. However, to just about everyone's surprise, Libet found that the readiness potential (the slow negative shift in electrical potential along the nerves that precedes voluntary motor actions) came first. Fascinating.

Equally fascinating, though, is what Libet and other scientists concluded from this discovery: *free will is an illusion.* Their work shows that awareness of making a decision to act comes *after* the nervous system kicks in to create a "readiness potential" to act. In other words, they concluded, so-called conscious choice must be illusory because it is caused by biochemical events in the brain and nervous system.

Libet's paper continues to be cited in journals and books decades later as scientific "proof" that consciousness or choice doesn't cause us to act—our "unconscious" *neurons* do. For example, in her book *Consciousness: An Introduction,* psychologist Susan Blackmore cites Libet and asks us: If a series of neurological events occured *before* a person consciously chose to act, then did she really choose? Did volition or free choice initiate the movement? And if not, if she is not the one who chose, who did? The results of Libet's experiment seem to show that consciousness comes too late to be the cause of the action.

Here's her actual quote:

> With Libet we may wonder, "If the brain can initiate a voluntary act before the appearance of conscious intention . . . is there any role for the conscious function?"* . . . That is the crux. These results seem to show (as did Libet's previous work . . .) that consciousness comes too late to be the cause of the action.[†]

She goes on to talk about an interesting twist to the free will debate:

> Unconscious brain events start the process of a voluntary act, but then just before it is actually carried out, consciousness may say either "yes" or "no"; the action either goes ahead or not. . . . Although we cannot consciously control having an impulse to carry out an unacceptable action (say, rape or murder or stealing sweets in the supermarket), we can be held responsible for consciously allowing its consummation—or not."[‡]

---

*Libet, "Unconscious Cerebral Initiative and the Role of Conscious Will in Voluntary Action," 536.
[†]Blackmore, *Consciousness,* 140.
[‡]Blackmore, *Consciousness,* 141.

Citing neuroscientist Richard Gregory, she quotes: "We don't have free will, but we do have free *won't*" (emphasis added).

I find it interesting how often authors use phrases such as "unconscious brain events" or "unconscious neurons" when clearly they mean *nonconscious* events or neurons. If our brain cells are actually *unconscious* (possessing low-grade sentience), then Libet's results do not warrant the conclusion that free will is an illusion. I'll explain why in a moment. On the other hand, if our brain cells are truly *nonconscious* (with *zero* sentience), then we slam right into the famous "hard problem": How could purely *nonconscious* events ever produce conscious experience? As I noted earlier, that idea is a nonstarter because it requires getting something nonphysical from purely physical objects and events—another case of "something from nothing."

As you've probably realized by now, the idea that Libet's data expose free will as an illusion hinges on the all-too-widespread confusion of the two meanings of *consciousness*—the *psychological* meaning contrasted with "unconscious" events and the *philosophical* meaning contrasted with "nonconscious" events. In short, they have confused "*un*conscious" with "*non*conscious" and, as a result, are confused about which meaning of *consciousness* Libet's work implies.

Blindspot: The idea that Libet's experiments disprove free will is a prime example of how confusion arises when scholars fail to distinguish between the *psychological* and *philosophical* meanings of *consciousness*.

If we pay close attention to what Libet (and Blackmore and others) are saying when they talk of "the conscious decision to move" coming after the neurological "readiness potential" or that "consciousness comes too late to be the cause of the action," we see the problem.

They are really saying that our *awareness* of the conscious decision to move (i.e., when the event rises from the body's unconscious processing to the level of conscious awareness) comes later. In other words, they are talking about consciousness *in the psychological sense* (distinct from unconscious, but not nonconscious, events).

Just because we are not *consciously aware* of decisions made at the level of our neurons does not mean that consciousness *in the philosophical sense* is not responsible for the decision to move or make things happen. To conclude that consciousness and choice result from prior purely physical neurological events is simply not warranted—not if we are talking about consciousness in the ontological or philosophical sense.

The fact that we are *unconscious* of our own neurological processes—*including conscious choices made at that level*—does not mean that consciousness (in the philosophical sense) is not the source of choice. Yes, consciousness in the *psychological* sense (i.e., our awareness of our own consciousness) may well come after the neurological events (as Libet's data indicate), but that does not mean consciousness per se (in the *philosophical* sense) also comes after.

That's the blindspot. And it keeps on happening. But we cannot legitimately draw conclusions about ontological consciousness from arguments based on psychological or neurological data.

As long as scientists and other authors fail to make this basic distinction, they will continue to make this error. Easy enough to correct, once you recognize it. And now you do, right?

COSMIC DEMOCRACY

I'm a Science of Mind practitioner, and my spiritual practice teaches us to use consciousness to call forth our good into tangible form, and that we can choose (or not) to use the laws of nature. The point is the laws work the same even if we use them out of ignorance (you will fall if you choose to jump, whether or not you know about the law of gravity).

In my forthcoming book, *Radical Science* (the third volume in my Radical Consciousness trilogy), I make a strong case for why choice and laws cannot mix in the same universe. How, then, might we account for the teaching that "we can choose (or not) to use the laws"?

What does that mean? If the laws still work the same (whether or not we choose to use them), what role or difference would choice make? If it makes no difference, choice would be an *epiphenomenon*—something that has no causal effect. But that doesn't sound like choice to me. It would be, at best, an illusion of choice.

It reminds me of the story of the little kid sitting in the backseat of his mother's car. He's got a toy yellow steering wheel, and he turns it this way and that, imitating his mother's arm movements as she steers the car. Sure enough, sometimes when he turns his yellow wheel the car turns in the right direction. He has the illusion that his choice (to turn his toy wheel) moves the car. But, of course, that's not what is happening. His toy wheel is an epiphenomenon—it makes no difference to the movement of the car.

If laws still work the same whether or not we make choices, then, like the kid's toy yellow wheel, our choices would make no difference. In your scenario, the most choice could do would be to either *accept* or *resist* the laws of nature (and, of course, resistance would be futile). But is that really so?

On the other hand, if choice *does* make a difference, then the "law" cannot be a *law*—because laws of nature (or divine command, or however you think laws are made) are supposed to act universally, *with no exceptions.* So whenever choice *makes a difference,* that means the "law" does not apply universally and, therefore, cannot be a law—instead, what we call "laws" are really *habits* of nature. They are deep-rooted *psychological* patterns, embedded in the universe as a result of countless repeated identical or similar choices.

As we know from human experience, some habits (e.g., addictions) can run so deep they override our ability to choose differently. When deeply ingrained habits kick in, we act mechanically. It's the same in the universe, where deep-rooted habits (for example, at the level of atoms or molecules) are so pervasive and persistent that they are indistinguishable from laws of nature. However, the crucial difference is this: Through acts of choice we can change even deep-rooted habits. And so, in a universe where consciousness tingles at the heart of matter, choices *can* change law-like habits (but this requires a consensus of the Cosmic Democracy).

From a psychospiritual perspective (and from simple observation of life experience), I think it is true that most of the time we are, indeed, like the kid with his toy wheel. Often, our intentions and choices don't seem to make the difference we aim for. This is because the greater force of the *habits* of *nature* (resulting from choices made by all the other innumerable sentient beings in the universe) override our (comparatively) puny little acts of volition. Have you noticed that?

However, that's not always the case. *Sometimes our choices do make a difference.* (Actually, they always make a difference . . . but I'll come back to that in a moment.) The point is this: If our choices make a difference, even if only sometimes, then, as explained above, that rules out the possibility of laws, which are defined as invariant and universal.

By substituting "habits" for "laws," we have language and ideas that not only match our experience of being choice-full organisms in a habit-filled universe (where our choices have to contend with our own habits plus the habits of all others) but also are logically consistent and coherent. *We can make sense of ourselves in the world.*

At every moment, we do have the ability to make choices; in fact, we do so all the time. The effectiveness of choice depends to a great degree on our awareness of *available options*. The more we are aware of what's actually the case and of what's possible, the more informed we are to make choices that could make a difference.

However, this is true of every other sentient being in the universe, too—all of whom are making choices all the time. Whenever we make a choice, then, it contributes to a universal pool of other choices, and only when our choice aligns with the universal pattern of choices do we get the result we aim for. Spiritual traditions call this universal pattern of choices *divine intention*. From a spiritual perspective, only when our intentions align with divine intention do our intentions achieve manifestation.

In the Great Cosmic Democracy, we all get to vote, but we don't get to decide.

DO ATOMS CHOOSE?

The idea that every individual atom makes its own choices challenges me. I agree to a point, and then it seems too odd. Yet I recognize that either they do or they don't—it cannot be both. Isn't it possible, though, that even if consciousness goes all the way down, choice emerges with the evolution of more complex organisms, such as animals with brains?

Think of it this way: Just as it is inconceivable for consciousness to emerge from wholly nonconscious precursors, it is equally inconceivable that the ability to make choices could emerge from wholly nonvolitional precursors (cells, molecules, atoms). If we have the ability to make choices, then it logically follows that whatever we are made of, all the way down, must also have that ability. I know it can take time to fully let this in, that we live in a world teeming with consciousness and choice at every level of existence. But once you get that, the world will never seem (or feel) the same way again.

I understand that the idea of consciousness and choice *all the way down* can be a challenge for minds educated to believe that consciousness requires complex organizations of matter (e.g., brains). However, as I've pointed out elsewhere, that materialist viewpoint is incoherent because if brains are conscious, then whatever brains are made of (cells, molecules, atoms, etc.) must also be conscious all the way down—otherwise, wherever we place the "consciousness cut," we are faced with exactly the same "hard problem" of explaining how it would be possible for consciousness to emerge from wholly nonconscious ingredients.

The only way around this is to accept that consciousness exists all the way down. And because consciousness always comes with the ability to make choices (see below), this means that even single molecules or atoms must be able to make choices—even though that idea may seem outrageously counterintuitive and anthropomorphic. However, the "counterintuitive" reaction is merely a result of our paradigm conditioning (materialism). Other traditions, such as those of indigenous peoples, have no such problem accepting the idea that consciousness pervades nature at every level, even in its tiniest particles.

THE PARADOX OF FREE WILL

The following dialogue is based on an exchange with my friend and colleague Peter Russell, a scholar who demonstrates a rare skill for blending science and spirituality.* He once studied physics under Stephen Hawking and now teaches a version of nondual meditation. The dialogue below draws mostly from his ideas, peppered with my comments and questions.

PR: One of my earliest ventures into philosophy, back in high school, concerned the question of free will versus determinism. If the world unfolds according to fixed laws, then everything that happens would be determined by events that have gone before. Because our brains are part of this world, their state would also be determined by preceding events—in which case, all our thoughts and experiences and, most significantly, our decisions would be determined.

CdeQ: And that is precisely how modern science views the situation. However, all of this assumes that thoughts and experiences *are* determined by the brain—which, to say the least, is extremely unlikely. How could the brain produce *experiences?*

---

*Peter Russell and I often meet for deep and rich philosophical discussions, which one or both of us records (we like to review our spontaneous insights later). Sometimes we draw on the content of our dialogues for blog articles or books, as I have done here. Peter has posted his own version of this exchange on his blog, without my contributions. You can find his blog at www.peterrussell.com/wordpress/index.php.

PR: On the other hand, we all experience making choices—from small things like what to eat to bigger issues like career and marriage. We live our lives on the assumption that we do indeed have free will. The two views seem incompatible. Hence the paradox—and the question of which is right: determinism or free will.

I suspect most people have pondered this question at some time or other. Many may have landed on the free will side of the conundrum, believing we do make choices of our own volition. On the other side, some believe free will is an illusion. Others, seeing validity in both sides of the paradox, may remain baffled or uncertain.

Over the years, I have revisited this paradox many times. In my mid-twenties I wrote a magazine article entitled "And the Opposite Is Also True," where I argued that it was not a question of whether free will or determinism is correct. I postulated they were like two sides of a coin, two very different perspectives of the same reality. From one perspective, determinism is true; from the other, free will is true. But as to what these two complementary perspectives might be, I wasn't clear.

Then last year, in one of those moments of insight, it all fell into place. I realized that the two fundamentally different perspectives stemmed from two fundamentally different states of consciousness.

But before I explain how this may resolve the paradox, we should first go a little deeper into the evidence for both "determinism" and "free will."

Determinism, in its original form, holds that the future is determined by the present state of affairs. But this does not imply that the future is fully predictable. For a start, we could never know the present state of affairs in sufficient detail to calculate the future precisely. Even if we could, chaos theory shows that the slightest uncertainty in the current conditions can, on occasion, lead to wildly different outcomes. Quantum theory added its own challenge to strict determinism, showing that events at the atomic level can be truly random.

CdeQ: Actually, I quibble with this. Quantum theory shows that quantum events are *unpredictable,* but whether the unpredictability arises from pure randomness or from choice is not decided in the theory. True, the vast majority of physicists opt for randomness, and, in fact, many don't even distinguish between unpredictability and randomness. From one perspective, this is understandable: to an *observer*, the unpredictability of randomness and choice is indistinguishable. Unpredictability could just as easily be the result of choice as randomness.

But to the *agent* making the choice, the distinction between randomness and choice is very clear. *Choice is the exact opposite of randomness*—it is the injection of order into randomness.

All we can get from quantum mechanics is that subatomic events are inherently unpredictable. Whether this unpredictability is the result of "quantum chance" or "quantum choice" is not decidable from the mathematics.

However, because we are all made of quanta, and because we have choice, it seems to me "quantum choice" accounts for more of reality than "quantum chance." If quantum events were really pure chance, it would be impossible to explain how choice could have evolved from chance.

PR: Today, scientists and philosophers alike accept that the future is neither predictable nor predetermined. But even though the future may not be fixed in a classical sense, this does not necessarily give us free will. The activity in our brain is still determined by preceding events— some random and unpredictable, some not—and so are our experiences, including our apparent experience of free choice.

CdeQ: From a panpsychist view, neurons have sentience and make choices. In fact, as I noted earlier, I'd say choice goes all the way down to quanta. Therefore, I'd say brain events are not random—even though many of them are unpredictable. But your point is more that events in the brain are *determined by preceding events*. I agree with this: Brain events are determined by prior events. However, I'd say they are not *fully* determined. The quanta, electrons, protons, atoms, molecules, and neurons are all making choices at every moment. The selections they make, of course, are constrained by the available options. Atoms, for instance, have fewer options available than complex molecules do, and neurons have even more options. I'd say that brain events involve both determinism and choice—whereas you would say that choice is merely apparent.

PR: In recent years, neuroscience has found interesting evidence to support this conclusion. In one oft-quoted experiment, subjects were asked to make a flick of their wrist at a time of their own choosing and to note the position of the second hand of a clock at the moment of choosing. However, simultaneous recordings of the subjects' brain activity showed that preparations for movement were occurring about half a second before the conscious decision to move.

Subsequent experiments have confirmed these findings. Scientists have been able to detect associated brain activity occurring as much as a second or more in advance of the conscious experience of making a choice. They conclude that our decisions are being driven by unconscious brain activity, not by conscious choice. But when the decision reaches conscious awareness, we experience having made a choice.

CdeQ: I've always been intrigued by such experiments (e.g., Libet's groundbreaking half-second delay between neuronal activation and conscious awareness of making a choice). As a panpsychist, I think the neuroscience and philosophical community have jumped to the wrong conclusion *precisely because of their materialist metaphysical assumptions.* However, if we accept panpsychism, then there's little or no mystery at all: Of course the neuronal event is registered before the person is aware of making a choice—*because the neurons are making choices!* I don't see that these experiments indicate that what appears as "choice" is nothing but neuronal determinism. As I say, *choice goes all the way down.*

PR: From the perspective of neuroscience, the apparent freedom of choice lies in our not knowing what the outcome will be. Take, for example, the common process of choosing what to eat in a restaurant. I first eliminate dishes I don't like, or ones I ate recently, narrowing down to a few that attract me. I then decide on one of these according to various other factors—nutritional value, favorite tastes, what I feel my body needs, and so forth. It feels like I am making a free choice, but the decision I come to is predetermined by current circumstances and past experience. However, because I do not know the outcome of the decision-making process until it appears in my mind, I feel that I have made a free choice.

CdeQ: I partly agree with this. It seems almost without question that a lot of *unconscious* processing precedes conscious choice. In which case, there's quite a bit of "predeterminism" going on. However, this "predeterminism" is not merely the result of mechanical physical processes (though those are happening, too). I'd say that as well as some (perhaps even a lot) of physical determinism, those unconscious neuronal processes also involve neuronal choices (and molecular, and atomic, and subatomic, and quantum choices). Every sentient being at every level, from quanta to queen bees, is making choices. Besides the determinism, *there's also a helluva lot of choosing going on.*

I've referred to this as the Great Cosmic Democracy. Every sentient being gets to *vote*. But none of us gets to *decide*. The outcome at every level, from quantum to cosmos, is decided by the countless gazillions of choices made at every moment by the system's constituents. Our human-level choices contribute to this process. And only when our choices happen to align with the most "influential voting bloc" do we get the outcome we aim for. So, when I happen to choose grilled salmon from the menu in a restaurant, I'm unaware that that choice surfs on top of a whole hierarchy of neuronal, molecular, and atomic choices that, based on various patterns of preferences and habits already laid down in my nervous system, happen to "vote" for grilled salmon. The collective has decided, and I'm content with that.

A SELF THAT CHOOSES?

PR: Whether biologically determined by insentient neurons or psychologically determined by sentient neurons, the experience of making choices of our own volition still seems very real. We live our lives on the assumption that we are making decisions of our own free will and directing our own future. It is virtually impossible not to.

Implicit in the notion of choice is the existence of a "chooser"—an independent self that is an active agent in the process. This, too, fits with our experience. There seems to be an "I" that perceives the world, making assessments and decisions, and making its own choices. This "I" feels it has chosen the dish from the menu.

CdeQ: Yes, and here we meet the $64 trillion question at the heart of most, if not all, psychospiritual traditions: *Who chooses?*

PR: The experience of an individual self is so intrinsic to our lives that we seldom doubt its veracity. But does it really exist in its own right? Two lines of research suggest not.

On one hand, neuroscientists find no evidence of an individual self located somewhere in the brain. Instead, they propose that what we call "I" is but a mental construct derived from bodily experience.

CdeQ: Of course it's no surprise that neuroscientists find no evidence for a self. How could they? Given their scientific method rooted in sensory empiricism, they will never find a "self"—*or any form of consciousness*—because the self is a subjective, nonphysical entity. Furthermore, when scientists claim that the "I" is nothing but a "mental construct," I have to ask: Where did that *mental* construct or bodily *experience* come from? Neither mind nor experience can be accounted for in neuroscience.

PR: Well, putting that aside for now, according to neuroscience, we draw a distinction between "me" and "not me" and then create a sense of self for the "me" part. From a biological point of view, this distinction is most valuable. Taking care of the needs of this self is taking care of our physical needs. We seek whatever promotes our well-being and avoid whatever threatens it.

CdeQ: This makes sense. Although I make a distinction between "I" and "me." The "I" corresponds with the sense of "self," the subjective feeling of "what-it-is-to-be *this* sentient being," while "me" corresponds with our "ego," which identifies with our objective body. Unlike spiritual traditions that attempt to get rid of the ego, I acknowledge its reality and the important role it plays in our lives. The ego has evolved to guide and protect "me" (this body) from the vagaries of an unpredictable and often dangerous world. I view "me" (ego) as the objectification of the subjective, witnessing "I." Neither "me" nor "I" falls within the scope of neuroscience.

PR: The second, very different line of research involves the exploration of subjective experience. People who have delved into the nature of the actual experience of self have discovered that the more closely they examine this sense of "I," the more it seems to dissolve. Time and again, they find that there is no independent self. There are thoughts of "I," but no "I" that is thinking them.

They find that what we take to be a sense of an omnipresent "I" is simply consciousness itself. There is no separate experiencer; there is simply a quality of being, a sense of presence, an awareness that is always there whatever our experience. They conclude that what we experience to be an independent self is a construct in the mind—very real in its appearance but of no intrinsic substance. It, like the choices it appears to make, is a consequence of processes in the brain. It has no free will of its own.

CdeQ: This brings us back to the question, who chooses? And I say, ultimately, *the cosmos chooses*—through what I have referred to as the Great Cosmic Democracy. So, even though "me" or any individual "I" might not choose, I still think that *consciousness* per se comes with the power of choice built in, as it were. I think we have good reasons for saying that choice is an ontological necessity.

Briefly, at every moment, every actual thing or event is *necessarily* surrounded by a cloud of possibilities or options. Call them quantum potentials, if you like. We know from quantum physics that the range of possibilities "collapses" into an actual event in the next moment *only in the presence of an observer* (i.e., of consciousness). For *anything new to ever happen, something has to choose which option or possibility to "collapse."* And because new things happen all the time, even if it's just a new "moment," it follows that *choice is inevitable.*

One other possibility, though—and from previous conversations, I suspect this might be how you view it—is that events *just happen* in consciousness without any choice or agency directing the process. We can think of these events as "ripples" in awareness, determined or caused by consciousness itself as it engages in "awaring." We might even call everything that happens "ripples of awaring." In short, in the process of "awaring," consciousness generates forms ("ripples") that, in turn, become objects of the "awaring" consciousness.

COMPLEMENTARY PERSPECTIVES

PR: Nevertheless—and this is critical for resolving the paradox—in our everyday state of consciousness, the sense of self is very real. It is who we are. Although this "I" may be part of the brain's model of reality, it is nevertheless intimately involved in making decisions, weighing up pros and cons, coming to conclusions, choosing what to do and when to do it.

CdeQ: For a brain to create a "model," it would also have to have a *mind*—without which the brain could never have a sense of anything, including and especially a sense of self or "I." It's the *mind* component of the brain-mind complex that is responsible for the sense of "I."

A side note: I find it useful to distinguish between "making decisions" (weighing pros and cons) and making *choices* (creative existential acts). Decisions are determined; choices are *creative* and undetermined. In one of my books, *Radical Knowing,* I point out that choice is the only instance in which an effect and its own cause coincide. As a creative act, when self-as-agent chooses it is simultaneously the cause and its own effect. The very act of choosing is implicated in generating the sense of self.

PR: In the state of consciousness where the self is real, we do experience ourselves making choices. And those choices are experienced as being of our own volition. Here, free will is real.

On the other hand, in what is often called the "liberated" or "fully awake" state of consciousness, in which one no longer identifies with the constructed sense of self, the thought of "I" is seen as just another experience arising in the mind. And so is the experience of choosing. It is all witnessed as a seamless whole unfolding before one.

CdeQ: Agreed. In *Consciousness from Zombies to Angels,* I have a chapter on this very topic—"I Think, Therefore I Am a God"—in which I develop David Bohm's idea that the ego (responsible for the sense of "me" as a separate, individual "I") is itself nothing more than just another *thought* in consciousness, another example of a "ripple" in awaring.

PR: When I appreciated the complementary nature of these two states of consciousness—one focused on the "I" and the other engaged in simply "awaring" or, as we have previously discussed, where consciousness is simply "am-ing"—the paradox dissolved for me. Whether or not we experience free will depends on the state from which we are experiencing the world.

CdeQ: I think our two quite different lines of thinking converge here. What you call "two states of consciousness" I describe in terms of two levels of being (the "voting" sentient organism and the Great Cosmic Democracy). In one of your "two states," consciousness identifies with the "voting self"; in the other, mystical state, it identifies with the All. I think we share the same, or at least a similar, insight.

PR: In one state of consciousness, there is free will. In the other, it has no reality.

CdeQ: Ah! We diverge again . . . I wouldn't say that choice per se dissolves in the mystical state. Even the Creative Ultimate has to choose—otherwise, nothing new would ever happen. I'm saying that even at the "ultimate" level, possibilities still exist. That means *differentiation* exists. Now, of course, if we go with the "insights" of nondual teaching (which I know you align with), such differentiations dissolve. However, to be consistent, the nondual "perspective" must also include the opposite: where the differentiations *don't dissolve.* So, the possibilities both exist and don't exist simultaneously. And lo! The paradox returns full force. The difficulty, of course, with the nondual "perspective" is that it cannot be a "perspective" and it cannot be *spoken* about without immediately falling into contradictions. Hence, *silence* . . .

PR: As I viewed the conundrum through the lens of the two states of consciousness, I saw that free will and determinism are no longer paradoxical in the sense of being mutually exclusive. Both are correct, depending upon the consciousness from which they are considered. The paradox appears only when we consider both sides from the same state of consciousness, that is, the everyday waking state.

I like to illustrate this with Hamlet pondering the question, "To be or not to be?" The character in the play is making a choice. And if we have not seen the play before, we may wonder which way he will choose. This is the thrill of the play, to be engaged in it, moved by it, absorbed in its reality with all its twists and turns. However, we also know that how the play unfolds was determined long ago by William Shakespeare.

So, we have two complementary ways of viewing the play. At times we may choose to live fully in the drama. Other times we may step back to admire his creative genius.

CdeQ: In this example, of course, the drama is *maya,** illusory.

A WILL FREE OF EGO

PR: So also in life. We can be engaged in the drama, experiencing free will, making choices that affect our futures. Or we can step back and be a witness to this amazing play of life unfolding before us. Both are true within their respective frameworks.

Although, in the liberated state of mind, there may be no free will in the sense in which we normally think of it, there is instead a new-found freedom far more fulfilling and enriching than the freedom of choice to which we cling.

CdeQ: I like that. And so, another aspect of the paradox: In the transcendence of surrender, we *choose to let go of choosing.*

PR: The will of the individual self is focused on survival. Its foundation is the survival of the organism, fulfilling our bodily needs, avoiding danger or anything that threatens our well-being. In other words, keeping us alive and well, fending off the inevitability of death as long as possible. Added to this are various psychological and social needs. We want to feel safe and secure, to feel stimulated and fulfilled, to be respected and appreciated. We believe that if we can just get the world to be the way we want it—and here the world includes other people— then we will be happy.

In the liberated state, the ego no longer drives our thinking and behavior. When it drops away, we discover that the ease and safety we

---

*Maya means "illusion" in Sanskrit.

had been seeking are already there; they are qualities of our true nature. But it is the nature of the ego to plan and worry, to seek the things it wants, to avoid the things it doesn't want. In so doing, it creates tension and resistance, which veils our true nature, hiding from us the very peace of mind we are seeking.

The life-changing discovery of the liberated mind is that it is already at peace. Nothing needs to be done, nothing needs to happen, nothing needs to change in order to experience peace. There may still be much to do in the world: helping others, resolving injustices, taking care of our environment, and so forth. But we are free from the dictates of the ego; we are free to respond according to needs of the situation at hand rather than what the ego wants. Here, our will is truly free.

At this point, Pete and I settled into silence, ending our conversation.

WHO CHOOSES?

In one of your lectures, you spoke about consciousness being able to direct the flow of events through choice, or free will. But we don't have a choice over consciousness, right? If I understood you correctly, the only choice we have is to go with or against the flow of events—to align our consciousness with the flow. So, how then can choices make a difference in the world?

I'm not sure what you mean by "not having a choice over consciousness." True, we don't have a choice in whether we have consciousness— it just comes with the package of being a sentient being.

However, choice is an essential ingredient of consciousness. Wherever there is consciousness, there is an ability to choose. And this involves a lot more than merely aligning with the flow of events or not. Whenever consciousness is presented with a range of options, we can choose among those options, usually selecting one aligned with our aims, goals, or intentions. If this were not the case—if consciousness could choose only to "go with the flow"—that would make it an *epiphenomenon,* without any causal potency.

So, I am saying that consciousness—*in every sentient being*—has the power to choose among available options. And in doing so, it causally impacts the flow of events, from collapsing quantum waves to sending rockets to other planets to affecting the environment. *Our choices do make a difference.*

Blindspot: I wonder if you had in mind what I had said about *intention:* Whenever we express an intention, it is, ultimately, not *our* intention that manifests—rather, it is the Cosmic Intention (or whatever you wish to call the purposeful aim of the Creative Ultimate). You could think of it this way: Cosmic Intention expresses itself through the innumerable "nodes" of consciousness (each sentient being). And only when the "localized" intention of an individual is aligned with the greater cosmic intention do intentions become manifest.

We, as individuals, have choice about where and how we direct our attention and form intentions. However, a great deal of psychospiritual practice focuses on developing awareness of the difference between desires formed by the ego, which tend to have self-serving goals, and intentions that are *expressed through* the individual self and serve a greater good. The spiritual koan, *who chooses?* directs our awareness to this.

Egoic desires (or personal intentions) are less likely to align with the transpersonal intentions of the Creative Ultimate because they are driven by the illusion of *separateness*—that our egos are isolated *individuals* and are our true *identity.*

I'm saying that when intentions are aligned with, and expressed on behalf of, the good of the whole, they are most likely to manifest.

Here's a question to ask ourselves many times a day: *When I make a choice, is it in service to my ego or is it a contribution to the well-being of the whole?*

GOD AND EGO

I once heard the Reverend Doctor Michael Beckwith describe the ego as "edging God out." How does that tie in with your views of ego as presented in your work?

It's a cute phrase. If by *God* he means Ultimate Reality, then, of course, it's impossible to "edge out" reality. The ego is real; it is a real part of reality. However, the ego makes a huge mistake when it believes it is the source and creator of itself.

I like to think of it this way: Reality, the Creative Ultimate, converges throughout the cosmos in a multitude of points in space and time and *expresses* itself through these points—you, me, and all sentient beings. Each point is like a little lens through which the Creative Ultimate perceives the light of itself.

Blindspot: However, every experience that passes through each lens leaves a mark, a trace—a kind of existential "scratch"—on the lens. These scratches are our "thoughts," "memories," and "beliefs"—the contents of consciousness. The ego is constructed out of these scratches. What happens is that we-as-egos focus on these scratches and *identify* with them. We think that reality *is* those scratches, we make up stories about ourselves and the world, and we confuse our stories for reality (i.e., we believe our beliefs).

All psychospiritual practice, it seems to me, is about learning to *see through those ego scratches* and to wake up to the realization that they are all just "likely stories."

Before ending this chapter, I want to highlight another frequently overlooked blindspot.

WE ARE ALL GODS

Blindspot: How often do you hear people say something like, "I have very few choices"? I hear it all the time. But that is hardly ever the case (except if they are about to die). What they mean to say is, "I have very few *options*." At any moment, we always have a range of options available; but at any moment, we have only a single choice.

I find it helpful, then, to distinguish between "choices," "options," and the act of "selecting."

Depth Alert: *Choice is an unconstrained, creative existential act of selecting from available options.* It is *necessarily* unconstrained and free; otherwise, it would be determined and, therefore, would not be choice at all.

Options are available circumstances and possibilities—the array of actualities and possibilities available to us. At every moment, we find ourselves in an ongoing stream of actual circumstances. We cannot change *current* circumstances or the range of possibilities that accompany them. In short, we have no control over options once they are present. They are given. All we can do is select among them by making a choice. Our options are given to us by the world around us, shaped by the entire history of the universe. They simply are what they are. And we must accept them as they are, if we want to remain sane and survive.

If that were the end of the story, however, we would be nothing more than "meat machines," biological robots compelled to follow the unfolding of the forces of nature *with no say in the matter.* But that's not the way it is. We do have a say. We do get to vote. *We can choose.*

We can choose to focus attention on specific circumstances, and, more important, we can focus awareness on, and then choose from, available *possibilities*. In doing so, our choices contribute to the unfolding of the actual circumstances in the next moment. *Our choices make a difference.*

However, for our choices to not only make a difference, but to make a *difference that makes a difference,* they must be aligned with the general, overall pattern of choices made by the Great Cosmic Democracy.

The point to note is this: Circumstances, including other people, can, and do, constrain or limit available *options*. But nothing can limit or constrain our *choices*. Even in the most constrained circumstances imaginable (e.g., imprisoned and chained up in solitary confinement) we still have the choice to accept or resist our circumstances. Others can, and do, limit our options, but they can never take away our choice (unless, of course, they take away our life and consciousness).

Choice is not only unconstrained, it is also *creative*—literally. It is the expression of the "divine spark" within each of us. And when we exercise choice, it creates a new actuality, or manifestation, from the combination of present circumstances and possibilities—our available options, always determined by others.

Selection is what happens once we make a choice. If it involves behavior, then selection is a physical act of taking one object or course of action, rather than any other. If selection does not involve a physical act, or precede a physical act, then it means we make a *commitment* to some way of being or thinking or to act in a specific way at some future time.

To give an example: Let's say you want to go to a movie and you check the listings to see what's currently playing. Those are your *options*. Now let's say all the films turn out to be blockbuster "blow-'em-up" dramas full of special-effects spectacle and violence, and you don't like that. You might be tempted to say, "I don't have any choices," when in fact what you mean is, "I don't like any of the available options." While that might be true, whatever movies are showing, you can always *choose* (or not) to *select* an *option,* the best of a bad bunch.

Whenever you say, "I don't have any choices," you disempower yourself. Even when your options are severely restricted, *you always have a choice.* At the very least, you can always choose to accept or reject the reality you find yourself in (never a good idea to fight reality, though—the universe is *much* bigger and more powerful than you are).

Blindspot: We can always make a choice. Circumstances might constrain our options, but no one can take away our ability to choose.

Choice is an expression of the creative "spark" within each of us, and it is always free and creative, never determined by circumstances.

If "choice" were determined, it wouldn't be choice, it would be "decision." Decisions are determined by weighing up the pros and cons of our circumstances.

When we exercise choice, we select a new or alternative possibility. And because we intentionally create something *actual* from a set of possibilities, we become like gods. In other words, choice expresses the power of intention to manifest a new reality.

Bumper sticker: *"Options constrain. Choices create."* Options are *given;* choices are *creative*. When we *experience* this difference and realize that we always have choice, we realize that, indeed, *we are gods*.

16

Consciousness Rules

"It's All in the Mind; Consciousness Is Everything"

Some time ago, I played philosophical ping-pong with a colleague who had sent me a link to an article: "Does Our DNA Demonstrate Intelligent Design?" Of course, the answer is "yes." But, equally of course, not in the way fundamentalists believe (see chapter 14, "Evolution by Design?").

The article explores the possibility that some alien intelligence tweaked our ancestors' genes. (What were they thinking!) Although that's plausible, it's not what caught my attention. My colleague made the following comment, and that set us off on a metaphysical detour . . .

He complained: "This article doesn't even consider the possibility that physical reality was created out of the nonphysical."

I replied: Well, for very good reasons. There simply is no way to even conceive how that would be possible. Getting matter or energy (anything physical) out of purely nonphysical ingredients would be just as inexplicable as the mainstream scientific claim that nonphysical mind or consciousness "emerges" from purely physical ingredients in the brain. In each case, an inexplicable ontological leap would be required.

NO FREE LUNCHES

To repeat a key theme throughout this book: You simply can't get something from nothing. Or, to be more precise, in this case: You can't get one type of reality (matter) from an entirely different kind of reality (*pure* mind). If your base reality contains *only nonphysical* ingredients, no amount of mental gymnastics or intentionality could *ever* produce *real physical* matter. That would require an inexplicable, miraculous, ontological jump. And that's a nonstarter. No one can even *begin* to explain how that might be possible.

Getting *real* matter/energy from *pure* mind/consciousness is no more likely than getting real mind from mindless matter. In short: no free ontological lunches.

Bear with me: All of this preamble relates to the idea of some alien intelligence tweaking the genetic structure of species on Earth—the original point of his e-mail. Like us, any "alien" would also have to be some kind of *embodied consciousness*—a sentient embodied being. This allows for the possibility of very different kinds of embodiment (e.g., so-called subtle or astral bodies). But a sentient being without embodiment of *some kind* would be incapable of ever *doing* anything. Doing requires energy, and energy requires physical embodiment. So, at the very least, we can be sure that any "alien intelligence" would be an *embodied* intelligence and could not have messed about with terrestrial genes from some idealized fictional disembodied consciousness.

He disagreed. "It seems to me," he said, "that science is discovering that the primary material is not matter (nor energy, which of course is more or less the same thing) but *consciousness*. I once had an experience— it lasted only seconds, almost certainly no more than a minute—in which I popped into another reality that was more real than the one we normally experience. No way I can defend that statement, let alone demonstrate it, but even though the source of the knowing is incommunicable, the knowing remains. This material reality is somehow *projected* from an underlying nonphysical reality." That's what he said.

Blindspot: Having spent a career studying the mind-matter (consciousness-energy) relationship, it is abundantly clear to me that no one can even begin to explain how mindless matter could produce mind (the standard science view) or how *pure* consciousness could ever produce *real* matter/energy (an idealist view). I am quite confident that my colleague is no exception—that is, he could not explain how an ontological jump could occur from *purely* nonphysical reality to one that includes *real* physical stuff.

Besides, I'd be really interested to know which science has discovered that the "primary material" is not matter/energy but consciousness. Because consciousness is *nonphysical,* and therefore not amenable to sensory detection, which is the basis of all science, science has absolutely nothing at all to say about consciousness—never mind declaring that the "primary material" is consciousness, an obviously self-contradictory statement. To even think of consciousness as some kind of "stuff" or "material" is to reveal a profound lack of understanding about the nature of consciousness. Consciousness is what *knows.* It is not "stuff." Consciousness knows, feels, or is aware of matter/energy, but it is not itself matter/energy.

Naturally, I have nothing to say about his personal experience—other than to urge caution in how he and others *interpret* their experiences. For example, the interpretation that physical reality is "somehow a projection" of some underlying nonphysical reality immediately raises questions, but it's unclear which version of idealism he adopts: (1) the maya hypothesis that matter/energy is just an illusion created in consciousness, or (2) the notion that real matter/energy *emanates* from pure consciousness. He seems to flip back and forth between these incompatible views of the mind-matter relationship.

If, however, he adopts the maya view, then I am quite certain that every day, every hour, every minute he is engaged in a *performative contradiction.* He, necessarily, lives and *performs* in the world in ways that clearly contradict the claim that matter is just an illusion—he doesn't walk through walls, avoids trucks on the freeway, doesn't eat or drink poisons, wears clothes, lives in a house, and so forth. In other words, *he treats the physical world as real even while claiming it is unreal.* He has no other option if he wishes to survive and remain sane.

Option 2, "real matter/energy emanates from pure consciousness," raises the problem of an inexplicable ontological jump and corresponding explanatory gap, as I mentioned above: Just *how* does nonphysical consciousness produce *real* physical matter/energy? Either way, both forms of idealism run into insuperable problems—just as standard scientific materialism does with its unsupportable claim that mind emerges from mindless brain matter or as dualism does when it claims that mind and body are separable yet "somehow" interact.

He responded that quantum physics has been driven kicking and screaming to the conclusion that consciousness is primary and creates the physical world. He cited a recent book, *Irreducible Mind,* from a research group at the Esalen Institute, in California, as a source of support.

As it happens, I am quite familiar with *Irreducible Mind* because I was involved in that research project in its early days. I am also no stranger to the conundrum in quantum physics regarding the role of the "observer" in collapsing the probability wave function. It is true (at least in the standard Copenhagen interpretation) that for quantum probabilities to "collapse" into an actual physical event, an "observer" must be part of the quantum system. Furthermore, any "observer" must be a *conscious* observer; otherwise, the idea of "observer" is meaningless.

In short: *somehow, consciousness collapses the quantum wave function.* This "somehow" is a big mystery in science, and yet physicists must acknowledge it because otherwise their equations don't work out. But they haven't the foggiest idea either how nonphysical consciousness impacts a physical system, even at the quantum level, or, of course, just what consciousness is or how it fits into their cosmology.

For the first time in four hundred years, since Descartes's infamous mind-body split, scientists have had to acknowledge the presence of consciousness as a decisive factor in science. They just don't know what to do about that. But none of this means, or even suggests, that consciousness is the "primary material" for the physical world to come into being. That is an unfortunate example of misguided and misinformed "pop" science eagerly embraced by wishful-thinking idealists.

Blindspot: Both physical and nonphysical ingredients, energy and consciousness, need to be present for the world to come into being, a world that consists of embodied sentient beings. Neither consciousness alone (the idealist view) nor matter/energy alone (the materialist view) can account for the actual world as we experience it. Every conscious observer is always an *embodied* conscious observer. Minds without bodies are fictions (the opposite is also true).

He objected to my statement "minds without bodies are fictions" and said: "I don't see how you can possibly prove that assertion."

He's right: I can't . . . and wouldn't want to, even if I could. The old idea of "proof" is just not empirically available. Science never actually "proves" anything. The best it can do is confirm or disconfirm some hypothesis (e.g., "all swans are white"). But no amount of positive confirmation of white swans can ever remove the possibility that the very next observation will reveal a swan of a different color. You might observe a million white swans, but all it takes is one black swan to disprove the hypothesis that "all swans are white."

I'm not interested in "proof," but I am interested in *conceptual coherence* and in coming up with the *most likely explanations* for what we experience. I know of no instance of any mind floating free, independent of a body. If he or you or anyone else is attracted to the idea of minds that could exist free of embodiment, I'd like to know why.

What "use" would a disembodied mind be—to itself or anything else? Without a body (energy) it could never *do* anything. The best a disembodied mind could do would be to generate intentions, but it could never *act* on them. Action and manifestation require *energy*. Minds without bodies are impotent. Bodies without minds are blind.

The actual world requires both consciousness (nonphysical) and energy (physical). Neither can be reduced to the other or arise from the other. No ontological "free lunches."

MINDS WITHOUT BODIES?

When I posted a version of the above, "No Free Lunches," online, not surprisingly some people were puzzled by my statement that minds without bodies are fictions, and some downright objected. They like the idea of minds floating free of our mortal coils. It matters to many people that consciousness continues on after we die. So if someone seems to imply otherwise, they don't like it.

Whenever I challenge the idea of "minds without bodies," people tend to get excited, even agitated. It matters to them that consciousness can separate from their bodies. And they let me know they've had "out-of-body" experiences (OBEs). I don't doubt it. I've had a few myself.

However, I also realize that whenever I experience an OBE, my body never goes away. It's always there, waiting for me when I wake up. The problem is not the experience per se. It's what we call it, or how we interpret it.

An OBE is more accurately called an ABE—an **a**lternative **b**ody **e**xperience.

Here's what I think happens: In certain states, consciousness shifts its locus of identity from our physiological bodies to what some traditions refer to as our *subtle bodies.* Composed of subtle energy (e.g., ch'i, ki, prana, mana), such bodies are much more fluid and exist in a different kind of space. Some call it *imaginal* or *dream* space.

The point is: *Subtle bodies have extension,* even if it's in subtle space. In other words, in addition to our flesh-blood-and-bone bodies, we also possess other, *alternative* bodies.

While ideas such as "subtle energy," "subtle bodies," and "alternative domains of reality" remain beyond the pale of modern science, other wisdom traditions—such as shamanism—frequently report entering these alternative "worlds." In nonordinary circumstances, consciousness can shift identity and associate itself with alternative subtle bodies. When that happens, we undergo an *alternative body experience* (ABE).

However, consciousness remains embodied—*always*. That's why I say "minds without bodies are fictions." Consciousness needs energy—embodiment—in order to make things happen. Without energy, or body, nothing could ever happen.

Give me consciousness and energy, and I give you a universe. Give me either one alone, and all I can give you is something stillborn.

IDEALISM AND PANPSYCHISM

In our spiritual philosophy of Religious Science, we believe that all things stem from consciousness (idealism), and that matter is real. We believe that through consciousness we can bring the invisible into the visible (is that panpsychism?). We believe there's consciousness in a rock and a blade of grass (panpsychism), yet all things are created in mind and consciousness (idealism). Can there be a blend of idealism and panpsychism?

In a sense, yes, and in a sense, no. "No," when idealism claims that all that exists is pure spirit or consciousness and that matter/energy is an illusion or dream in consciousness. This is maya idealism.

"Yes," when idealism claims that spirit or consciousness gives rise to or "emanates" real matter/energy. This is *emanationist* idealism. In this version of idealism, *matter is real,* it but is created or produced by mind.

Emanationist idealism is consistent with panpsychism because, since all matter/energy (physical domain) emanates from spirit/consciousness, then all matter/energy necessarily is imbued with its source (spirit/consciousness). In other words, emanationist idealism implies a form of *consequent panpsychism;* panpsychism is an inevitable, or logical, *consequence* of emanationist idealism.

However, a conflict between panpsychism and emanationist idealism remains. Almost always, people who profess emanationist idealism state not only that consciousness/spirit creates matter/energy but that *pure* consciousness/energy creates *real* matter/energy, where "pure" means *nothing but* consciousness—the *complete absence* of anything physical or material.

Philosophically, this claim is incoherent because it would involve an ontological jump—getting from one state of reality (pure consciousness) to a radically different state of reality (where *real* matter exists). Such a leap between two radically different kinds of reality is inexplicable and, therefore, would require a miracle to be true.*

Now, of course, just because we can't explain something doesn't mean it isn't true or couldn't happen. If miracles do happen, it just means we can't *explain* them. But if we are interested in providing explanations, as science and philosophy are, then miracles are not permissible. If we wish to invoke miracles *in place of* explanations, we are doing religion, not philosophy or science.

We just need to be consistent: If we wish to *understand* or *explain* something, then invoking a miracle doesn't help.

As a companion to the bumper sticker, "Laws and consciousness just don't mix," here's another one: "Science and miracles don't mix." Likewise, philosophy and miracles don't mix.

Zooming in more precisely on your question: Yes, the belief that "all things stem from consciousness" is idealism. However, as noted above, if you mean "all things stem from *pure* consciousness," including real matter, here's a question for you: Can you *explain*, step by step, how *pure* consciousness could ever make the ontological leap to produce the miracle of *real* matter? Of course you can't. No ontological jump is open to explanation. How could you bridge the gap between one state of reality (*pure* consciousness) and a radically different state of reality (*real* matter)?

You guessed it: *You can't get something from nothing.* If you begin with a cosmos or reality in State A (with *zero* matter/energy), then you can never get to State B (a cosmos with *any* real matter/energy).

This is merely the mirror image of the problem facing scientific materialism (a.k.a. "metaphysical materialism")—the claim that pure

---

*A *miracle* is an insurmountable gap in explanation for something that is supposed to truly happen. If, on the other hand, we *could* explain it, then it wouldn't be a miracle.

matter/energy gives rise to consciousness. It is assumed that consciousness *emerges* from *wholly* nonconscious matter. Of course, this claim resists any attempt to even begin to *explain* how such an event could happen.

Both emanationist idealism and scientific materialism face an identical and insurmountable explanatory problem, only in reverse. To be true, each requires a miraculous ontological jump. While importing a miracle is not inconsistent with idealism (where, by definition, everything is ultimately transcendent and therefore miraculous), scientific materialism does not have that luxury.

Emanationist idealists might resort to miracles instead of filling in gaps in explanation. However, in doing so, they give up any claim to being a science or philosophy. Getting real matter from pure mind is logically inconsistent. But that is not a problem for a *spiritual* or *mystical* cosmology rooted in direct experience and doesn't rely on coherent explanations.

However, this option is not open to modern science—which is in the business of providing explanations, or at least aims to. And because miracles are "gaps in explanation," they have no place in science.

Because science begins with the metaphysical assumption of *complete materialism* (everything is ultimately reducible to matter/energy), it leaves no room for anything supernatural to intervene in the course of natural events. And that is precisely what a miracle is: an inexplicable supernatural intervention into the course of natural events.

Science denies the existence of anything supernatural; everything is natural, and everything natural is physical. Therefore, science rejects the possibility of miracles. But the claim that consciousness emerges from *wholly* physical interactions in the matter of brains and nervous systems *requires* a miracle. Remember, you can't get from a universe in State A (nothing but matter/energy) to State B (brains with *minds that feel and choose*) without a miracle.

Blindspot (major): Scientific materialism is in the embarrassingly awkward position of denying the possibility of miracles yet requiring a miracle when it claims that purely physical brains produce minds, or consciousness.

Bottom line: *In order to be true, scientific materialism must be false!* Try getting your head around that one.

Science ought to be deeply embarrassed by this, but it's not. Why? Because very few scientists pay attention to, and have not been trained in, metaphysics (in the philosophical sense). They do not take time to explore the basic assumptions that underlie what they take for granted to be real. Even less do they follow through on the logical implications of those metaphysical assumptions. If they did, they could not avoid being embarrassed by the huge contradiction embedded in the heart of their worldview—which is this:

In order to exist, science needs scientists, and scientists need minds, or consciousness, to observe the world and to experience and think about their methods as well as the results of their experiments. But scientists are utterly incapable of explaining how their own or anyone else's consciousness could possibly exist—given their basic starting assumptions. Without consciousness, without experience, science could not exist. Yet consciousness and experience are precisely what science cannot explain.

Now, science is in the business of explanations, and it cannot explain the existence of consciousness; therefore, it cannot explain the existence of scientific data; therefore, it cannot explain the existence of science . . . and presto! another bumper sticker: "Science is fundamentally unscientific." (Another cause for deep embarrassment—if only they paid attention.)

The way out of this, of course, is for scientists to radically change their fundamental metaphysical assumptions about the nature of matter and mind. Instead of rooting themselves in *materialism,* or *physicalism,* the belief that everything is ultimately physical, a shift to *panpsychism,* the assumption that matter is intrinsically and naturally imbued with mind, would immediately dissolve all those deeply embarrassing dilemmas.

If we assume that consciousness and energy exist at the starting point, then we don't have to try to explain how either one "emerged" into existence from the other. This neatly sidesteps the "hard problems" facing both scientific materialism and emanationist idealism.

Depth Alert: Finally, your last point: "We believe there's consciousness in a rock and a blade of grass (panpsychism), yet all things are created in mind and consciousness (idealism)."

Panpsychists would not claim that consciousness exists in rocks, in the sense that rocks have "rock consciousness." A rock is an aggregate of molecules, a "heap," not a unified whole. In panpsychism, only whole organisms (from apes to atoms, and from quahogs to quanta) possess *unit consciousness.* Rocks *as rocks,* then, don't have rock consciousness. Heaps don't have unit consciousness. However, the individual *molecules* that compose rocks do have their own *molecular consciousness.*

A molecule is an "organism" in the sense that each of its parts is interdependent and *internally related* to all its other parts. "Internally related" means that *the being of one part is wholly entangled with, and partly constitutes, the being of all the parts in the network that make up the whole.* That's not true of rocks or sand castles or thermostats or computers.

The claim that "all things are created in mind or consciousness" is idealism, not panpsychism. It conflicts with the idea that consciousness and energy always go together. As a spiritual belief, it could be consistent with the spiritual experience of miracles. However, it defies *explanation* and, therefore, does not qualify as science or philosophy. It is logically and communicatively incoherent—at least in symbolic language.

If you want to think or talk about the deepest nature of reality, about the relationship between mind and matter, between consciousness and energy, then the "most likely story," the most consistent explanation, is panpsychism.

By claiming that everything is created in consciousness, you deny the ultimate reality of matter/energy as having any existence *in its own right.* I am not inclined to accept a worldview that inherently diminishes the reality or significance of matter/energy, and, therefore, of *embodiment.*

Denying the reality of either matter or mind is fraught with serious psychological, social, and environmental (not to mention philosophical) dangers. I want us humans to honor both mind and body, to recognize that they are inseparable, and, thereby, to instinctively honor and respect the sacredness of the natural world that, after all, has given birth to us, and to which we all return.

17
Quantum Consciousness
"Quantum Physics Proves Consciousness Creates Reality"

I hear it all the time: "Quantum physics tells us that consciousness creates reality." Close, but no cigar. That's just a popular fiction. The real story is pretty amazing, nevertheless.

Quantum physics does tell us that consciousness plays a decisive role in the physical world by turning possibilities into actual reality. Without it, nothing would ever actually happen. Of course, few practicing physicists would put it that way. They like to use more technical jargon such as "the observer collapses the Schrödinger probability wave function."

That's a fancy way of saying: Until a quantum system is observed (usually by a trained scientist), it stays suspended in a state of multiple probabilities, all present simultaneously. And then, the moment the quantum system is observed, the probability waves "collapse" into a single actual reality, for example, a subatomic particle such as an electron or proton—building blocks of the physical world.

In other words, without an observer, without consciousness, nothing would ever actually happen. That's *big* news. Why isn't it blazed across the media?

QUANTUM HEADLINES

Let's pause for a moment to note a few important points:

1. Any "observer" implies a *conscious* observer; otherwise, the idea of "observation" is meaningless.
2. Therefore, somehow, consciousness is necessary for the physical world to come into being. (Big news!)
3. For the first time in four hundred years, science can no longer ignore the reality and causality of consciousness. (More big news!)
4. Science hasn't the faintest idea how consciousness works its "magic." But quantum physics can't avoid the fact that consciousness does so. (Yet more big news—if only science and the media really paid attention!)

As noted previously (p. 226), the "somehow" mentioned above in item 2 is a big mystery for science.

BEYOND POP SCIENCE

Blindspot: But none of this means, or even suggests, that consciousness alone is enough to bring the physical world into being. Consciousness operates on preexisting probabilities and states of energy. In other words, every moment of awareness, every intentional act, always takes place in an *already existing* actual world. Both physical energy and non-physical consciousness must exist in a world populated by embodied sentient beings.

The idea that "consciousness creates reality" is misguided pop science—a misinterpretation of complex quantum events. Yet the bottom line is clear: Without consciousness, the physical world would remain suspended in a tangled mesh of quantum probabilities.

Of course, that's not the case. Actual events do happen all the time. When you flip a coin, toss dice, or make a choice, something actually happens. Probabilities collapse into a single outcome. Chance responds to choice.

Consciousness co-creates reality. That's much more accurate.

Neither consciousness alone (the idealist view) nor matter/energy alone (the materialist view) can account for the actual world as we experience it—a world with bodies and minds. Every conscious observer is always an embodied conscious observer. Minds without bodies are fictions—the opposite is also true.

A MIND-MATTER SPECTRUM?

I found an illustration online of the scientific model of reality, from large-scale matter (like tables and chairs, rocks and mountains) to what is called the "Planck scale" right down at the quantum level. It shows dense matter at the top and then moves downward, getting less and less dense, until we reach the quantum level. On that scale, at 10^{-35} meters, the smallest particles exist. Beyond that, matter disappears and we are in the domain of quantum waves. As I looked at the scale, it suddenly hit me: Science has the whole thing inverted. If consciousness is primary, then we should place the less dense levels at the top of the scale and matter at the bottom. Here's my question: Doesn't that spectrum, from gross matter all the way down to nebulous quanta, reveal how matter shades off into waves—showing that matter and mind exist on the same spectrum? Isn't the quantum domain, then, an entrance to the nonphysical dimension of consciousness?

Short answer: I think you are barking up the wrong tree when you try to place consciousness and matter on the same spectrum. They are two completely different kinds of reality. The idea of "inversion" is a red herring. Putting either matter or mind at the top and its opposite at the bottom of a scale makes no sense.

Blindspot: First, every piece of data coming from quantum physics is about the *physical* world—and tells us nothing about *nonphysical* consciousness. The notion that particulate matter "dissolving" into waves opens the door to nonphysical consciousness is confused and mistaken. Both particles and waves are *physical*. Both occur in space. As I've explained, consciousness does not exist in space in any way whatsoever. It is *nonlocated*.

Second, matter and energy are essentially (i.e., ontologically) identical—they are both *physical*. Matter is just "denser" or "slower" energy; that's all. Think of energy as water and matter as ice. Ice is just frozen water. Similarly, matter is just "frozen" energy. And just as you will never produce mind from melting ice or from the vapor of boiling water, you will never get mind from waves of oscillating energy down at the quantum level.

The Planck scale is still 100 percent in the physical domain. It describes the smallest possible units of *physical* reality and has nothing to do with consciousness.

The idea that physicality stops at the Planck scale and beyond that it transitions into consciousness is pure nonsense. It completely misunderstands the essential nature of consciousness—and of matter/energy. Remember: "Consciousness *knows*. Energy *flows*." As I keep pointing out, consciousness does not exist as an object. Subjective consciousness is what *knows* objective matter/energy. The idea of "measuring" consciousness is absurd. Measurement applies to objects that exist in space. Consciousness does not exist in space because it is *subjective*.

Third, the idea that "consciousness is primary" is ontological idealism—and is deeply problematic (as explained in *Radical Nature*). If consciousness were primary, then how did *real* matter/energy ever come to exist? You cannot get something *physical* from purely *nonphysical* precursors. The idea that consciousness is primary is just as confused as the materialist notion that matter/energy is primary. In idealism, it is impossible to explain how to get *real* matter/energy from *pure* consciousness/spirit. In materialism, it is impossible to explain how to get *real* mind from *wholly* mindless matter/energy. *No ontological jumps.*

In place of the idealist's *primacy* of consciousness, panpsychism asserts that both consciousness and energy are *primordial*. That is, both *always* existed from the "beginning" of time (except there never was a beginning to time). Consciousness and energy (mind and matter) are inseparable and irreducible to each other. They *always* go together. You never have one without the other. Why? Because there are not "two things"—there is just the one, unified, ontological foundation to the universe: *sentient energy.* That is, energy is intrinsically *sentient*—it has an innate capacity for feeling, knowing, awareness, and choice. Energy per se is physical. The ability of energy to feel, know, be aware, and choose is *nonphysical.* Thus, everything physical incorporates a non-physical "interiority"—sentience or consciousness.*

A GATEWAY TO CONSCIOUSNESS

We are fortunate to live in a time when quantum science is evolving. This new science offers a language and a framework within which to explore consciousness beyond the limitations of classical physics, and it has resulted in new cosmologies with the potential to shed more light on the subject of consciousness. Do you agree that quantum physics is, finally, the scientific gateway to exploring consciousness? I have in mind the cosmology of Arthur Young.

In a word, "no." I don't think quantum science is an open sesame to the mysteries of consciousness. Quantum physics does not give us a language for talking about consciousness—other than metaphorically, just as classical science does. Remember, quantum physics is just that: *physics.* It studies the physical world. Indeed, it is called quantum *mechanics* for good reason.

Quantum physics has nothing to say about consciousness—except the fact that, somehow, consciousness is involved in the collapse of the probability wave function. That's it. The fact that consciousness has

---

*I explore the relationship between quantum physics and consciousness in *Consciousness from Zombies to Angels.*

reared its strange presence in quantum physics—the first time in science since Descartes split mind from body four hundred years ago—is a complete mystery to quantum physicists and other scientists. They have no way to account for this inconvenient fact.

All they can do is put a place marker (the Greek letter psi—ψ) in their equations, but they have no idea what it is, or how or why it is essential for their equations to work out.

Blindspot: Popular New Age thought is rife with misconceptions that see quantum physics offering, or on the verge of, a breakthrough into consciousness. It's not. Like all sciences, quantum physics deals exclusively with the objective physical world and has nothing to say about the subjective domain of experience and choice. For that, science will need to radically expand its methodology beyond its current reliance on sensory empiricism.

As I discuss in *Consciousness from Zombies to Angels* and in my forthcoming book *Radical Science,* a true science of consciousness will have to include nonsensory and nonrational ways of knowing, such as feeling and intuition, if it is ever to plumb the depths of consciousness or understand the intimate relationship between mind and body.

However . . . I want to expand on what I just said: I think I can see why you say quantum science offers a language that sheds light on consciousness. You referred to the work of cosmologist and renegade visionary Arthur Young, in particular his book *The Reflexive Universe.* Young's work clearly draws on science, especially quantum physics, to make sense of a universe in which both matter and consciousness are real. However, just as with physicist Amit Goswami's blending of quantum theory and consciousness, Young makes the connection by breaking away from the accepted metaphysics of modern scientific materialism.

Young, like Goswami, begins with consciousness as an existential given—primordial, if not primary. This cosmology is radically at odds with standard science and its foundational metaphysical assumption of universal materialism. Only because Young makes this metaphysical shift can he then go on to make sense of consciousness in relationship to quantum physics.

Young starts out by proposing that the quantum of action is purposeful—in other words, it is intrinsically conscious or intelligent. He doesn't discover consciousness (or a language for consciousness) in the details of quantum science. Rather, he imports the language of consciousness ("purpose," "choice") into quantum physics.

Despite his wide-ranging knowledge of science, Young was not a scientist. He was a mathematician and a metaphysician. His work paves the way for open-minded scientists to shift their metaphysical prejudices in ways that could begin to make sense of the connection between consciousness and the physical world through a revised understanding of quantum physics. Young's is not your "grandfather's" quantum physics.

Quantum Mysteries and Pop Myths

The implications of quantum science are vast. It tells me that whatever I unconditionally focus my attention on becomes real.

This does not follow at all from quantum physics or even from the "pop" version of it that makes the rounds in New Age circles—in movies and books such as *What the Bleep Do We Know!?* and *The Secret*.

Just because consciousness is required for the collapse of quantum probabilities into some actual, manifest event does not mean, therefore, that whatever we focus attention on becomes real.

Blindspot: For one thing, that idea seriously misconstrues and misapplies the data of quantum science, which deals with infinitesimal subatomic regions of space-time and does not translate to gross macroscopic bodies, such as humans, houses, hippos, or Humvees.

Second, even in quantum experiments, the observer does not focus attention on the outcome of the quantum event, such as an electron or photon radiating from an atom. One of the core tenets of quantum physics is that single quantum events are inherently unpredictable and unknowable in advance. Therefore, what "manifests" or becomes "real" following an observation is definitely *not* what the observer focused on.

The observer focuses on the experimental setup as a whole. The observer's consciousness does not "create" that setup. The quantum system already exists as a combination of actual entities: human researchers, technological devices, and sets of quantum possibilities.

All we know from quantum science is that, *somehow,* only when the quantum system as a whole is observed, which includes the observer and his or her consciousness, does the set of quantum probabilities "collapse" into a single actual physical event.

In no way can we claim that the observer "created" the reality of that event. All we can say is that, somehow, the observer's consciousness participated in the outcome. That "somehow" is one of the biggest mysteries confronting modern physicists. They haven't the faintest idea how to explain what happens. They can't—because their entire science deals exclusively with investigations of objective, measurable things or events, and consciousness is not objective, measurable, or physical. It is subjective, unmeasurable, and nonphysical.

Next, let's shift focus from the minute domain of quantum events and look at the bigger question of what it means to say that "nature has a mind of its own."

18

Nature

"Rocks Have Consciousness, Too"

The philosophy of panpsychism tells us that physical reality possesses some degree or kind of mind at every level—that consciousness goes all the way down to cells, molecules, atoms, and subatomic particles. In brief, matter tingles with sentience.

It's the only way to make sense of the fact that we are embodied physical beings composed of cells, molecules, and atoms and that *we are sentient, or conscious*. But because this view seems "counterintuitive," it is often ridiculed by mainstream philosophers and scientists.

German philosopher Arthur Schopenhauer famously wrote: "Every truth passes through three stages before it is recognized. In the first place, it is *ridiculed*. In the second, it is *opposed*. In the third, it is regarded as *self-evident*."

Back in the early 1990s, I gave a talk at the Toward a Science of Consciousness conference in Tucson, sponsored by the University of Arizona. During a presentation by professor Stuart Hameroff, he referred to *panexperientialism* as "de Quincey's theory of consciousness" (a month or two earlier, I had published a paper in the *Journal of Consciousness Studies* on panpsychism).

While it would be an exaggeration to say my views on panpsychism were "ridiculed" at that conference, they mostly fell on deaf ears. However, the fact that Hameroff, one of the conference organizers, endorsed my ideas nudged some folks to sit up and take notice.

Then, a year or so later, philosopher David Chalmers came out with

The Conscious Mind, in which he made a case for a quasi-panpsychist view (or, as he likes to call it, *proto-panpsychism*). By that time, many more conference participants and others in the academic world were beginning to take panpsychism more seriously and to spend time actually discussing and debating it—elevating it to Schopenhauer's second phase of being "opposed." At least it was now on the map.

In the intervening years, I've noticed more and more philosophers and scientists (though, of course, by no means all or even most) are willing to talk about the plausibility of consciousness all the way down. Major exceptions include staunch materialists such as Richard Dawkins, Daniel Dennett, John Searle, and Patricia and Paul Churchland. (They remain at phase 1: for them, panpsychism is something to be ridiculed and dismissed out of hand.)

However, it is clear to me that people who object to the panpsychist idea that some degree of consciousness exists even in atoms, electrons, and protons cannot have thought through their objections. Instead, they react from deeply biased metaphysical assumptions, most notably the idea that the ultimate nature of reality is nothing but "dead" insentient matter/energy.

Instead of knee-jerk protests like "don't be absurd," if they just stopped to *think,* they could see that "consciousness goes all the way down" is, after all, *self-evident.*

Making the Absurd Self-Evident

Here's a seven-step science-based logical proof that nature has a mind of its own:

1. We (humans) are sentient beings made of atoms and molecules.
2. There are no "unique human atoms or molecules." As I've noted before, you won't find any special "Hu" atom in the table of elements. Any atoms or molecules that exist as part of us also exist elsewhere in the universe.

3. No intrinsic difference exists between atoms of any kind; they all consist of electrons and protons.

4. That means there is no difference between the *atoms that make us* and *atoms elsewhere* throughout the universe.

5. *It is impossible for sentience to evolve or emerge from insentient atoms . . .**

6. Therefore, all atoms and molecules throughout the universe must also be sentient.

7. And, therefore, because the cosmos is permeated by sentient atoms and molecules, we can confidently conclude that *nature must have a mind of its own.*

It's that simple!

How else could we explain the fact that we are embodied sentient beings made of atoms and molecules, if those atoms and molecules were not themselves also sentient?

BEYOND THE MYTH OF EMERGENCE

The central message here is this: For something to "emerge," some version or degree of it had to be there from the beginning. As I emphasize in step 5, *it is impossible for sentience to evolve or emerge from insentient atoms.*

That point is crucial because even if people agree with the logic of the preceding steps, a lot of folks are likely to object along the lines of, "Well, yes, every kind of atom in the human body, nervous system, and brain can be found elsewhere in the universe, but that doesn't mean all those other atoms must be sentient, too." Logically, that's true—except for a pervasive and persistent *blindspot . . .*

---

*See *Radical Nature* for a detailed account of the insuperable problems facing the scientific materialist notion of consciousness emerging from nonconscious atoms and molecules.

Blindspot: The materialist's objection depends on the ungrounded and unscientific assumption that it is possible for insentient atoms to combine and evolve into sentient organisms. That's a foundational assumption in modern scientific materialism. As I have shown in detail in *Radical Nature,* the idea of mind or consciousness "emerging" or "evolving" from nonconscious, insentient ingredients just doesn't cash out. It is incoherent and makes no sense.

If atoms—or anything else—were insentient to begin with, then they, and everything they compose, would also remain insentient *forever.* But, obviously, that's not so. We know with certainty that we are sentient, conscious beings. Reminder: If you doubt or deny that fact, you have just contradicted yourself—because only a being with consciousness can have doubts about anything.

In short, the undeniable fact that we experience anything at all, even doubts, flies in the face of standard scientific materialism, including neuroscience and most modern philosophy of mind.

Folks who claim mind "emerges" from mindless matter either haven't thought through their assertions or should be prepared to offer a step-by-step *explanation* of just *how* insentient ingredients could "squirt out" consciousness, as Berkeley professor of philosophy John Searle famously said.

If anyone challenges my seven-step "proof," then I simply ask them to point out where they think the argument is flawed. Most likely they will focus on step 5. In that case, I invite them to then provide their own seven-step (or twelve- or twenty- or two-thousand- or two-gazillion-step) counterargument *without any explanatory gaps*—especially not skipping over how insentient atoms could have evolved into sentient organisms. You see, I know they can't—*and never will*—provide any such explanation.

Bottom line: We can be confident that consciousness goes all the way down and, therefore, that nature does indeed have a mind of its own. Where else do you think *our* minds came from?

FOR THE LOVE OF MATTER

I just had a very interesting discussion with my partner on love and the material world. I took the approach that all things have some level of consciousness, but she denies that any material object has consciousness, especially at the level of atoms and molecules. To her, that just seems ridiculous. But isn't it true that we, the Earth, and the universe are all made up of the same atoms and molecules? Someone who denies that all matter has consciousness cannot show love for material creations. Right?

I'm not sure; it depends on what you mean by *love*. Lots of people "love" material possessions, indeed are addicted to them. Yet most of these would also deny that matter has consciousness. Perhaps your friend is someone who "loves" material possessions but doesn't really *love* matter because she neither believes nor experiences the deep and innate sentience and sacredness of all matter—whether animals, plants, bacteria, viruses, molecules, or atoms.

People who deny sentience in matter deny that atoms and molecules have any level of consciousness. That is the dominant paradigm of scientific materialism. But, as I point out in my books and lectures, it makes no sense—because it cannot account for the fact that *we* have consciousness and we are made of atoms and molecules.

If your friend denies that atoms have consciousness, then ask her how come *she* has consciousness—after all, she is made of atoms. Can she explain how mindless atoms could ever come together to produce her mind? Of course, she cannot. Nobody can. It would require a miracle.

I suspect, however, that if you did ask her this, she would reply that science *can* explain how mindless atoms and molecules form into brains. But if that's her response, it merely shows how deep her confusion is—she's not even aware of the crucial difference between *minds* and *brains*. She thinks that by showing how presumed insentient matter evolves into brains also explains how matter evolves into *minds*. Her big blindspot would be not to see the fundamental ontological difference between *subjective first-person minds* and *objective third-person brains*. The central "hard problem" remains: Can she explain how *purely* objective matter could ever produce *subjective* experiences? And, of course, the answer is a resounding "no."

Yes, you are quite right: We humans are made up of atoms and subatomic particles found elsewhere in the natural world. There are no special "human atoms" or "human molecules."

Blindspot: If we have consciousness (we do) and if we are made of atoms and molecules (we are), then, unless some inexplicable miracle has happened, it follows that the atoms and molecules we are made of must also have some degree of consciousness as well. And, because there is nothing special about human atoms and molecules, it follows that *all* atoms and molecules must also have some degree of consciousness. The logic is plain and straightforward.

People who deny this either (1) do not think things through clearly enough or (2) believe in some inexplicable miraculous process that can produce minds from mindless matter. Ironically, this option is not available to materialists because, by definition, they deny the possibility of anything supernatural like miracles.

Generally, people who deny that matter has its own consciousness have just unthinkingly bought into the dogma of scientific materialism—which is based on the metaphysical assumption that the ultimate nature of reality is "dead" matter. However, that assumption is not in any way scientific or supported by scientific evidence. To put it bluntly: *Science has absolutely nothing to say about consciousness one way or the other.* Why? Because science restricts itself to studying the *physical* world, and consciousness is *nonphysical*.

If your friend is truly interested in clearly thinking things through, then you might want to pursue this kind of conversation with her. If, however, she just unthinkingly adopts the "standard dogma," then I'd say don't even waste your time.

But be patient and compassionate. People in our culture have been educated ("brainwashed" is appropriate) to believe that only humans—or, at best, animals with complex brains—could possibly have minds or consciousness. There are long and complex reasons for this. Essentially, it all comes down to the need to believe that *humans are special.* We're not. We, like everything else in nature, are composed of matter and mind, or energy and consciousness.

Interestingly enough, people who truly love matter—let's call them "radical materialists"—tend not to be in love with *material consumption.* They recognize that all of nature is sacred. Indigenous cultures recognized this a long, long time ago.

Rocks and Minds, Heaps and Wholes

In Radical Knowing *you wrote: "Mountains* per se *do not have 'mountain consciousness' or 'rock consciousness'—but their constituent molecules and atoms do have molecular and atomic consciousness. It's an important distinction."*

I understand that rocks and mountains are not organisms with metabolizing abilities. But I'm puzzled to know just what we are tapping into if the mountain as a whole does not have consciousness? I am confused with what I have read and heard from shamans in regard to listening to the language of the mountains, rivers, and wind. I do comprehend that sentience is the ability to perceive or feel. What, then, are the shamans (or others having these experiences) perceiving—what are they interacting with or receiving that they then translate into wisdom for the rest of us? If, as you say, "nature has a mind of its own," why wouldn't these marvels of the natural world have a mind of their own, too?

Shamans, some mystics, and others do report experiences in which they claim to have communicated "intersubjectively" with aspects of the natural world such as mountains, rivers, rocks, clouds, winds, and so forth. Yet according to the philosophy of panpsychism, these don't have their own consciousness—so how do we accommodate these apparently conflicting views? That's essentially what you are asking.

Given my approach to philosophy, where I acknowledge and honor different ways of knowing—the Scientist's Gift of the *senses*, the Philosopher's Gift of *reason* and *language*, the Shaman's Gift of *participatory feeling*, and the Mystic's Gift of *direct knowing* or *intuition* through sacred silence, I have two ways of dealing with this kind of question.

First, it could be (*philosophically*) that shamans and mystics experience intersubjective communion with the *molecules* of the mountains, rivers, rocks, and clouds, which they then *interpret* in language as if the "heaps" had their own unit consciousness. Without denying or questioning their intersubjective experiences, it is possible that their linguistic expressions of those experiences are deficient or even inaccurate. *Philosophically,* they could be in error.

However, as I write in *Radical Knowing,* one of the great gifts of reason is that it tells us that reason is neither the end of knowledge nor the edge of reality. Reason tells us that beyond reason other ways of knowing exist and that these could give us access to other domains of reality. So, there may well be domains or aspects of reality that lie beyond the capacity of reason and language to accurately express. Even though the idea of heaps or aggregates manifesting unit consciousness is *philosophically* problematic, that doesn't mean it can't be true. It could be philosophically incoherent yet shamanically or mystically coherent and true.

The problem arises when we attempt to *talk* or *write* about experiences that occur in realms of feeling or intuition, rather than in the domain of reason and language.

It depends on what our objective is: Do we wish to think and talk with *philosophical coherence,* in which case the "heaps and wholes" distinction is worth paying attention to—and any intersubjective experiences with rocks, rivers, or mountains would really be with their constituent molecules? Or are we more interested in communicating insights based on feelings and intuitions that may not be amenable to accurate expression in language or ideas? If we wish to communicate shamanic or mystical truth, then it doesn't serve us to get too concerned about philosophical and linguistic coherence.

How can you say that molecules can think, yet at the same time say that rocks cannot? You lose me there.

First, I have never said, and would never claim, that "molecules can think." However, I would say, and do claim, that molecules and atoms can *feel*. That is, they are sentient; they have an ability to subjectively "prehend," or take in and know about, events in their environment.

I am aware that the idea that molecules and atoms could possess some trace of consciousness (an ability to feel) is likely to boggle the minds of some folks. Well, let the mind boggle, at least for a while. Even more mind-boggling is the idea that consciousness could evolve from wholly mindless ingredients. Once again—I *really* want to drive this home—here's why I say molecules and atoms *must* have some trace or degree of consciousness, or sentience:

1. You and I are made of molecules and atoms.
2. We are conscious beings.
3. Therefore, *whatever we are made of*—at every level, all the way down to molecules and atoms—must also possess some trace of consciousness, too. Otherwise, we face the mystery and miracle of the ontological jump described earlier.

You may ask why, then, would I say that rocks don't have consciousness? After all, they too are made of molecules.

The simplest answer relies on an important distinction I discussed earlier between *heaps* and *wholes*, or *aggregates* and *individuals*. Let me tackle this from a different angle: Rocks are "heaps," made of molecules just scrunched together under pressure. Individuals, like you and me, are "wholes"; our molecules are organized into interdependent systems and hierarchies, where the whole is dependent on the maintenance of this organization.

Molecules, too, qualify as "individuals" or "wholes" because every molecule relies on the organized coordination of its constituent atoms. Rocks are not like this—they are unorganized heaps.

Because of their interdependent coordinated organization, individuals, or wholes, have *unit* consciousness. That is, the unit as a whole—whether human organism, cell, or molecule—is coordinated in such a way that the "little consciousnesses" of its constituent parts combine into a unified monad of consciousness. Rocks are not like this—their molecules are not internally organized to form a unified individual, where the functioning of all the parts depends on how they are *internally* related to each other. The molecules in rocks are jumbled together in *external* configurations.*

Moroccan Rock Experience

I sometimes tell a personal anecdote on this topic: Many years ago, I spent some time on a beach in southern Morocco. One night, I set up camp beneath a large overhanging boulder. As darkness descended, and the sky sparkled with countless points of light, I lay in my sleeping bag staring up at the heavens seeing and *feeling* the looming presence of the giant silhouette between me and the rest of the universe. I was convinced I was communing with the rock, having an "intersubjective" experience, as I would later come to describe it.

This was years before I became a philosopher. At that time, all I knew was that the experience was undeniable. Years later, when I learned about the difference between "heaps" and "wholes" in process philosophy, I remembered and wondered about that experience on my favorite Moroccan beach. I concluded I must have been having

---

*For a more detailed explanation of the difference between "heaps" and "wholes," look up "individuals" and "binding problem" in *Radical Nature*.

an intersubjective connection with the *molecules* in the rock.

However, that is not what it felt like at the time. If I had a time machine and could go back to the 1970s and talk with my twenty-year-old self, I probably would have rejected the idea that I was experiencing "molecular consciousness." It felt like *rock consciousness* to me.

The point is that the philosophical distinctions—even if they are accurate and right—were not all that interesting to me at that time. What mattered to me was the *experience,* which I would now call "shamanic" or "mystical."

Blindspot: Wearing my philosopher's hat, I would talk of "molecular consciousness"; wearing my shaman's hat, I would talk of "rock consciousness." It would depend on what I most wished to communicate—either *coherent ideas* (philosophical) or *meaningful feelings* (shamanic).

From the larger perspective of "state-specific knowing" (which I also write about in *Radical Knowing*), both the philosopher's and the shaman's accounts of the experience would be true. Each is addressing a different level of knowing and reality—where different epistemologies are appropriate for different ontological levels.

Finally, one way of talking about such experiences that honors both the philosophical insight and shamanic experience is to describe intersubjective connections with natural processes as instances of what the Taoist sages called *no-knowledge*—the silent knowing of nature knowing itself (beyond all our categorizing distinctions).

Animism or Panpsychism?

I've wondered for a long time about the difference between animism and panpsychism. Does animism necessarily project human qualities onto the nonhuman world, or do animists simply see individual beings as sacred, as gods?

Depending on the form of animism, I think some do project human qualities onto the "more-than-human world," as author David Abram prefers to call it in *The Spell of the Sensuous*. A case in point would be children conversing with their dolls or teddy bears. A more common modern example, of course, is when we shout in frustration at our misbehaving computers or cars! To the extent that animism views objects as endowed with spirit, all of nature is sacred.

Depth Alert: Animism differs from panpsychism in a couple of respects, depending on the form of animism:

1. In animism, *all* of nature is endowed with spirit or spirits—including inanimate phenomena such as rocks, rivers, clouds, mountains, winds, rain, places, and so forth. By contrast, as I noted earlier, panpsychism distinguishes between *individuals* and *aggregates* (or *wholes* and *heaps*). Only individuals, or whole organisms, from atoms to apes, have unit or "monad" consciousness. Aggregates, such as rocks, beer cans, or computers, are not organized as "individuals." Their parts are not related *interdependently* and with *internal relatedness,* in which the being of each component is mutually constituted by its interdependent relationships with the network of other components.

   Animism is a worldview, cosmology, or spiritual belief system; panpsychism is a philosophy or metaphysics. They do, of course, overlap to a great degree.
2. Many forms of animism view matter as imbued with spirit that can enter or leave the object. This, as you know, is *dualism,* not panpsychism, in which matter and spirit are inseparable.

A central part of my work is to expand the epistemology of science, philosophy, and everyday life by including and cultivating nonrational, nonsensory ways of knowing. Shamans and mystics do it all the time and have enriched our understanding of the wider and deeper dimensions of existence.

That said, we always need to remain alert to the temptation, conscious or unconscious, to project our own experiences beyond ourselves and attribute to other beings or objects states of consciousness we are familiar with. Anthropomorphism is always something to watch out for. However, accusations of *anthropomorphism* need to avoid equally problematic *anthropocentrism,* the assumption that consciousness and certain kinds of experience are uniquely human.

Is Science of Mind Panpsychism?

> *I was reading* Radical Nature, *where you write about different worldviews on mind and matter. From what I understand, I probably hold a "combo worldview"—a combination of emanationist idealism and dualistic panpsychism, as well as panentheistic panpsychism, and radical materialism. I see some truth in all of them. In Science of Mind, we hold that nature is sacred and believe it is a reflection of the One Power and One Presence—kind of like panpsychism, but still probably idealism or a form of panentheism, the idea that God is in all of nature. What would you say is the worldview of our philosophy?*

Good question. Keep in mind, though, that there are only four distinct worldviews on the mind-matter relationship, and that any "combo" probably indicates some inherent contradiction in the "combined" worldview.

Depth Alert: Given that we are dealing with two fundamental aspects of reality, mind and matter, we can have a maximum of four worldviews that can account for how mind and matter relate:

1. Everything is ultimately *matter;* mind is an emergent epiphenomenon (materialism).

2. Everything is ultimately *mind;* matter either emanates from mind or it's an illusion (idealism).

3. Everything is ultimately **separable** *mind and matter,* and each interacts from within its own separate domain (dualism).

4. Everything is ultimately **inseparable** *mind and matter;* together they constitute *sentient energy,* the ultimate unified nature of everything (panpsychism).

The examples of "combos" you give above are not really combinations of different worldviews. *Emanationist idealism* and *consequent panpsychism* are really forms of idealism that recognize the reality of matter (i.e., that matter is not just an illusion). So, there's really no combo. *Dualistic panpsychism* means that the unity of sentient energy includes two aspects: sentience and energy. *Panentheism* is a theology, not specifically an ontological worldview. It is, essentially, the theological version of emanationist idealism.

So, which worldview do I think is embraced by Science of Mind (based on the teachings of Ernest Holmes)?

Clearly, as you note, it's not *materialism* . . .

Nor is it *dualism* . . .

Sometimes it sounds similar to *panpsychism* . . .

Mostly, though, it is *emanationist idealism.*

Now, because it is emanationist idealism, which means it acknowledges the *reality* of matter and the physical world—the world of "forms"—it turns out to be what I have called *consequent panpsychism.* Although I explained earlier what I mean by this, let me clarify again:

In emanationist idealism ultimate reality is considered to be "pure spirit" (Level 1 in both Holmes's and Young's cosmologies). Spirit then expresses itself ("pours forth" or "emanates") in stages of involution—three stages in Holmes, four in Young. The final stage of involution in both models is matter.

Now, because matter is a product of spirit—that is, a *consequence* of spiritual emanation—all matter ("all the way down" and "all the way up") is inherently spiritual. Therefore, all matter is inherently *sentient.* Hence: consequent panpsychism.

This is why in many places Holmes's writing *sounds like* he's espousing panpsychism. However, if, as seems to be the case, Holmes's starting point is the idea of *pure* spirit that produces *real* matter, his version of emanationist idealism runs right into the core problem facing all forms of emanationist idealism: How does *pure* spirit produce *real* matter? How could any such miraculous ontological jump occur? Remember, an *ontological jump* is getting from one state of reality (*pure* spirit) to a very different state of reality (one that now contains something completely new and different—*real* matter).

If, however, the claim is made that matter is just a form of spirit, then that means it is not *real* matter, and we would be dealing with *maya idealism,* which claims that matter is merely an illusion, or "form," created in the mind of spirit. And that worldview, as we have seen, runs smack into the problem of a performative contradiction. People just don't (and can't) live in the world in ways consistent with the claim that matter is illusory. Everyone, without exception, treats matter as though it is real. And for very good reason.

It seems to me that Holmes wants to acknowledge the reality of matter and does not claim it is just an illusion. That's why his version of idealism is emanationist, not maya or absolute.

Now, as I emphasized in *Radical Nature,* a major problem lurks at the heart of emanationist idealism: the jump from *pure* spirit to *real* matter is simply not explicable; no ontological jump is. It is essentially the same kind of problem facing materialism, only in reverse. In the case of materialism, how does one explain the jump from one state of reality, pure matter/energy, to a radically new and different state of reality, one that now contains real mind, or consciousness? In both cases—emanationist idealism and materialism—the ontological leap resists all attempts at coherent explanation. In short, if it were true, it would require a *miracle.*

"Well, what's wrong with that?" you might ask. "I believe in miracles. So that's not a problem for me."

If this happens to be your response, then fine. Of course, you are entitled to believe whatever you wish. However, I would point out two things: (1) Just because you *believe* something doesn't make it true. (2) If miracles do happen, and that is a possibility, by definition they are inexplicable; if we could explain them they wouldn't be miracles. *Miracles can't be explained.* Therefore, they have no place in either science or philosophy, which are in the business of providing coherent explanations.

The most appropriate and probably the best response to a miracle would be to just remain quiet, not say anything that might suggest we understand anything about it, and allow ourselves to just be awed by and reverent toward the event. If miracles happen, it means something *supernatural* has just intervened in the course of natural events.

As a panpsychist, I don't see any need to invoke the aid of anything supernatural. I see nature (i.e., the cosmos) itself as wholly capable of providing everything the universe and all its inhabitants need. I see mind or consciousness or spirit as *wholly natural* elements in the cosmos—a cosmos that doesn't involve anything supernatural.

A major difference between the cosmologies of Young and Holmes is that while Young, like Holmes, sometimes refers to "pure consciousness" or "pure spirit" as the ultimate or first cause, which would qualify his model as emanationist, Young also, and more emphatically, insists that the ultimate is the photon, the unit of light, which is identical to the *quantum of action*. Now, he is also clear that the quantum is *purposeful* action.

Young's ultimate cause, then, is not pure consciousness or spirit because *action* is essential to its nature. And action is *energy*—the capacity to makes things happen, to manifest. Thus, Young's ultimate contains both *consciousness* (purpose) and *energy* (action)—which qualifies his model as a form of panpsychism. From this starting point, Young then continues with an emanationist cosmology of involution, turn, and evolution. So, we could say that Young's cosmology is a form of emanationist panpsychism.

However, coupling "emanationism" and "panpsychism" together

is contradictory. The whole idea of emanationism is an attempt to explain how *pure* spirit produces *real* matter, and, of course, because it involves an ontological jump, the explanation inevitably breaks down. By contrast, because panpsychism begins with the assumption that *both* consciousness and matter are real and that neither comes from, or is produced by, the other, no emanation is required to account for the existence of real matter; and, contra materialism, no emergence is required to account for the existence of real mind.

Blindspot: In the final analysis, emanationist idealism and panpsychism are not compatible. Either one or the other could be true, but not both. Either reality, the cosmos, begins with *pure* consciousness or it does not. Emanationism claims it does, panpsychism claims it doesn't. Any worldview that attempts, either consciously or unconsciously, to incorporate both emanationism and panpsychism reveals some underlying confusion and contradiction.

One way to resolve the contradiction lurking in the emanationist cosmologies of both Holmes and Young is to either (1) redefine *pure spirit* or (2) drop the adjective *pure*. The redefinition of *pure spirit* would distinguish it from *pure consciousness*. In this new understanding, *pure spirit* would be *pure sentient energy* (or pure consciousness and energy). Less confusing, I think, to simply drop the adjective *pure*. It doesn't help clarify any meaning.

If, then, we think of spirit as sentient energy (Young's "purposeful action")—and that spirit consists of both consciousness and energy—we avoid the contradictions between emanationism and panpsychism and gain the benefit of being able to explain the relationship between consciousness and matter. Note that in this panpsychist view, *spirit is embodied*. It is not pure consciousness. Spirit also contains *energy*, a capacity for making things happen, a capacity for manifesting intentions.[*]

---

[*]See appendix 2, "Science of Mind and the Reflexive Universe," for some further comparisons between the evolution of consciousness models of Holmes and Young.

Now that you are more equipped to weigh the alternative world-views and align with one that best matches your experience and understanding of the world, *which is it for you?*

Whichever worldview you choose, I leave you with this nugget of inspirational wisdom from Plato: "It's all just a likely story." I encourage you not to be too attached to any particular worldview. Use it, work with it, see how it serves you. And always be willing to let it go.

Most of all, I don't want you to *believe* any worldview. And I certainly don't want you to believe anything I have said or written. In the end, I want you to trust your own *experience*. Cultivate experience beyond belief—the path to wisdom.

19

The Living Universe
"Everything Is Alive"

Life isn't everything. As anyone knows who has ever been present when someone dies, whether a human or some other animal, the difference between a living and a dead organism is palpable. We need a meaningful way to distinguish between "life" and "death."

The idea that "everything is alive" misses something important: Life does not equal all that exists.

While all matter/energy in the universe is sentient (has some degree of consciousness), not all forms of matter are "alive" or "living."

Blindspot: We need to distinguish between "life" and "sentience." While everything alive is sentient, not everything sentient is alive. Stop and take that in. It's important, with profound implications for science, philosophy, and day-to-day living. Molecules and atoms, for instance, are sentient (it feels like something to be an atom), but they are not alive—they do not metabolize energy. That's the distinction between "life" and "death" and between "life" and "prelife"—*metabolism.*

Let's be clear: Life is a biological process based on metabolism of chemical energy. Living systems take in parts of their environment; process the energy; build up tissue, transforming external energy into embodied energy; and then eject residual waste back into the environment. When metabolizing ceases, the organism dies.

WHAT HAPPENS
TO CONSCIOUSNESS?

While an organism is alive, its matter/energy, in the form of cells, is organized coherently and interdependently in ways that form a unified whole. When an organism is unified, its associated consciousness is also unified. That's why we experience ourselves as "individuals."

When we die, however, the organic unity of our body breaks down, and so the organism as a whole no longer experiences unified, individual consciousness. At the moment of death, consciousness "retreats" to—or, more accurately, continues to exist at—the level of cells. A shift happens from "organism consciousness" to "cellular consciousness."

Next, the cells decay and lose their coherence and unity. At that point, consciousness "descends" to the level of the molecules that compose the cell. In time, these too break down when exposed to energy (e.g., sunlight or chemicals). When that happens, consciousness "descends" to the level of atoms.

Except in cases of nuclear explosions or radioactivity, that's the end of the decay process. Most atoms remain stable for hundreds of thousands of years. Protons apparently can remain unchanged for around fourteen times the life of the universe!

After death, some of our atoms or molecules may get recycled into the bodies of another living organism. Could be a plant, worm, bird, cat, fish, or human . . .

EXPERIENCE IS NEVER DESTROYED

In physics the law of conservation of energy states that energy is never created or destroyed. A similar "law" exists in panpsychism: Every experience you've ever had is recorded holographically in every cell, molecule, atom, and subatomic particle of your body. When you die, the atoms and molecules that were once part of "you" continue to hold the memories of your life experiences until they, too, decay—at which time consciousness "descends" to the level of subatomic particles such as electrons, protons, or quanta.

In time, when one or more of "your" atoms or molecules has been recycled—let's say it becomes part of some future human being—then that person, in a sufficiently sensitive state of consciousness, can reexperience the experiences recorded in "your" atoms and molecules.

When that happens, the future person might well think he or she had a "past-life experience." But that would not be an accurate description of what actually happened. That person never lived as "you"; he or she merely "relives" some of your experiences.

That's one form of *immortality,* or consciousness surviving biological death. But it's unlikely to satisfy our egos because they don't survive the disintegration of our bodies. What does survive is impersonal, or *transpersonal,* consciousness and the experiences it records.

The universe wastes nothing. Think of it as the Great Cosmic Recycling Program.

For many people—including scholars, scientists, and philosophers—consciousness and life are synonymous. "Everything is alive," they say, "and all is an expression of consciousness in varying degrees."

LIFE IS NOT CONSCIOUSNESS

In my work, I make a distinction between "life" and "consciousness." As I noted above, life is a biological phenomenon that involves metabolism of chemical energy. When metabolism ceases, the living system dies. However, while death by definition is the cessation of life, it is not the end of consciousness.

Let's review: From a panpsychist view, when we die, the life in our body expires. So does the egoic unit of consciousness we call "me." This unit of consciousness depends for its unity on the coherence of the body. When the body decays, the unit of consciousness dissolves. It decays into its constituent cells, and at that stage consciousness as "me" no longer exists. However, what remains is the consciousness of the cells of the body—a transformation from "organism consciousness" to "cellular consciousness." In time, these cells also decay into their constituent molecules, and at that stage what is left is "molecular consciousness." Except in very rare instances (e.g., a nuclear explosion), the process of decay stops at the molecules (in nuclear explosions molecules are broken down further into atoms and subatomic particles).

So, while all life (metabolizing, living systems) has consciousness or sentience, not all sentient beings are alive. Molecules and atoms, for instance, are sentient, but not alive. They are not biological systems. This distinction between "life" and "consciousness" is important so we can make sense of the difference between a "living" organism and a "dead" organism.

Clearly, this difference exists. I often think of my experience sitting with my father as he was dying. I was holding his hand when he took his final breath (it was such a privilege to be there). At that moment, and for the succeeding hours as his body lay in the hospital bed, it was palpably clear and real to me that a profound difference existed between my living father and his dead body. We need some way to account for this difference. To me, the idea that "everything is alive" makes no sense and is contradicted by the facts of our experience. Some things are alive, others are dead, and others never were alive (e.g., rocks, beer cans, computers). However, every organism is sentient (i.e., has consciousness)—this includes all living systems, as well as the molecules and atoms in nonliving systems (e.g., in dead bodies, beer cans, computers, sand castles, pools of water).

This seems worth noting because so many people talk about "life" and "consciousness" as though they were the same. They're not, and the difference is both significant and profound.

And, by the way, this applies equally to another common blindspot. I often hear people (including many of my professional colleagues) talk about the "living universe." When I probe a little deeper, however, I find that what they really mean is a *sentient* universe. Big difference.

20

Science Reigns

"Everything Is Governed by the Laws of Physics"

If you have a passion for deep questions about the nature and origin of consciousness, whether the universe or evolution has purpose, or the relationship between spirituality and science, you might want to put aside about an hour to watch a YouTube video called "Dangerous Ideas."* The video is mostly in English. If you don't speak Spanish, you might want to skip forward about fifteen minutes.) The video features a take-no-prisoners debate between spiritual author and physician Deepak Chopra and archmaterialist Richard Dawkins. After I watched it—a little dismayed at the immense gulf between their respective dogmas—I posted my own views on my Facebook page, "Consciousness for Life."

As you might expect, neither succeeds, even slightly, in shifting the other from his perspective. Nevertheless, their interaction turned out to be a dramatic illustration of what I call the Metaphysical Gulf War— the gaping divide between worldviews, one in which consciousness is primary and one in which matter/energy rules the universe.

If, like me, you understand why brains made of mindless matter could not produce minds or consciousness, be prepared to feel impatience or frustration when Dawkins says to Chopra with 100 percent self-assured conviction (and I'm paraphrasing here): "You don't honestly believe that atoms, or even single cells, have consciousness or sentience!"

Even though I "knew" that is what Dawkins would say, what most

---

*See www.youtube.com/watch?v=f4c_CrQzUGw.

scientists would say, it still stopped me in my tracks. It shocked me to see and hear Dawkins express this dogma with such total conviction.

So . . . be prepared.

However, as I watched these two men battle it out across the gaping metaphysical divide and felt the strong convictions each possessed, I observed my own reactions.

At first, I felt my blood heat up listening to Dawkins—and, at times, to Chopra. Then I decided to shift my perspective and attitude. Instead of rehearsing my own responses to either man, especially Dawkins, I decided to listen to what each had to say with a clear intention to understand as deeply as I could—not just "what" he had to say but also "why" he was saying it. What was motivating him?

I found the experience highly instructive. It reminded me to really *listen* and let in the other—to feel the meaning intended and to process it—before responding with my own understanding. Unfortunately—or, perhaps, fortunately—the format of the show didn't allow the speakers time to go deep.

Had I engaged with Dawkins, I would have focused on finding whatever common ground might exist between us—perhaps not much. From there, I would try to identify how and why and at what point our shared understanding began to diverge toward different conclusions. I think that would be illuminating—and probably much more satisfying than trying to rattle him with intellectual counterpunches.

It would mean, of course, staying "grounded" and attentive to my own embodied understanding and awareness, and responding from there—rather than merely reacting to whatever I happened to disagree with.

CHANGING THE SUBJECT

At one point, Dawkins forcefully declared something like: "I don't believe the universe itself has purpose or consciousness." To which Chopra inquired: "What is this 'I' you are talking about?"

Dawkins's reaction amused me: He accused Chopra, and not for the first time, of "changing the subject" (no pun intended) and clearly missed any irony.

So, who won the debate? That doesn't really matter. In my opinion neither man won, but their interaction revealed, in a dramatic way, the depth of the science versus spirituality paradigm war.

Me? I'll put my money on finding a way to integrate both.

Though not expressed in these terms, the key question underlying their debate, of course was: How could purely physical processes in the brain ever give rise to nonphysical minds or consciousness?

I am confident Dawkins cannot answer that question. In fact, he admitted this to Chopra, preferring, instead, to offer scientific faith in "promissory materialism." Like Chopra, I'd say: don't bank on it.

Dawkins's likely response to my question would be along these lines: "Only physical things and events exist; therefore mind, or consciousness, is just another emergent physical property."

To which I would reply: (1) what do you mean by *physical?* and (2) what characteristics of mind, or consciousness, qualify as physical?

Notoriously, mind, or consciousness, is subjective; it is first person; it cannot be observed; it cannot be measured; it has none of the key characteristics of physical things or events such as mass, charge, or location . . . I could go on.

The point is that consciousness has none of the characteristics we attribute to physical things and events and has many that are intrinsically inexplicable in terms of physical events—such as feelings, qualia, experience, sensation, subjectivity. Therefore, it is safe to conclude that consciousness is nonphysical.

At that point, it would be up to Dawkins (or Daniel Dennett or any other scientific materialist) to explain in what sense consciousness could be physical. Failing such an explanation—an inevitable result—the best Dawkins could do would be to shrug and try to change the "subject." Hmmm . . .

In a moment, we'll take a close and detailed look at why modern science harbors a major blindspot—in fact, it's so huge, it's more like a psychological black hole! Preview: It's got to do with the fact that every piece of scientific knowledge—*including all its "laws"*—exists because scientists *observed and experienced* some aspect of the natural world. In other words, because of the fact that every scientist has *consciousness*. No consciousness, no science—or any other form of knowledge. That's clear and straightforward. However, what's not so clear, at least to the scientific community, is that *because their consciousness exists, scientific laws cannot exist*. Big blindspot, as I will explain.

First, though, I want to acknowledge what *is* useful about science—it tests ideas, hypotheses, and theories. And it has a method for doing so.

Briefly, modern science has developed a set of observational procedures—called the *scientific method*—for testing hypotheses and theories, and for sharing results with a community of peers who can then do further testing—that's one reason why science builds on past successes.

However, this method of testing is not unique to modern science. Indigenous knowledge, too, accumulates through careful and attentive observations of nature, and the results are shared with peers—this works as a way to check whether the knowledge stands the test of time.

Modern science differs, however, by focusing on a process designed to yield "objective" (measurable, quantifiable) knowledge, which, necessarily, restricts scientific data to purely *physical* things and events. Scientific knowledge, then, is *mechanistic*—literally a *machine* at odds with the natural world because it has lost its connection to the *organic* and *intersubjective* matrix that characterizes indigenous science.

Laws and Consciousness Don't Mix

To a certain extent, I think I understand why Dawkins so forcefully resists any attempt to include a spiritual or nonphysical dimension, and why—for him—consciousness *must* be a product of brain chemicals: If consciousness is nonphysical (which it is), then that would play havoc with the entire metaphysical superstructure of materialism that undergirds modern science (which it does). But Dawkins cannot accept that. After all, he has built a career betting on the paradigm of scientific materialism. If he were to accept that consciousness is not just some epiphenomenal "electrochemical ooze" squirted out by brains, then he would be forced to open up to the idea that not only is consciousness real, it is *causal*—consciousness makes things happen.

Now *that* would be a difficult pill for him to swallow. It would mean that the so-called laws of physics (Dawkins's version of the biblical Ten Commandments) would fall apart. Why? Well, as we have already seen, consciousness and laws just don't mix—and that's because consciousness comes with *choice.* The moment choice enters the picture, scientific laws break down. Let's look more closely at this.

As we know from quantum physics, consciousness (an observer) is involved in shaping the manifest physical world through what is called the collapse of the quantum wave function. In simple terms, this means:

1. Every quantum system exists in a state of multiple coexisting *possibilities,* described mathematically as "probabilities" in the form of "wave functions."
2. When a sentient being *observes* the quantum system, the various possibilities, or probabilities, "collapse" into a single actuality, a tiny piece of the manifest physical world, such as an electron or proton, the building blocks of all matter.

In other words, *until* a sentient being observes the quantum system, all probabilities of that system remain "suspended in possibility." Only when an observation is made—which, necessarily, involves the presence of consciousness—does the "collapse" happen, and what was previously merely *potential* (unmanifest) becomes *actual* (manifest). In this way, *consciousness participates in manifesting the physical world.*

A similar understanding of the relationship between possibility and actuality (between unmanifest and manifest) is explained in Alfred North Whitehead's process philosophy, which provides a rigorous metaphysical foundation for *panpsychism.*

So far so good. However . . . we cannot conclude from this that "consciousness *creates* physical reality." Dawkins and I would agree on this, though Chopra, being an idealist, would not. Besides the *possibilities that surround every actual event* (specifically quantum events, but the same is true for *all* events), each actual event also has a history or a past. Nothing happens from nothing. The domain of all past events *is* the physical world—of *energy.*

Depth Alert: Everything that *actually* exists has two distinct, though always coupled, components: *energy* and *consciousness.* Consciousness does not "create" energy (the physical world); it *shapes* it by making choices from the cloud of possibilities that surround every actual occasion. In other words, energy always *precedes* every moment of consciousness, or choice. And energy unfolds and evolves into new forms only because of consciousness, or choice—which always acts *now,* in the present moment.

Consciousness always needs something to work with. It needs both unmanifest possibilities (quantum potentials) and manifest actualities (matter/energy). Without energy, pure consciousness could never manifest anything. By itself, the most *pure* consciousness could achieve would be to generate intentions. But to make intentions manifest, something has to happen. Spirit must *act.*

Spirit, therefore, cannot be *pure* consciousness; it must also possess the ability to act—and *action is energy.* Therefore, in order to manifest anything, spirit must possess both consciousness to create intentions and energy to express intentions through action. *Without action, nothing could ever happen;* spirit-as-pure-consciousness would forever remain suspended in a realm of eternal possibilities.

This explains why it is inaccurate to say "consciousness creates reality." Rather, a more accurate and coherent statement would be to say that by choosing from already existing actualities and from among present possibilities, *consciousness participates with energy in co-creating the next moment.*

To create a manifest actual world, both consciousness and energy are needed. Neither one creates the other. This preamble lays the groundwork for understanding why consciousness and laws don't mix. First, though, let's take a little time to remind ourselves just what a scientific law is.

WHAT IS A SCIENTIFIC LAW?

A law is assumed to be a description of *invariant* and *universal* patterns or forces in nature. In other words, laws *inflexibly determine* the course of events in the world. By definition, nothing can contradict or contravene the laws of nature. They hold for all time, everywhere. No exceptions.

Furthermore, in science, every law is assumed to describe *purely physical causality.* Everything that happens, it is assumed, is caused by physical forces or events. No other form of causality is acknowledged—including, of course, the causality of consciousness. *Causality is always physical,* according to science.

If true, this means that everything is completely *determined* by physical causes. A wholly determined universe would operate like a machine, purely mechanically.

Now, if reality *were* fully determined by physical laws and causes, then there would be no room left, no possibility, for anyone ever to make a choice. All nonphysical causes (*choices*) would be ruled out.

WHAT IS CHOICE?

Choice is a *nonphysical, unconstrained,* and *creative* existential act. By definition, choice is *totally free.* If it were otherwise—if choice were *determined* by laws of nature—then it couldn't possibly be free, and it couldn't be *choice.*

This is not to deny "facts" or actualities of nature. As we saw above, consciousness manifests something new by selecting from the array of *past* actualities (the facts that compose the physical world) and from the spectrum of possibilities that surround every actuality (in the *present*), thereby generating some novelty, something new (shaping the *future*).

More simply: If the universe were governed by *invariant* and *universal* scientific laws that are true everywhere for all time, everything that ever happens would be *fully determined* by those laws. The universe would be a giant machine. But machines don't have consciousness and don't make choices.

As soon as we accept that consciousness, or choice, is part of reality, present in the universe, which is obviously so, this means that *something other than pure determinism,* pure mechanism, is at work, guiding the unfolding of events.

If something truly new, truly creative, ever happens through consciousness, or choice, then it follows that universal mechanism, or determinism, cannot exist.

We can't have it both ways: *Either* the universe is fully determined by laws *or* choice exists.

Yes, it is the case, as explained above, that consciousness works with "facts" of nature, with actualities, with things as they actually are. It does so by selecting among already existing actualities—the objective, physical world of matter/energy—and by choosing from available possibilities.

If either of these actions were fully governed or determined by laws, then real choice could not be possible—because, by definition, *choice is necessarily free* and *undetermined.* If choice were determined by laws, then, as already noted, it wouldn't be *choice.* At best, it would be an *appearance* of choice—not true choice. Creativity would be impossible.

Creativity is possible only because consciousness exists to truly *choose* from among the possibilities present at every moment. In a universe of wall-to-wall laws, consciousness and choice would be squeezed out.

HABITS OF NATURE

So, if *either* laws of nature *or* consciousness exist—but not both—what, then, are we to make of the regular patterns we observe in nature? Clearly, some regularities do occur in the natural world.

Scientific laws are supposed to describe these patterns of regularity. That's what enables science to accurately predict what will happen. If we accurately know this pattern *now,* then based on knowledge of the laws of nature, we can accurately predict how this pattern will unfold. And, clearly, science has been tremendously successful at this.

Why, then, doubt the existence of laws if science is so successful?

The answer involves a slight, but fundamentally important, shift in understanding once we acknowledge the presence of consciousness in nature, in the universe. A universe where consciousness exists is a place where *choices* can, and do, happen. If, by definition, choices are unconstrained and free (undetermined), then it follows that they cannot be governed (determined) by laws—otherwise they wouldn't be free.

Yet we know that reality—the universe—does contain consciousness, and therefore it does contain choice. Therefore, at least *some events* are not fully determined—because they result from choice. Therefore, if *some* events are undetermined and unpredictable because of choice, they cannot be the result of laws. Remember, by definition, laws are *universal* and *invariant*—with *no room for exceptions.*

Yet we still have to account for the observed *regularities* in nature. How? Well, by making the "slight shift" in understanding I mentioned above. Instead of *laws* of nature, we think and speak of *habits* of nature.

Remember, a world governed entirely by deterministic laws would be a "world machine," with no room for consciousness. It would be entirely *mechanical.* However, a world with consciousness, where choices are made, would be *psychological,* not mechanical.

Once we recognize that consciousness is involved in the unfolding of events, we realize that enduring patterns and regularities of nature are more meaningfully described as *habits* (psychological processes or patterns) than as laws (mechanical processes or patterns).

This shift of perspective is the difference between seeing the world as a giant machine and seeing it as a great sentient organism.

Unlike nonconscious mechanisms determined by laws, habits can be changed by exercising choice. *That's a fundamental and major difference.* Laws, if they existed, would be unchanging everywhere for all time. If a law could change as a result of choice, then it wouldn't be a law—it would be a *habit.*

Laws govern machines. But they cannot govern or constrain organisms or sentient beings—beings with *consciousness and choice.*

We live in a universe with consciousness, where *choice* is possible. This same universe is also *determined* to a great extent by the force of accumulated past events, or past actualities. Therefore, we live in a world where both mechanical determinism and conscious choice operate.

And, because of the presence of conscious choice, mechanical determinism is always subject to the operations of choice. In other words, with consciousness present, mechanical determinism cannot be the whole story; it cannot be the only source of causality, or what causes things to happen. Therefore, mechanical determinism cannot be *universal.* This eliminates one of the two key components of scientific laws—their supposed *universality,* or the idea that they govern or operate everywhere.

And, because of the existence of consciousness and choice, mechanical determinism cannot be *invariant.* New, unpredictable events can and do happen, *caused by consciousness and choice.* This eliminates the second key component of scientific laws—their supposed *invariance,* or the idea that they operate in the same way in all circumstances for all time.

Therefore, because mechanical determinism is neither universal nor invariant, it cannot rise to the status of law, which, remember, by definition, is universal and invariant.

Given the above, and our certainty that consciousness is a fact, then it follows that the cosmos unfolds *psychologically,* through acts of consciousness, and is governed by a series of *habits*. And, as we know from our own experience, some habits can be so deeply ingrained that they become almost indistinguishable from mechanisms. It is the same in the rest of nature: Some habits of nature are so deeply ingrained, stuck in deep repetitive grooves, that for all intents and purposes they function and appear as mechanical laws—the familiar laws of physics.

However, when we make the shift from "laws" to "habits," we realize that even deeply ingrained *habits can be changed* through focused intention and choice. In this way, the so-called laws of nature can change over time, depending on the choices made by the innumerable sentient beings that inhabit the cosmos.

Brightspot: Habits can be changed through choice. Laws, by definition, cannot be changed. A universe that involves the *causality of consciousness,* where choice causes things to happen, therefore cannot be governed by laws that describe purely, and exclusively, physical causes.

I have given a long and detailed explanation here of why laws and consciousness cannot mix. Before wrapping up this chapter, I'd like to turn the spotlight on one more scientific venture, from the field of cognitive science, that generates a lot of excitement these days.

ARTIFICIAL INTELLIGENCE

Most blindspots show up in phrases or full sentences, such as "the universe exploded from nothing in a big bang," "time is an illusion," or "our souls leave our bodies when we die." However, some blindspots are *so blind* that the very idea itself makes no sense. Artificial intelligence (AI) is a case in point. It is an oxymoron—a contradiction in terms. The idea not only assumes way too much, it assumes the impossible.

For example, all AI researchers or advocates I know assume that the building blocks of computers and robotics—silicon microchips and software programs—are made of "dead" insentient matter and information. They assume that when they integrate chips and programs into highly complex data-processing systems, with lots of algorithms and feedback loops, *somehow* these "dead" insentient components will produce conscious, intelligent machines. And remember, if the machines *aren't* conscious, then they can't be *intelligent,* either. At best, machines can be designed to *behave* intelligently—but, as explained earlier, intelligent *behavior* is not the same as *intelligence* (see p. 189).

It's really another version of the absurdity in neuroscience we looked at earlier: brains, made of mindless meat, "miraculously" produce minds and consciousness. Here, in AI, instead of mindless brain cells, engineers work with mindless integrated circuits and chips and assume, or hope, that one day these highly complex electronic circuits will begin to "think" and "feel." Dream on.

In both cases—whether it's the idea that minds emerge from mindless brain cells or that intelligence emerges from dumb computer chips—the underlying blindspot is the absurd idea that something can come from nothing.

Blindspot: If you don't have mind or intelligence to begin with, all the way down to the most fundamental components in the system, you will *never* get mind, consciousness, intelligence, or sentience *no matter how complex the system becomes.*

Think about it: If you begin with "dead," insentient, mindless stuff and then make it more and more complex, all you will end up with is more and more complex mindless stuff. We looked at the fallacy of "emergence" earlier, in chapter 8, "Brains and Minds." Yes, new forms, even new properties, do emerge—as when we combine the gases of hydrogen and oxygen to produce H_2O. The gases at room temperature exhibit none of the properties of liquids, but water does. Therefore, liquidity or "wetness" *emerges* from ingredients that didn't have any wetness to begin with. Similar kinds of new properties emerge throughout nature and evolution.

So what's the problem with the idea that minds can emerge from mindless brains or that intelligence can emerge in complex machines? Because, as we saw in earlier chapters, the comparison of water emerging from the gases of oxygen and hydrogen has *no relevance* to the idea of minds emerging from brains. It's a false analogy.

To remind you: In the case of water from gases, both the starting ingredients (molecules of hydrogen and oxygen) and the end product (water) are *physical*. The "before" and "after" are all objects that can be detected and measured in space. They all belong to the same "ontological bucket"—*physical* reality. But that's not the case with the idea of minds emerging from mindless matter. Minds, consciousness, intelligence, sentience—these are *nonphysical* (see chapter 4, "Consciousness").

You simply cannot get something nonphysical from purely physical ingredients. That would require an inexplicable ontological leap—a jump from one state of reality (purely physical, zero mind) to a new and radically different state of reality (with nonphysical minds). How on Earth (or anywhere else in the cosmos) could that happen? Short answer: it couldn't. Or, if it could, it would require a miracle—some kind of supernatural intervention that supersedes all the so-called laws of physics, chemistry, and biology that are assumed to govern the natural world.

The metablindspot here, as elsewhere, is the idea that *something comes from nothing.* As we saw in chapter 1, that idea makes no sense at all. If you begin with *true nothingness,* then that's all you'd ever have—*nothing.*

Well, clearly that's not the case. We know we live in a world of something—indeed, a great many somethings. *Something does exist.* Therefore, there could never have been a time when nothing existed.

But I've already covered that ground. Let's spend the rest of this chapter, then, looking specifically at why the idea of artificial intelligence is likewise a nonstarter. I'll begin by clarifying what I mean by *intelligence.*

WHAT IS INTELLIGENCE?

Let's review the discussion of intelligence from chapter 14, Evolution by Design (p. 190):

Intelligence is a characteristic of consciousness. You simply cannot have intelligence if you don't have consciousness. Anyone who attempts to define *intelligence* as a "problem-solving ability" and tries to avoid implying consciousness is likely to produce something far removed from anything the word *intelligence* typically means.

The very words *problem* and *solving* already imply consciousness. Nonexperiencing entities (such as rocks, beer cans, hammers) never experience problems and never discover solutions. A problem arises only when some experiencing entity has a goal or purpose in mind that is thwarted or perceived to be thwarted. And only creatures with consciousness can have goals or purposes. Nothing purely physical can have a goal or purpose.

And remember: IQ tests don't measure intelligence—they measure *behaviors.* Then the observer or interpreter of the behavior infers (or not) some intelligence guiding the behaviors.

AI investigators working with computers can at best design processes in their software and hardware to produce behaviors that *they,* the investigators, or others interpret as "intelligent" using *their own intelligence.* The best AI can do is *simulate* intelligence.

It is important not to make the error of equating "intelligence," which is a *subjective* phenomenon, with "intelligent behavior," which is based on evaluations of *objective* behaviors. Being a subjective phenomenon, intelligence simply is not observable or measurable. There's no getting around that. As noted earlier, we don't have a "mindalyzer" to detect and measure mental events. Only consciousness can observe consciousness.

So, again, here's my definition of *intelligence:* "having a purpose and the means to creatively move toward fulfilling that purpose" or "having a purpose, perceiving possibilities, and choosing actions that realize a goal."

Intelligent Robots

An automaton (computer or robot) can be programmed to have a goal (e.g., to move around objects it encounters), and, with sufficient programming, it can achieve that goal over and over again, despite obstacles placed in its way. Isn't that an example of artificial intelligence at work?

Blindspot: Note what you said: the robot or automaton is *programmed* to "solve" problems. Programmed by what or by whom? By an *experiencing* human programmer, of course!* Both the problem and the solution exist only because of the awareness of the programmer.

Computers or robots don't "solve problems"; that's just a colloquialism. They *compute,* a mechanical operation, based on *instructions* embedded in the machines by conscious human beings. The goals that computers achieve are not goals for the *computer;* they are goals originating in the minds of human beings.

DIGITAL IMMORTALITY

In his Big Think blog, Orion Jones wrote about futurist Ray Kurzweil's vision of digital immortality:

By 2019, computers will have an emotional intelligence comparable to humans, making them indistinguishable from us on essential levels of being. By the 2030s, humans will have millions of nano-sized robots coursing through our bodies, which will effectively eliminate

---

*Even in cases where computers can "learn" from interactions with their environments (one of the key advances of AI)—and even when computers can use what they "learn" to modify their own programming or programs in other machines—without the original *human* programming, none of the "learned programming" would occur. Without human intelligence, so-called artificial intelligence is, at best, *simulated* intelligence. AI, then, would be more accurately called SI—or AIB for "artificial intelligent behavior."

disease. By 2045, computers will be one billion times more powerful than the human brain. And by the 2050s, it will be possible to create an entire human body out of nano-machines, completely blurring the line between man and machine. Such are the bold predictions made by futurist, and . . . lead engineer at Google, Ray Kurzweil.

Kurzweil believes the day will come when technology will have advanced to the point that it will be possible to "upload" an entire replica of a living human brain—and then later "download" it again into a highly sophisticated android or robot. Presumably the process could be repeated forever.

Blindspot: Kurzweil—like so many other AI enthusiasts—clings to the naive illusion that consciousness and the subjective experience of "self" emerge from complex matter such as brains or advanced computers. But that's just science fantasy.

Even if it becomes possible to "download" exact replicas of our brains, how would that ever result in *subjectivity,* the *feeling* of being? Exact copies of our brains would be merely exact copies, in digital form, of *physical* neurons, synapses, and so forth. No amount of replication of *physical* objects could ever result in subjective experiences. It would be like taking a series of photographs of someone and then downloading them into 3-D printer, expecting to produce a living, breathing, feeling being. Not gonna happen. The "immortality" that folks like Kurzweil look forward to is a mirage. "They" won't be there to *experience* the duplication of their own brain states—any more than your great-grandmother springs back to life whenever you look at her photograph.

Digital immortality would really be nothing more than "zombie immortality." Now, who on Earth wants that? Bring on the singularity . . .

21

God

"God Created Everything from Nothing"

And so we come full circle: from Big Bang nothingness to divine nothingness.

Is spirituality a sign of something amiss? Typically, spiritual practices that lead to experiences of "unity," "divinity," "transcendence," or "transformation" are considered a mark of superior or special human consciousness. But here's something to think about:

Couldn't it be that we humans feel a need to engage in psychospiritual practices precisely because we are constitutionally out of sync with the rest of nature? I've never met a parrot who needs a priest, a rabbit longing for a rabbi, a gorilla searching for a guru, or a dog howling for the divine.

What we assume to be a great achievement of human consciousness may, in fact, be a magnificent expression of profound pathology. Actually, this is not such a radical or revolutionary insight. It forms the basis of Buddhist enlightenment—especially Zen.

Being on a spiritual path implies that something is amiss where you are right now. Enlightenment is not something to aim for (try it, and you'll always miss your target). Rather, enlightenment is waking up and simply accepting *what is*.

Okay, so what about God? Don't we need some spiritual practice to cultivate or deepen a relationship with the divine? Well, let's take a look at what we mean by this baggage-laden word.

If *God* means anything, it refers to some variation of "the source or creator of everything." Well, then, wouldn't that also apply to the scientific notion of the Big Bang—also assumed to be the source or creator of our entire universe? However, few people would feel comfortable equating the Big Bang with God. Something else besides being the "Source" needs to be included in the divine job description.

For one thing, God is also believed to be eternal, if not timeless. But, clearly, the Big Bang that started our universe was a one-time event, and all the matter, stars, and galaxies it produced will vanish in about one hundred billion years, give or take, when our universe comes to an end. That hardly counts as eternal—a *long* time, yes, but not forever.

Here's another thing most people attribute to God—*personhood.* God is believed to be a *conscious person*—the most powerful, even omnipotent, dude in the cosmos. In a moment, we'll take a look at this notion of divine personhood and what it implies. One thing it doesn't imply is that God is some guy with a long white beard sitting on a golden throne somewhere "up there" above the clouds, watching down on us, checking every move we make (we can leave that to the NSA—who apparently think they are gods). Whether or not God is a person, the common habit of using the personal pronoun *he* for the divine is an absurd anachronism. The whole idea of attributing gender to the Source of All Creation is laughable. Yet I can understand why many people feel uncomfortable referring to God as *it* or even *It.* Probably much better, and more accurate, to refer to your personalized God as *I,* as mystics throughout the ages have, and as contemporary Rastafarians do when they say, "I and I."

In any case, who or whatever God is, it cannot be the Big Bang if God not only is the source of everything but is also eternal and personal.

As frequently happens, some of my more nuanced insights arise during conversations with my philosopher friend Eric Weiss. Here's another snippet of one of our dialogues. He believes that God, or what I prefer to call the Creative Ultimate, is personal, whereas I tend to think of it as impersonal, much like the Taoists or Buddhists.

GOD, DON'T TAKE IT PERSONALLY

EW: I've been thinking more about our discussions concerning God as personal. I've realized that I think of actuality, *the totality of All That Is, as personal. That is, I think of* persons *as entities that integrate the past into unity and choose possibilities to actualize for the sake of value. In other words, I think of all actual occasions as personal in some sense. After all, how could* personalities* *be made out of elements that are not "personal"?*

Your technical definition of *personal* makes sense to me, and because God is an actual occasion, it would qualify as personal. Nonetheless, I don't find your technical definition persuasive in making a case for a "personal God." First, it sounds a bit like a rationalization for an aesthetic or pre-philosophical bias. And, of course, I can understand why someone so passionate and committed to a rational account of the world would be moved to do so.

Here's how it seems to me: By defining *personal* in such a technical way, it strikes me that the very experiential essence of a *personal relationship* is lost. If personal and personality can be fully accounted for in terms of "entities that integrate the past into unity and choose possibilities to actualize for the sake of value," the definition seems far too abstract and generalized to capture the essence of what people *experience* when they speak of having a personal relationship—with God, another human, or some other creature.

Blindspot: Your definition of *personal* seems to reduce or equate it to "sentience." If all sentient beings are personal, which is what I think you are saying, then the distinction between *personal* and *impersonal* evaporates. And so, having a *personal* relationship—with anything—seems to

---

*Eric Weiss uses Whitehead's technical phrase "personally ordered societies of occasions" to describe personalities.

lose that special quality that people appear to be referring to when they say, "I have a personal relationship with X."

Now, while I do accept that the cosmos as a whole is sentient, I don't feel or think it is personal. For me, a *personal* relationship involves something more than a mere intersubjective or intersentient relationship. What is this "something more"? I think it involves a level of consciousness and intentionality that *communicates a reciprocal sense of caring—between individuals.* I may care about the cosmos, but if I don't experience, or imagine, the cosmos caring specifically about me, I don't consider myself to have a personal relationship with it. I am not denying intentionality to the cosmos; I'm just saying that its intentions are far too "generalized" and not specifically directed at me as an individual. I speculate that the generalized intentions of the cosmos involve something like a deep and intrinsic urge to explore its own innate potentials; this is the great "adventure of evolution." I am part of this great adventure, and, at least some of the time, I am grateful for this opportunity and experience.

I am an individual; the cosmos is the totality of all individuals—but it is not itself an individual in its own right. The totality of existence cannot be an individual because an individual becomes or qualifies as individual only *in contrast to some actuality it isn't.* An individual is a demarcation of some subset of the totality of being. I don't see how this can apply to the notion of God—meaning the Supreme Being, or Brahman, or Creative Ultimate. While God may care about God, and even the totality of its creation, it doesn't make sense that God would care specifically about *me.* Whatever I do, the great adventure of evolution will continue to unfold, and so God's grand intention will be fulfilled *no matter what I do or what happens to me.* "Someone" who doesn't care about what I do or what happens to me does not meet my criteria for a "personal relationship."

I wonder if, or how, equating personhood and actuality satisfies your sense of, or need for, a personal relationship with God. Is it *sufficient* for you just that God is actual? What, then, differentiates your sense of personal relationship with your actual wife and with the actual car parked in the driveway next door? Doesn't something *very significantly more* than mere actuality characterize the quality of your personal relationships?

I don't see the problem you seem to think exists in the idea of personalities or persons emerging from impersonal precursors. There is no ontological jump involved. Impersonal actualities (atoms, molecules, cells) are composed of sentient energy, and as bundles of sentient energy evolve some of them become more aware of their individuality—their personhood. That is, there is some degree of a subjective sense of a "self boundary" that distinguishes this self from nonself. As this sense of individuality evolves and becomes more complex, at some stage it achieves a sufficient level or degree of awareness to recognize not only its own individuality but also that it is surrounded by, and is in relationship with, other individuals.

To the extent that I can value the experienced individuality of others, I can consider them "persons," and to the degree that this value is reciprocated, I consider myself to have a personal relationship with those individuals. For the reasons I've outlined above, I don't see how this view of relationship can be attributed to the Cosmic Totality we call God.

IS GOD ENERGY?

I had been using the term energy *for God . . . but now I often simply use* spirit. *However, I still resonate with "source" and "energy" to refer to God. I use* energy *not as a scientific term, but how it's used in shiatsu and Oriental medicine. For example, when I do bodywork, I know I connect with something far greater than I am and that I make a difference and influence the flow of ch'i. Isn't ch'i the flow of God's energy?*

As you probably know by now from my work, I would not equate God with energy. Here's why: In order to be creative, God must also possess consciousness, intention, purpose. Likewise, God could not be just pure consciousness either. God also needs energy in order to act on its intentions. I would say God is *sentient energy,* or *purposeful action.*

Blindspot: If you stop to think about the terms *source* and *energy,* you will see that they are not at all the same. A source is an origin of something. It could be energy flowing from a source or a river from a spring. But a spring is not a river.

You say your use of the word *energy* comes from Oriental medicine and not from science. However, *energy* in Oriental medicine is an English translation of the Chinese *ch'i* or the Sanskrit *prana.* And the English word *energy* used to translate these other terms is borrowed directly from nineteenth-century Western science. Whether you are aware of it or not, when you use the word *energy,* you are using a term borrowed from mechanistic science—"energy talk."

Besides all that, even in Chinese cosmology, ch'i is not the same as consciousness. As I explain in *Radical Nature,* the ancient Chinese always coupled ch'i, or energy, with *li,* an innate organizing principle, or consciousness. Ch'i is not the same as li, though they always go together, just as energy is not the same as consciousness, though they always go together.

Yes, when you do shiatsu, you connect with something greater than you. I would say that you are connecting with ch'i and li, or sentient energy. You are not just influencing the flow of ch'i, or energy, but also connecting with the li, *consciousness* or *meaning,* that guides the flow of ch'i. In my experience, healing has less to do with exchanges of energy (ch'i) and more to do with connecting through *shared meaning* (li); see chapter 10.

I'm also not clear how you relate the notion of ch'i with your discussion of God-as-energy above. Are you implying that ch'i equals God? I don't think you'll find any support for that idea in the literature. God is more than ch'i, or energy; it is also li, or consciousness.

TRANSCENDENT GOD?

God is the great "I Am" of existence. Yet as the source and end of everything, God is also more than the material world. Reality transcends the physical.

Yes, reality "transcends the physical" because reality also includes *non-physical* consciousness. But that doesn't make God transcendent in the sense that that word usually implies—above and beyond *nature*.

Nature is just another word for reality, and is equivalent to God. And because nature consists of both energy and consciousness, the fact that God is more than physical doesn't make it "transcendent." Nature, too, is more than physical. But it would be absurd to say nature is transcendent—meaning nature transcends nature.

Why God Exists

In one of her blog posts, science journalist Lynne McTaggart approvingly offers a summary of an article by William Lane Craig in defense of the existence of God—a response to the militant atheism of the late Christopher Hitchens.

In a nutshell, here are the four key points of her summary:

(1) The cause of the universe must be transcendent and supernatural. (2) The cause itself could not have been caused by anything—because if it had to start somewhere that would lead to an impossible "infinite regress" of causes. (3) It must be eternal because it created time. (4) It must be nonphysical because it created space.

Let's take each point one by one:

1. *The cause of the universe must be transcendent and supernatural.* It's not clear to me that this is so. In fact, I would not say that

the ultimate cause is transcendent, in the sense of being super-natural. When we factor in *consciousness* as an intrinsic element of reality—that is, accepting that nonphysical consciousness is natural—then the universe and all its spiritual leanings, long-ings, and awareness are wholly *natural*.

2. *The cause must not have been caused by anything.* I agree, except I'd add this qualification: It could only be self-caused. I would say that the cosmos (All That Is) never started anywhere. It always existed (call it the Creative Ultimate, even God, if you like). Our 13.7-billion-year-old universe began as one event within an eternal cosmos of an infinite number of such events, occurring over unimaginable stretches of time.

3. *It must be eternal because it created time.* Here, I have difficulty with Craig's logic. To say that something must be "eternal" because it created time involves another contradiction, or at least a tautology—a common *blindspot*. If by *eternity* we mean "endless time" (which is what the word means), then it could not have "created" time. Why? Because, by definition, endless time *already* existed. If, however, *eternity* is supposed to mean "time-lessness" (which is a contradiction), then it deepens the puzzle. How could something wholly *without* time ever produce time? You don't get something from nothing (where have you heard *that* before?). It's exactly the same kind of problem facing scien-tific materialists who claim that *wholly mindless* matter generates minds. So, while I agree with Craig that the Creative Ultimate, the cosmos, is eternal, or never had a beginning, I don't follow his reasoning that it "created time." As we have seen in earlier chapters, time, necessarily, always existed. Besides, because cre-ation is an *act*, it *requires time*. No act, event, or process could happen without time.

4. *It must be nonphysical because it created space.* Here, again, his logic seems to be inverted. I would say: "If the Creative Ultimate created space, then it could *not* be nonphysical." Only something

physical (e.g., energy) can produce something physical (e.g., more energy or matter). Similarly, only something nonphysical (e.g., consciousness) can produce something nonphysical (e.g., minds). Being physical, space—the domain where matter and energy exist—can come only from *physical* precursors. Following Leibniz and Whitehead, I would say that space is formed by the *relationships* between actually existing entities. No entities, no space. So, if the Creative Ultimate did in fact create physical space, as Craig says, then the Creative Ultimate itself must be at least partly *physical*—not nonphysical. Furthermore, if the Creative Ultimate created nonphysical consciousness, then the Creative Ultimate must also be *nonphysical*. In other words, because the actual world we live in consists of both physical matter/energy and nonphysical minds/consciousness, then the Creative Ultimate must also be both physical and nonphysical.

Blindspot: I make these observations because Lynne McTaggart says that William Lane Craig's logic "made mincemeat" of Christopher Hitchens. That surprises me because Craig's logic is actually very weak, or worse, full of holes. Had he lived, Hitchens, a man of great intellectual caliber, would undoubtedly have characteristically and unmercifully attacked those weak spots. But perhaps not. After all, Hitchens's bullying atheism revealed a mightily self-limiting intellectualism, as does any mind that obsessively clings to the metaphysics of scientific materialism. Given his intellectual biases, *Hitchens could never have accounted for the fact of his own consciousness,* his own ability to feel, be aware, and make choices. Yet he made effective and demonstrative use of these capacities. He, like all scientific materialists, was a walking performative contradiction. His very way of living and acting contradicted what he claimed: that anything nonphysical didn't—*couldn't*—exist. His own mind was never to be found anywhere in the world of the physical objects he held so dear. Yet he used it all the time, often to dramatic effect.

The following is a much more robust argument in favor of God, if we define God as the source or ground of all that exists—both physical and nonphysical:

1. Fact: we live in an actual world where both matter and mind, or energy and consciousness, the physical and the nonphysical, are real.
2. Therefore, whatever the unmanifest source of the actual world is, it must be brimful of possibilities for the existence of manifest matter and mind.
3. Therefore, the Creative Ultimate must be both *potentially* and *actually* physical and nonphysical.

Clearly, this is not your "grandfather's God," yet it gives us a way to respond to the world, to the cosmos and all it contains, as sacred. In other words, the "spiritual" domain (nonphysical existence) and the physical domain (material existence) always exist together in some form. We can justly call this God. God-as-spirit is always God-embodied. Spirit expresses itself as consciousness, and embodiment expresses itself as the physical cosmos.

KNOWING THE MIND OF GOD

One of the founding myths of the Enlightenment seems to be that cosmic rationality is at work in the universe. And because human beings also have this faculty of reason, there is no difference in quality between human rationality and cosmic rationality. If so, then, through the use of reason, we can know the mind of God. Does any difference exist between cosmic creativity and individual creativity?

Great question. First, I think a major difference exists between cosmic creativity and human creativity—a difference in degree and quality of expression. Human creativity exists only because of, and as an expression of, cosmic creativity. But human creativity is incomparably less in scope and capacity than cosmic creativity. To think otherwise is the height of hubris. Also, I am not inclined to single out *human* creativity as anything special. Cosmic creativity expresses itself not just through us—it is expressed through all species, including what modernity considers purely deterministic inorganic processes.

Regarding the Enlightenment perspective and the assumption that human rationality is a special way to penetrate the mysteries of the universe: I simply do not share that perspective. As Immanuel Kant so persuasively argued, there are *limits* to human reason. But (as I argue in *Radical Knowing*) the limits of reason are by no means the limits of knowledge, and most certainly do not mark out the limits of reality. There is far more to reality than reason can access. We do, however, have other ways of knowing beyond reason that can give us access to these other domains of reality, such as feeling and intuition.

One way to understand why reason is so limited is that it works with ideas, thoughts, concepts, beliefs—and these are all *abstractions,* "frozen fragments of consciousness" literally *abstracted* ("taken from") the ongoing flow of experience and awareness, as reality itself unfolds from moment to moment. Reason alone—the manipulation of conceptual abstractions—necessarily and inevitably *distorts* our knowledge of reality. We need to complement reason with other ways of knowing if we wish to reduce these epistemological distortions.

Regarding the relationship between individual consciousness and universal, or cosmic, consciousness, I would say that as long as we are operating from our rational, concept-based egoic minds, then we have virtually no meaningful access to ultimate reality, just to its fragments. However, in certain states of consciousness, such as mystical and other spiritual states, "individual" consciousness transcends its limited individuality and becomes "transpersonal," or consciously *intersubjective.* When that occurs, the consciousness that finds expression through an "individual," such as the Buddha, is no longer individual consciousness, but universal consciousness itself. As the Buddha showed, this state of consciousness is best communicated in *silence,* beyond the distortions of language and thought.

Before ending this chapter, I want to explore a question that has stumped theologians and philosophers for centuries.

THE PROBLEM OF EVIL

What do you think of evil? Is it part of nature, just magnified on the human level? Is it something alien or a result of "devolution," some negative cosmic process at work counterbalancing evolution? I suppose I'm really asking: Is God responsible for evil?

Evil is part of nature because *everything* is part of nature. Evil results from choice and, therefore, is a product of consciousness. But what *is* evil? Ultimately, I think evil consists of intentions and choices—and the *acts that follow from those choices*—that impede, damage, or destroy the ability of sentient beings to fully experience, enjoy, and realize their natural potential. So, by this definition, the world is rife with evil, at all levels, and none of us is free of it.

But there is, of course, a great divergence in the range of evil intentions, choices, and acts. Two of the most prominent these days are the consistent and deliberate "strategies of evil" and "campaigns of terror and torture" emanating from the current White House administration, targeted at Muslims abroad and at U.S. citizens and residents at home. The other is the annual slaughtering and almost unimaginable torture of hundreds or thousands of innocent dolphins committed by Japanese fishermen and sanctioned by the Japanese government, along with Denmark. If you want to see evil in action watch the Academy Award–winning documentary *The Cove*. It's horrendous, but explicitly reveals just how evil and barbarous some humans can be.

Is God Evil?

At first glance, this might seem like a strange question—but is it? Of course, how you answer depends on how you define *God* and *evil*.

Typically, *God* refers to the source or creator of All That Is (see where I'm headed?).

God, then, is the ultimate source of all our preferences and values, as well as all our actions. Most theists would accept this—in fact, insist on it. However, we would be right to ask: Are "ultimate values," such as integrity, truthfulness, justice, equity, benevolence, peace, and love, more than projections of our own preferences onto the world? Perhaps these "good" values are our own creations, as Nietzsche dramatically expressed in *Beyond Good and Evil.*

And evil? Well, at the very least, evil is whatever violates our deepest values. If the violation is intentional, the evil is inexcusable. If evil exists as more than our projections onto whatever violates our deepest values— if it is inherent in the world—then it, too, must be sourced from God.

Killing twenty small schoolchildren and innocent adults with a semiautomatic assault rifle, as happened in Newtown, Connecticut— along with the manufacture and sale of such weapons—strikes me as a clear example of evil, and insanity.

Who, then, is ultimately responsible?

Epicurus—the ancient Greek philosopher who "taught that pleasure and pain are the measures of what is good and evil; death is the end of both body and soul and should therefore not be feared; the gods do not reward or punish humans; the universe is infinite and eternal; and events in the world are ultimately based on the motions and interactions of atoms moving in empty space"—said it well (if we ignore the absurd anthropomorphic attribution of gender to God and his explicit denial of the role of consciousness and choice in natural events . . . otherwise, he said it well):

> *Is God willing to prevent evil, but not able? Then he is not*
> *omnipotent.*
> *Is he able, but not willing? Then he is malevolent.*
> *Is he both able and willing? Then whence cometh evil?*
> *Is he neither able nor willing? Then why call him God?*

Final Exit

"Human Ingenuity and Technology Will Save Us"

Let's wrap this up by zooming in on what is likely the "mother of all blindspots"—the looming environmental crisis and catastrophe. Not only is this one real, but its effects are already upon us.

Greenland and Antarctica are melting. Before we know it, sea levels will rise dramatically, swamping whole islands, coastlines, towns, and cities around the world. The devastation has already begun; just ask the people of the cyclone-ravished South Pacific islands of Vanuatu. Globally, the impact will be vast. Think of Greenland as a nearly two-million-square-kilometer iceberg just waiting to strike. We are all on a sinking Planet Titanic.

Some of us are rushing for the lifeboats; some of us are trying to plug the holes; some of us are doing whatever we can to deny the reality; and some of us are facing the likelihood that no matter what we do, it's all too late anyway. In that case, the best we can do, like a terminal cancer patient, is to be grateful for each remaining moment we have and choose to live it with joy, compassion, and gratitude.

A while ago, I had a long conversation with Peter Russell, author of *Waking Up in Time,* who has been closely tracking the details of climate change for many years—long before Al Gore brought the issue to mainstream attention. I asked him:

"We're living on a knife edge, in times of great uncertainty. One way lies systemic collapse into ecological disaster. The other, perhaps involving some degree of the first, is a path to collective waking up and the transformation of our species. Which side do you lean to when you wake up in the morning?"

His response stunned me:

"Without a doubt, I see us falling into total systemic collapse."

I probed a little deeper, and he revealed that he didn't just mean some temporary setback for civilization, but the inevitable extinction of our species—within a few generations!—involving, of course, the great extinction of vast numbers of other species.

I questioned him more, and he talked about how, within 100 to 150 years, climate change will be so rapid and so vast that a band of desolation and desert will circle the planet, with only small regions remaining hospitable for life in places such as northern Europe, Alaska, parts of Canada, and Antarctica. He thinks that all mammalian species will be wiped out, and perhaps most reptiles and amphibians. Possibly only plants and insects will survive.

I had never encountered such a bleak scenario based on what I understand to be a clear reading of the available data. It overshadows even the most pessimistic scenarios I've heard elsewhere. Worse, this may not be a reversible process. It's not as if the Earth will quickly spring back to life and the deserts will bloom once again. No, in this scenario, we are already in the early stages of human-induced climate change that will turn our beautiful globe into a planetary desert for many millions of years. And if all the water boils off, it could even be permanent. It happened on Mars.*

We could well be living through the end days of our species, and for all practical purposes, the end of life on Earth. Sobering.†

---

*The Mars scenario is only one possibility, an extreme one. Over millions of years, our planet may well recover. A similar hothouse period occurred in the Eocene, thirty-four to fifty-five million years ago. However, even if the deserts do bloom again, the chances of humans surviving the furnace are highly unlikely.

†See Peter Russell's essay "Blind Spot" at www.peterrussell.com/blindspot/blindspot.php.

WHAT WOULD YOU DO?

Given this, what are we to do? What's the point of spreading such a message of hopelessness?

Pete's response: There is no point. There is *nothing* we can do now to change what is inevitably coming—very soon. He then told me how waking up to this reality has changed his life. For a time, he experienced the existential angst of despair and total hopelessness. And then his "aha" moment struck:

"Yes, it is hopeless. But by letting go of all sense of hope, I discovered that I still had a choice: about how to live out my life knowing that it is all over for all of us. I choose to live with compassion and to savor every moment—just like some cancer patients do when the bad news finally sinks in."

For a few brief moments, I let it in and felt a deep wrenching sickness in my gut, a profound sorrow for our species and for the millions of other species we will take down with us. But within a few hours, my own denial defense mechanisms kicked in. I find I can no longer actually *feel* the total demise of our species. Intellectually, though, I know it is a strong possibility.

How would you live your life in the light of this knowledge?

What would you do when we discover that our planetary Titanic is holed and that we are rapidly and inevitably going down? Do you dance? Do you panic? Do you rush for the lifeboats? (Are there any lifeboats?) Do you pray? Do you offer comfort and solace to your neighbors? Do you head for the bar and get mind-blowingly drunk? Do you stuff yourself with food from the cafeteria? Do you find beautiful partners and make passionate love? Do you heroically start giving swimming lessons (knowing they won't help)? Do you jump overboard before the ship goes down?

What would you do?

Pete has decided that the most heroic response is for individual members of our species—better, for our species collectively—to immediately stop extracting *any* resources from the planet, so that, at the very least, we spend our last days minimizing our contribution to the acceleration of systemic collapse. Of course, this would mean not extracting food or water, and so our species would vanish very soon. In doing so, we may give a few more years, perhaps another generation or two, for other species to enjoy. We might, for instance, leave the planet habitable for species that inhabit the oceans, who just might survive the ecological devastation that will sweep the land. However, as he pointed out, the oceans may be in an even more precarious predicament. "They may collapse first. Coral reefs are already dying fast, and the increased acidity of CO_2 is making life very hard for the microscopic creatures at the base of the food chain. No plankton, no shrimp, no humpback whales."

It's hard to grasp, isn't it?

FINAL EXIT?

Perhaps ecological collapse is the fate of any planet when evolution produces a species with advanced intelligence coupled with the means to manipulate its environment to suit its own needs (e.g., an opposable thumb). Add language into the mix for spreading ideas and knowledge far and wide, and we are blessedly cursed with an inevitably fatal combination. That's what Pete thinks.

One ray of "hope" in the face of such dire hopelessness, he believes, is an opportunity for a profound transformation in consciousness— along the lines envisioned by French philosopher and paleontologist Teilhard de Chardin and fictionalized in Arthur C. Clarke's sci-fi novel *Childhood's End*.

The pressure of breakdown either wipes out the species or pushes it to evolve. Planets, then, serve as seedpods for launching consciousness to higher levels of evolution.

At this point, though, such scenarios begin to sound like spiritual science fiction—the human mind's ultimate creative response to the realization of radical hopelessness.

What else can we do?

THE BIG SURRENDER

Well, we can *surrender*. Perhaps that is the hidden gift of being shocked, of waking up to our predicament. All the world's great spiritual traditions teach us about the power of surrender, of letting go and trusting in some greater intelligence or process beyond anything mere mortals can ever imagine.

When we do finally and fully surrender, we open up to the possibility of some unforeseen, unimaginable event that transforms what seemed like a dire and hopeless situation into an opportunity for a new beginning. The great mystics call this entering the "dark night of the soul" before the dawn of spiritual enlightenment.

Today, we might be facing an unprecedented "dark night" of the collective soul. We may be called on to let go of attachment, not just to our petty personal needs and desires, but to the very survival of our species, and to accept the impending "death" of our beautiful planet—the Big Surrender, followed, perhaps, by the Big Breakthrough. Perhaps.

This is just one perspective—but I think it is worth paying attention to. Do you?

BLIP! PUTTING IT ALL IN PERSPECTIVE

A BBC TV series called *Walking with Beasts* traces evolution from the dinosaurs to whales and humans. While I was familiar with the general outlines of the origin and transitions of species, this particular account of our deep animal history helped to put it all in perspective.

Our earliest mammalian ancestors began to come into their own about sixty-five million years ago, after the end of the Age of Dinosaurs. Our *Australopithecus* ancestors (somewhere between chimps and humans) lived about three million years ago. That's an almost unimaginable span of time—from the earliest mammals to the first humanoids, more than sixty million years!

And then, less than fifty thousand years ago, Neanderthals and Cro-Magnons walked in Europe. The evolution of humans, from Stone Age nomads to modern techno civilizations, all packed into fewer than ten thousand years! Truly a blip compared to the millions of years our mammal ancestors roamed the forests, plains, and tundra and swam the oceans—and no more than a "blink" since the birth of life on our planet more than four billion years ago.

And, now, here we are today, in the twenty-first century, watching videos about our ancestors on iPads and TVs. It's no wonder we sometimes feel so special.

Yet each generation is really no more than an infinitesimal "blip" in this immense temporal progression. Our individual lives seem so important to us (and they are), but in the greater scheme of things we are no more than a crinkled leaf falling from a tree in autumn. We splutter and spurt into being and just as quickly splutter out again.

Every species is eventually replaced. It is both an awesome tragedy and a miraculous gift. When you think about it: *Here we are, then . . . blip! It's all over.* Let's enjoy and celebrate it while we are here!

APPENDICES

○ ○ ○ ○ ○

The following appendices started out as exchanges with students from my online graduate course Mind in the Cosmos for the Holmes Institute. While these dialogues address questions mostly in connection with the spiritual philosophy of Science of Mind, based on the teachings of Ernest Holmes, they also tackle issues relevant to any spiritual cosmology that aims to be consistent with modern science—for example, the work of visionary mathematician Arthur M. Young.

If you've ever wondered about the role of miracles in life (or elsewhere in the universe), or how the cosmologies of Holmes and Young compare, or have ever been confused about the difference between *pantheism* and *panentheism,* and how these relate to *panpsychism,* you might find the following chapters illuminating.

Miracles

You say I shouldn't believe what you or anyone else has to say and that it's better to focus on my own beliefs. Nevertheless, I still wonder where the mysteries of the universe fit into your picture of reality. You say panpsychists don't believe in miracles because that would require belief in the supernatural—for them, everything is natural. Because nature has its own mysterious ways of operating, why aren't mysteries part of the panpsychist view?

First, I'd like to clarify an important distinction: When I invite people not to believe what I or others say, I do not suggest that you focus on your own *beliefs* instead. In fact, I emphatically suggest that you do not do that. I do, however, encourage you to focus on your own *experience*.

In my work (especially in *Consciousness from Zombies to Angels*), I point out that beliefs are "frozen fragments of consciousness." Beliefs are composed of thoughts, and thoughts are *abstractions* plucked from the ongoing stream of in-the-moment experience. As such, every thought, every belief, is anchored in the past and is out of touch with what is *actually happening* right now. *Beliefs distort reality*—inevitably. Every belief—whether it's yours, or mine, or Young's, or Holmes's, or Einstein's, or the Dalai Lama's—disconnects us from reality.

However, because experience always happens *right now,* and reality likewise always happens *right now,* experience gives us a direct "hotline" to reality. Beliefs can be wrong or more or less accurate; however, an experience can never be wrong. Every experience is exactly what it is. And then we *interpret* (think about) our experience. That's when things begin to roll off the rails.

Once more, here's the "secret" they didn't tell you in *The Secret*:

Experience → Interpretation → Belief → Dogma → Ideology . . . → Action

Notice all the "stuff" that happens between experience and action. No wonder, then, that so much of what we do is often out of sync with reality. Instead of acting from our beliefs, I recommend that we learn to act directly from our experience. That way, our actions are connected with, and flow from, reality (see *Consciousness from Zombies to Angels* for more on this).

MYSTERIES OR MIRACLES?

Now to your point about mysteries and miracles. You ask: "Why aren't mysteries part of the panpsychist view?" Short answer: they are.

Panpsychists don't shy away from *mysteries,* but they do reject *miracles* as a substitute for explanation. I wonder if you equate mysteries and miracles? They are very different.

Blindspot: Remember, a *miracle* is a *gap in explanation* that, by definition, cannot be filled in; if we could fill the gap, if we could explain the phenomenon, it wouldn't be a miracle. A *mystery,* on the other hand, is something that is, in principle, explainable but has not yet been explained. For example, as in the rest of life, science is full of mysteries (e.g., what is the nature of dark matter and dark energy; does the Higgs boson really exist?), but science has no room for miracles.

The scientific method is explicitly and exquisitely designed to explore unexplained mysteries systematically in attempts to reduce or remove some of them. However, as both scientists and lay people are well aware, the moment we resolve one mystery, a host of new mysteries pops up. While the universe is deeply mysterious—and most likely will forever remain so—we can, nevertheless, advance in knowledge step by step as we remove specific mysteries. That's the march of science.

Mysteries are part of nature; "Nature loves to hide," as Heraclitus famously said. They indicate areas of knowledge yet to be illuminated. But *mystery* is not the same as *mystification*—which results from confused thinking and by making things more complicated and ambiguous than they need to be. Despite its remarkable progress, science has not done so well in removing *mystification*.

Blindspot: *Nature creates mystery. People create mystification.* Mysteries are natural; mystification is manufactured.

With this distinction in mind, let's now take a closer look at miracles.

FAITH IN MIRACLES

I'm still a little bothered about the way you define a miracle as a supernatural occurrence, without explanation, and therefore a sign of ignorance. I can understand why science would think this, but I believe faith can explain miracles.

Let's be clear: Science deals with the *natural* world, not with the supernatural. And because science unquestioningly accepts the metaphysical dogma of materialism—the idea that everything that exists is both natural and physical—the very possibility of a supernatural intervention is rejected out of hand. However, science can't really tell us anything about miracles, including whether they occur—it just *assumes* that's the case.

Philosophy, however, does its best to examine the language we use to express our ideas, insights, and experiences. It's *philosophy*, not science, that defines a miracle as a supernatural intervention. By the way, that is also how theology and religion define a miracle—as something "supernatural."

For some reason (I'm not really clear why), you don't want to accept this. You go on to say:

From my faith-based knowing, miracles are explainable because I believe in the Supreme Power of the universe, which science can't explain, just as science can't explain emanationism or panpsychism. Because I am one with this Supreme Power, I can use spiritual laws to set a cause in motion, through the law of cause and effect, to produce an outcome that could be deemed a miracle. It seems to me this is what happens in the process that causes a quantum jump (collapsing a wave through observation and bringing "it" into manifestation)—that's a "miracle" as well, right?

Blindspot: First, the fact that you *believe* in the Supreme Power of the universe doesn't mean that any such Supreme Power actually exists. The universe is under no obligation to conform to your (or anyone else's) beliefs. The fact that we believe something has no necessary relationship to what is real.

So, something much stronger than belief is required as a foundation for knowledge—for example, *experience*.

Second, you are correct: science cannot explain either emanationism or panpsychism for the simple reason that both of these worldviews include *consciousness*, which is nonphysical, and science deals exclusively with physical events.

You then go on to say you are one with the Supreme Power and can use spiritual laws to set a cause in motion. What does it mean to say you are "one" with the Supreme Power? Do you mean you are *identical* to the Supreme Power? That seems a little grandiose—and inaccurate. After all, you, as an embodied human being, will grow old and die, but I doubt you would claim the same fate awaits the Supreme Being. So to be "one with" cannot mean you are *identical* with. It must mean something else.

Perhaps you mean your being exists entirely within the reality of the Supreme Power? Well, yes, that must be the case. Where else could you exist? But just because you form a part of the Supreme Power does not mean you have access to all the power of the Supreme Being. By analogy, each cell in your body forms a part of you, but no individual cell has access to all the power that you, as a human being, possess.

Blindspot: You say you can "use spiritual laws to set a cause in motion." What do you mean by this? What are these "spiritual laws," and how do you know whether (1) they are "spiritual" and (2) they are "laws"? How do you *know* this? Because someone told you? That hardly counts as knowledge. At best, it is *rumor.* This is a good example of what I mean in this book when I encourage people to "think before speaking." How often do people use phrases like "spiritual laws" without ever really *thinking through* what they mean?

Even if it were true that you could use "spiritual laws" to set a cause in motion, are you, in fact, saying anything different than *you can make choices that cause things to happen in the physical world?* In other words, you use your consciousness to direct the flow of energy in the world?

Good. Well, we all do that all, or almost all, of the time. And by "we" I mean all sentient beings—not just humans. That's what any being with consciousness can do. We are aware of options and possibilities, and we make *choices* that affect the physical world. *Consciousness manifests physical reality by actualizing possibilities.* This is what we know from quantum physics. And every possibility exists as an alternative option available to some actual event,* and every actual event consists of both consciousness and energy. This is what we learn from process philosophy.

But to call the effect of consciousness on matter a "miracle" is to buy into scientific materialism. It would be a miracle only if (1) the natural world consists exclusively of physical events (matter/energy), because then (2) that would mean something *supernatural* intervened in the course of natural events.

---

*I'm aware this phrase is a bit of a mouthful, so let me unpack it: I'm saying that every actual thing or event (everything that *actually* exists) is surrounded by a halo or cloud of *possibilities,* and that each possibility is, by definition, an alternative option to what actually exists right now (otherwise it wouldn't be a *possibility*). Hence: "every possibility exists as an alternative to some actual event."

But that view assumes mind or consciousness is not natural. Unlike materialists, panpsychists claim that consciousness is wholly natural. It is a *natural* nonphysical ingredient of all physical phenomena. When consciousness acts through choices and makes things happen in the physical world, it is not a supernatural event. It is a *natural* event. Therefore, it is not a miracle.

Blindspot: Consciousness and choice are miraculous only if we assume they are not natural.

When, in quantum physics, an observer (i.e., consciousness) collapses the wave function, it is a case of nonphysical mind causing something to happen in the physical world (a quantum collapse). Again, that would be a miracle only if consciousness were considered supernatural or the event completely lacks explanation *in principle.*

Now, science doesn't accept the existence of anything supernatural, and yet it is utterly at a loss to explain how consciousness collapses physical events into existence. And that's because consciousness is, *by definition,* a complete mystery to science. Remember, science defines reality as consisting of wholly objective physical events. But consciousness is *subjective* and *nonphysical.* Hence, the inexplicable mystery.

Science cannot avoid acknowledging the reality of consciousness—because all scientific knowledge requires consciousness and because of the necessary presence of an observer for quantum collapse to occur—yet science hasn't a clue what consciousness is, how it exists, or how it interacts with matter/energy. Therefore, the reality of consciousness looms large as a huge gap in scientific explanation. *Science simply cannot explain the existence or nature of consciousness; yet it cannot, without contradiction, deny its existence.* In short, from the perspective of science, something "supernatural" intervenes in the course of physical events, even though science denies the possibility of anything supernatural existing.

Blindspot: Put another way, science claims that mind, or consciousness, is (and must be) part of the natural world *and* that it is produced by the complexity of nonconscious brains. But science cannot even begin to explain how this could happen—how nonconscious brains could produce nonphysical consciousness. So, faced with a gaping "explanatory gap," science finds itself in the awkward position of needing a miracle, yet denying the possibility of miracles. In order to be true, scientific materialism must be false! Confusing, eh?

However, as soon as we adopt the panpsychist view—that both matter and mind are wholly natural and that neither one produces the other—we no longer need to call on a miracle or anything supernatural to intervene in the course of events. Because the ultimate nature of reality is *sentient energy*—energy that "tingles with the spark of spirit"—the mystery is removed.

In panpsychism, *consciousness is the intrinsic ability of matter/energy to know, feel, and purposefully direct itself.* In other words, energy has a native and natural ability to make *choices* and direct itself as it flows through the world. That ability, to be aware and make choices, is *consciousness*—and it is wholly natural. We don't have any looming "explanatory gaps" between mind and matter, between the nonphysical and physical domains, between sentience and energy. They are unified, though distinct.

So, back to your question: Why would you think that because you can make choices that impact the physical world that you are, thereby, creating an "outcome" that "could be deemed a miracle"? If you accept that both your consciousness and the physical world are wholly natural (part of nature and intrinsic to the cosmos), where's the miracle?

Why is it important for you to call this a miracle? Why, in a larger context, is it important for you to claim you live in a universe where miracles are possible? Why would you not be content to live in a magnificent world full of natural mysteries, some of which can, in time, be explained by science and philosophy, and some that require other ways of knowing (such as shamanic states of consciousness or mystical experience) to penetrate the mystery?

Me? I prefer to live in a cosmos where all of this happens naturally. I don't need to diminish the capacity of the natural world by claiming the existence of something supernatural. Nature or the cosmos is good enough for me. I'm content to know that I live in a reality where "mind in the cosmos" creates all kinds of wondrous mysteries—mysteries without miracles. Mysteries are natural; miracles are supernatural and, therefore, have no place in the natural world.

MIRACLES BEYOND REASON

I accept your argument against the use of a miracle in a cosmological view. But do we not fall under the danger of positivism if we accept only what seems reasonable to us?

I want to be clear about this: I am not suggesting that miracles don't happen; they might. However, because—by definition—a miracle is a supernatural intervention into the natural course of events, it is not something that can be *explained*. Miracles are *gaps* in explanation.

So, if miracles happen, we simply cannot *explain* them. That's all. It means they are beyond the scope of both philosophy (rational explanation) and science (empirical evidence and rational explanation). The point is this: If we want to explain something, such as the mind-matter relation, then resorting to miracles doesn't help—because it doesn't inform us one iota about the mind-body connection. For all I know, dualism *could* be true—perhaps the world is split between minds and bodies that somehow mysteriously come together and interact. It's just that if that is the case, we cannot explain the connection. The "miracles" of materialist emergence and idealist emanationism are equally inexplicable, too.

I am not suggesting that we accept only what is "reasonable" to us, meaning only what can be explained. Our lives are often graced with experiences that transcend rational explanations. However, we can know them and feel their meaning using other appropriately valid ways of knowing, such as feeling and intuition.

Nevertheless, I encourage us to develop and use our gift of reason as best we can by taking it as far as it can go before yielding to other ways of knowing. One of the wonderful things about reason is that it can tell us that reason has its limitations (e.g., paradoxes). Reason can also tell us that there is no good reason to decide that beyond the limits of reason there is nothing else to know. Reason tells us that beyond reason there are other valid ways of knowing that give us access to domains of experience reason cannot penetrate. Reason tells us that reality does not end at the limits of reason—and it tells us that in order to know what lies beyond the limits of reason we must shift to some other way of knowing. You see, reason can be very reasonable!

> *The same argument you use against the idea of miracles applies to alternative forms of knowing, such as feeling and intuition, does it not? I have examples in which I or friends made decisions based on some "feeling" or "intuition" that then caused real problems because of an imagined misunderstanding. We can't always rely on our intuitions or feelings because they, too, can mislead us, just like poor reasoning. Worse, these other ways of knowing are* beyond rational explanation *and, therefore, automatically involve some kind of miracle, according to how you define the word.*

Note that I am not arguing against the possibility of miracles—it's just that if we assume that a miracle has happened, then it means we cannot explain the event. If we want to *explain* an event, then resorting to miracles is out of the question.

Blindspot: As I make very clear in my work, I am definitely not making a case against the validity of nonrational ways of knowing, such as feeling and intuition. The practical difficulty we all face when using other ways of knowing is that inevitably and invariably as soon as we have a nonrational experience, we automatically *interpret* it. That is, we overlay the experience with language and reason. But when the experience is extrarational, we run a real risk that our interpretations will be inadequate and inaccurate. Part of the value of psychospiritual practice is that it equips us with an awareness and ability to discern our feelings and intuitions from our interpretations of them. But it does take practice.

I would caution you and your friends to keep in mind that *feeling* and *intuition* are not the same as *imagination* or, more to the point, *fantasy*. Just as reason and our senses can lead us astray or misinform us, so too can we misinterpret our feelings and intuitions—especially if we let our imaginations run away with us.

> *I have difficulty shaking the need for a* higher source *of mind. Panpsychism tells us there is mind in every bit of matter and that collectively all these "little minds" direct the flow of events in our lives and throughout the universe through what you call the Cosmic Democracy. How, then, do we account for those individual spiritual human beings such as Jesus and Buddha who seemed to operate on a* higher spiritual *level than others?*

It all depends on what you mean by a *higher source of mind*. If by *higher source* you mean "transcendent"—a level or quality of consciousness that is *supernatural,* or beyond the natural world—that would not be compatible with the panpsychist view I have offered in this and my other books.

However, if by *higher source of mind* you mean a level of intelligence that transcends (is greater than) that of individual human beings, that would be consistent with panpsychism. Panpsychism would say that the collectivity of minds guides life (and nonlife, too). I refer to this collectivity as *intersubjectivity* (see *Radical Knowing*).

In this view, folks such as Buddha or Jesus would be examples of enlightened beings who had found a way to let go of identification with their personal egoic minds and opened up to receiving wisdom from the collective or universal mind of the cosmos. Essentially, they were channels for expressing the intelligence of mind in the cosmos.

Science of Mind and the Reflexive Universe

The worldviews of idealism and panpsychism seem different to me, but I find it interesting that Ernest Holmes's Science of Mind blends emanationist idealism and panpsychism—which I'd call panpsychist idealism. *Also, the levels of Arthur Young's reflexive arc and Ernest Holmes's V look very different. Holmes's model has three levels, Spirit, Soul, and Body, whereas Young's arc has four levels, Spirit, Soul, Mind, and Matter.*

Actually, the levels in the models of Holmes and Young are not all that different—both are versions of the Great Chain of Being. The difference is mainly the number of levels. Holmes goes for the most basic "chain of being," or "continuum ontology," as I like to call it: Spirit, Soul, Body. These three levels are included in Young's model: Spirit, Soul, Mind, and Matter.

Both put Soul at Level 2. In Young's model, time comes into being at Level 2, and this is the realm of Soul—that is, Soul exists in time, not in space.

Holmes's Level 3 (Body) is Young's Level 4 (Matter). *Body* and *matter* are two terms for the same physical reality existing in time-space.

That leaves Young's Level 3 (Mind) unaccounted for in Holmes's model—which is curious, because he called his teaching Science of *Mind*.

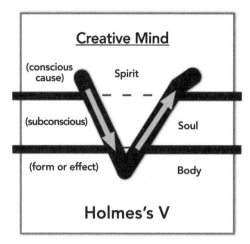
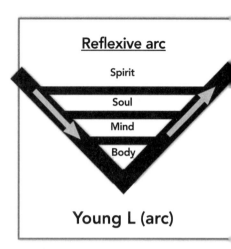

Figure A2.1. Involution and evolution:
Holmes's V compared with Young's L or reflexive arc

PANPSYCHIST IDEALISM

The coupling of panpsychism and idealism does not qualify as a fifth worldview, and it's not really a worldview "combo" (see p. 255). The critical distinction between idealism and panpsychism still stands. In idealism, pure consciousness, or pure spirit (minus any physicality or materiality whatsoever), is the ultimate. Not so in panpsychism, in which the ultimate is both mind and matter, both consciousness and energy—in the form of *sentient energy* (see below).

Yet there is some overlap between the two worldviews. Emanationist idealism claims that the ultimate is *pure* consciousness, or *pure* spirit, that then "emanates" or shines itself forth in involution to create the domains of Soul, Mind, and Matter.

Now, because all levels are ultimately made of spirit, or consciousness (according to emanationism), it follows logically that all matter "contains" something of the nature of spirit. In other words, all matter is conscious, or sentient—just as panpsychism claims.

In short, panpsychism is a natural and inevitable *consequence* of emanationist idealism. In some of my books, I refer to emanationist idealism as *consequent panpsychism* to distinguish it from *ontological panpsychism.*

Because consequent panpsychism is a form of emanationist idealism, the ultimate is assumed to be *pure* spirit, or *pure* consciousness (without any trace of physicality or materiality). Of course, this is not what ontological panpsychism assumes. In this true form of panpsychism, as I noted above, the ultimate is both matter and mind in the form of *sentient energy.*

PURPOSEFUL ACTION

Is the ascent/descent process of Arthur Young's reflexive arc similar to or the same as the description of the involution/evolution process described in the emanationist worldview? I imagine the arc of evolution as a V shape, similar to the Science of Mind symbol, which Ernest Holmes referred to as the involutionary and evolutionary process of God.

I have already addressed this above, but let me add a few more points. In many ways, Young's cosmology matches emanationist idealism—especially the coupling of *involution,* the descent of spirit to form matter, and *evolution,* the homecoming journey back to spirit. And, yes, this is also similar to Ernest Holmes's model.

However, as you might expect by now, nothing is ever quite as simple as it might first appear. While Young's reflexive arc *resembles* Holmes's V, it is different in some important respects. Young is quite clear and explicit, for reasons he gives in his books, that his arc is not a V shape; it is an L shape, with a *right angle,* turned on its side. The 90-degree angle in the arc plays a significant role in the mathematics of Young's overall theory, and a 45-degree angle in a V shape would not work in his model. Also, the Holmes model has three levels, whereas Young's has four.

The question of whether Young was an idealist often comes up.

This is understandable because, on the face of it, his model certainly looks like a form of emanationism. He does say that it all begins with Spirit,* and Spirit then "involutes" through progressive self-constraints to create the levels of Soul, Mind, and Matter, before evolving back up through those levels to its homecoming in Spirit at Level 1. This certainly smacks of emanationism.

However, there is a crucial difference—I refer to Young's model as *quantum emanationism.* Let me explain the difference.

QUANTUM EMANATION

Typically, emanationist idealism claims that all matter derives from *pure* consciousness, or *pure* spirit. But then we have the problem of explaining how it would be possible to get *real* matter from *pure* consciousness, or *pure* spirit. An alternative (Arthur Young's "quantum" variation of emanationism) is to posit the photon, or *quantum of action,* as fundamental. His *quantum emanationism* is really a form of *panpsychist emanationism.*

Young's fundamental photon, or quantum, is *purposeful* action. It is simultaneously *consciousness* and *action.* The "action" component is crucial for Young's ontology because otherwise it would fall victim to the same critique leveled at other forms of emanationism. The photon, then, could be described as *sentient action.* That way, we can account for the fact that reality is both mental and physical—originating with quanta, or photons, that are bundles of purposeful, sentient action or energy.

If, as is the case in Young's model, Spirit is the creation point, then it follow that Spirit is *sentient energy*—it is not just consciousness, or sentience; it is also energy, or action.

---

*In Young's model, he equates "Light," "Spirit," and "Consciousness." He also explains how light, which consists of photons, is a quantum of action. Therefore, in his model, the terms "Light," "Photon," "Quantum," "Spirit," and "Consciousness" are synonymous.

Spirit needs *consciousness,* or purpose, to account for subjectivity, and it needs *action* to account for objective energy—to *make things happen.* Without energy, or action, Spirit would be pure consciousness and would not be able to manifest anything. It could create all kinds of great *intentions,* but without energy, it could not act on them—it could not manifest its own intentions.

So, bottom line: *Spirit must be sentient energy.* This notion of sentient energy or sentient action is fully consistent with the panpsychist view that mind and matter, sentience and energy, are inextricably united, though not equated. Mind is always embodied; matter is always ensouled.

As just pointed out, if Young is consistent, then Spirit must include both *action* and *consciousness.* It cannot be *pure* consciousness, which is what idealists claim. In other words, action, or energy, must also be present in the nature of Spirit, or the Creative Ultimate, which is what panpsychists claim.

If we view Young's model through the lens of panpsychism, the cosmos begins with pure *sentient action.* Both components are eternally present: *sentience* (consciousness or spirit) and *action* (energy). Young's fundamental photon, the building block of the universe, is a quantum of *action* as well as a quantum of light, spirit, or *consciousness.*

We cannot conveniently ignore the action component of the quantum. If anything, as a scientific concept, action is more basic than consciousness. But, of course, standard quantum physics doesn't know what to do with consciousness, so it ignores it or assumes it arrives much later on the cosmic scene. Not so in panpsychism, where consciousness (spirit) and energy (action) always go together all the way down and all the way back.

Because we *know* we live in a world of *energy,* we need a worldview that accounts both for the capacity to know (*consciousness*) and for the fact that things change and work gets done (*energy*). Idealism accounts for only one aspect of reality. Panpsychism accounts for both.

QUANTUM COSMOLOGY
AND PANPSYCHISM

I notice a subtle discrepancy between your beliefs about consciousness and Arthur Young's cosmology. In The Reflexive Universe, *Young draws heavily on quantum physics and places the* photon *at Level 1, Light/Spirit. You have cautioned us against using third-person science, which quantum physics is, for discussing or explaining consciousness. At best, you say, we should use quantum science as a source of metaphors for consciousness, not as a means for providing literal explanations. But Young uses the quantum of action to develop a deeply personal, and therefore first-person, account of the cosmos. He uses physics to explain the role of consciousness in the cosmos. Does Young's cosmology, then, qualify as a first-person exploration of consciousness and not just another third-person account, like other theories derived from quantum physics?*

Specifically, I'm puzzled by the fact that, as you say, Young's Spirit should not be understood as pure *consciousness—because it contains action, or energy, which is physical. Doesn't Young's work show that at its deepest, quantum level, matter/energy fuses with, or dissolves into, consciousness, or Spirit? In other words, at its deepest level, doesn't quantum matter approximate the characteristics we reserve for mind (e.g., nonlocality)? How, then, do you reconcile Young's photon-based cosmology with the panpsychist idea that mind and matter are distinct yet inseparable?*

I'll start with a brief summary to answer your question, then follow with a more detailed explanation.

SHORT ANSWER

1. Young posits the "photon" as the cosmological ultimate.
2. Young equates "photon" and "quantum of action" with "Spirit."

3. The photon is a quantum of *purposeful* action.

4. Therefore, "photon," "quantum," and "Spirit" include both *consciousness* (purpose) and *energy* (action) as fundamental to reality.

5. This is precisely the claim made by panpsychism.

LONG VERSION

Here's how I reconcile Young's cosmology and panpsychism. First point: Young has offered us a *cosmology*, not a *science*. He provides a theoretical model for how to integrate first- and third-person perspectives, but he does not provide an experimental protocol. However, reading between the lines, his work does suggest an approach that is compatible with both first- and third-person perspectives.

Second, Young quite explicitly departs from mainstream quantum physics by insisting, correctly, that any comprehensive cosmology must account for the fact of consciousness; standard quantum models do not do this. Thus, from the outset, Young includes consciousness as a primordial element in reality. His photon, or quantum of action, is a quantum of *purposeful* action. That little word *purpose* carries a big philosophical punch. It means that consciousness is intrinsic to action, or energy, right from the start.

Because of this, Young's cosmology opens the way for a first-person approach to studying consciousness—by paying attention to our own subjective experience of purpose and how it relates to our own actions. Young's cosmology is, of course, also a third-person approach because it deals with ideas, abstractions, words, and formulas—all of which are objective.

Things get very tricky very fast when talking about the quantum of action. Here's the main point to keep in mind: There are two aspects to the quantum—one is the domain of quantum potential, or unmanifest reality, and the other is the domain of quantum actualities, or manifest reality. We only ever detect matter/energy in the manifest domain of quantum actualities—that is, in the domain of locatable, quantifiable, spatial extension. In its unmanifest form, the quantum, or photon, is not yet matter/energy—it is *potentially* energy—and does not occupy space, is unquantifiable, and is nonlocated. Quantum potential is *inferred,* not observed.

Because of Heisenberg's uncertainty principle, at the quantum level, matter/energy loses "fixed" attributes such as location and quantity, and this is why many who popularize quantum physics get excited about its implications for consciousness. However, none of the properties of the quantum as an object studied by physics can even begin to account for or explain the existence of subjective, sentient, experiencing beings. Consciousness is not explicable in terms of quantum physics, even though quantum physicists can no longer ignore the causality of consciousness in collapsing the probability wave function. The fundamental distinction (not "separation") between matter and mind, or energy and consciousness, remains.

Arthur Young does identify the quantum, or photon, with Spirit. And although, at times, it might seem like he equates Spirit with pure consciousness, it is also very clear that he describes the quantum, or photon, as a "quantum of action"—to be even more precise, as a "quantum of *purposeful* action." In other words, Spirit (as quantum) has two fundamental ingredients—purpose and action. Now purpose is an expression of consciousness, and action is energy expressed. Therefore, Spirit consists of both consciousness and energy; that is, it is not pure consciousness.

If Spirit were pure consciousness, then the most it could do would be to create intentions, but it could never act on them—it could never manifest its intentions. For manifestation to occur in the physical world, Spirit also needs action, or energy. The action, or energy, component of the quantum, or photon, is guided by the purpose inherent in Spirit.

In other words, we could conceive of unmanifest Spirit as combined unmanifest consciousness and energy, or unmanifest purposeful action. Because both components exist in the unmanifest domain, it is then possible for Spirit to express consciousness and energy in the manifest domain without a mysterious ontological jump. Measurability, objectivity, location, and so forth belong to manifest energy, not to unmanifest energy (dark energy, perhaps?) and not to either manifest or unmanifest consciousness.

It is fine to use the quantum as an analogy for consciousness as long as we are careful not to slip into taking the analogy literally. I would say that matter and consciousness are always *distinct* because the former exists in space and the latter does not. This holds whether we equate Spirit with consciousness or Spirit with consciousness and energy or purposeful action. The distinction between purpose and action, consciousness and energy, or mind and matter remains in every case. Consciousness is what knows, or is aware of, and purposefully directs forms of energy that flow through space. While consciousness and energy always go together, they are, nevertheless, always distinct, like the shape and substance of a ball. Unity does not equal identity. Unity contains distinctions.

We could conceive of Spirit not only as purposeful action but also as sentient energy, whether manifest or unmanifest.

Earlier in this book, I described consciousness as *the intrinsic ability of matter/energy to know, feel, and purposefully direct itself.* Evolution, then, is the grand adventure of matter/energy exploring its own unfolding potentials. There is no separation between consciousness and the flows of energy it directs from within. Yet energy and consciousness always remain distinct; one is physical, while the other is nonphysical.

SENTIENT ENERGY

The term *sentient energy* occurs frequently in *Radical Nature*. It refers to the ultimate rock-bottom essence of reality. As I explained previously, *sentient energy* refers to energy that intrinsically feels its own being, or energy that "tingles with the spark of spirit."

In panpsychism, unlike in materialism or dualism, energy is intrinsically sentient—it has a built-in, innate capacity to feel, to know, to be aware, to choose. *Sentient energy* refers to energy that pulses with consciousness.

While sentient energy forms an inseparable unity (sentience and energy always go together), sentience, or consciousness, and energy are *conceptually* distinct. Energy is the capacity to do work, the capacity for *action*; it's what makes things *happen*. Consciousness, or sentience, is the capacity for feeling, knowing, and choosing.

Neither the capacity to do work (action or energy) nor the capacity for feeling, knowing, or choosing (consciousness) can be reduced to, or explained in terms of, the other. That is, consciousness/sentience and matter/energy are *distinct* (but never separate). Hence the bumper sticker: "Consciousness *knows*. Energy *flows*."

GOD TALK

Whatever any person or tradition might say about God, the undeniable fact is this: Ultimate Reality exists. Reality rules!

The key question, of course, is not whether reality exists; that is indisputable. It is: What is the *nature* of reality? Then the next question is: Is reality intrinsically conscious, aware, and purposefully creative?

That is where theological "God talk" begins to veer off from scientific or philosophical "reality talk." On one hand, religion says that God is Spirit, or consciousness: On the other hand, modern science says "no," reality is not intrinsically conscious or aware; consciousness emerges during evolution.

The way out of this impasse is to change our fundamental assumptions about the nature of reality. Instead of a reality ultimately composed of "dead" insentient matter, we may assume that reality (matter/energy) is intrinsically sentient or conscious *all the way down*.

God, then, is all of reality, the sum total of all sentient energy (as we find in panpsychism or pantheism), or God is *greater than, but includes,* the sum total of all sentient energy (as believed in panentheism).

APPENDIX 3

Panpsychism, Pantheism, and Panentheism

I frequently get asked to clarify the difference between *panpsychism* and *pantheism*—and also between both of those and *panentheism*. Here's a simple way to grasp the distinctions.

First, pantheism is a *religion*. Panpsychism is a *philosophy*. *Pan* is an old Greek term that means "whole" or "all of"—so, theologically, pan-*theism* means, essentially, "God *is* all," or "God *equals* everything," or "God is *in* everything," and "everything *is* God." And philosophically, pan-*psychism* means "all (of nature) possesses mind," or "mind is everywhere," or "mind is in all things."

Pantheism is a belief about the nature of God (or gods). It holds that God and nature (the cosmos) are the same. God equals nature. All of nature is imbued with spirit, with divinity. Nothing exists beyond nature. Nature is all there is, including God. God is wholly *immanent* in nature, and nowhere else.

Panentheism is also a belief about the nature of God (or gods). The additional "en" in the middle of the word indicates that God is "in" all of nature—but also beyond nature. It differs from pantheism by claiming that nature does not exhaust the limits of God. In other words, all of nature is divine, but not all of the divine is accounted for by nature.

Nature *does not* equal God. God is both *transcendent* and *immanent*.

In pantheism, if all of nature were obliterated, God would vanish, too. In panentheism, if all of nature were obliterated, some of God would still exist. In fact, because God is assumed to be infinite, even if part of God were obliterated, *all* of God would still remain.

Panpsychism is a set of metaphysical assumptions about the nature of reality, essentially the relationship between mind and matter or consciousness and energy. It holds that nature is intrinsically sentient, or has consciousness. All matter/energy "tingles with the spark of spirit." Matter is always sentient, and consciousness is always embodied. Mind and matter always go together. They are inseparable. "Consciousness goes all the way down" means that some degree of mind, or consciousness, is present at every level of the physical world.

Panpsychism is a coherent philosophy that gives support to both pantheism and panentheism. If God and spirit are the same, and if spirit and consciousness are the same, pantheism and panpsychism become variations of the same worldview. However, the *transcendent* God aspect of *panentheism* is not wholly consistent with panpsychism because, in panpsychism, consciousness/spirit is never separable from matter/energy. Consciousness/spirit is never "transcendent" to nature or matter.

> *You mentioned that in* pantheism, *if both God and nature became extinct simultaneously, nothing would be left; whereas in* panentheism, *if nature vanishes, God continues—an infinite and eternal presence, as opposed to the possibility that either could cease. I don't see how something eternal could ever come to an end.*

When I referred to the possibility of God or nature ceasing, that was simply to contrast *pantheism* and *panentheism*. It was *hypothetical*, a thought experiment. It couldn't really happen. If nature were to vanish, where would it go? I raised the question as a conceptual device to show how pantheism and panentheism differ. *If* (remember, it's an "if") nature were to disappear in panentheism, God would still persist because God is not fully accounted for by immanence in the natural world.

Again, hypothetically, in *pantheism,* if either God or nature were to vanish, nothing would be left because God equals nature, which equals all that exists. In pantheism, God is fully immanent, with nothing left over beyond nature.

However, in *panentheism,* if nature were to vanish, God would still exist because in that theology, God is also *transcendent* to nature. In panentheism, all of nature is in God, but not all of God is in nature. God is both immanent *and* transcendent. So if all "immanent God" were to go away, "transcendent God" would still remain.

As a philosophy, panpsychism is more aligned with pantheism because it takes the view that all that exists is the natural world. In panpsychism, there is nothing left over, nothing supernatural. That's one way panpsychism differs from both dualism and idealism. As soon as you slip in anything supernatural, which is what *transcendent* means, then explanations go out the window, and we're left to invoke the convenience (or inconvenience) of miracles. Because both science and philosophy are in the business of explanations, that rules out miracles.

To sum up: *Pantheism* is a theology consistent with the philosophy of panpsychism, which holds that nothing exists beyond nature. In *pantheism,* there is no room for anything supernatural.

By contrast, *panentheism* is a theology consistent with emanationist idealism, which holds that nature is an "emanation" or "extension" of God. In panentheism, room is left over for a transcendent supernatural being.

But remember, if we go for that last option, we jettison all hope of explaining reality. We give up science, philosophy, and coherent, non-contradictory communication. Why? Because if *transcendent* means anything, it means not only "beyond the natural world" (an *ontological* state) but also "beyond reason and language," beyond anything we could think or talk about (an *epistemological* limitation).

In my work, I adhere to the philosophy of panpsychism and I'm less concerned with theologial distinctions between pantheism and panentheism. However, panpsychism—which I also refer to as "radical naturalism"—recognizes that the sum total of all sentient embodied beings throughout the cosmos constitutes the Creative Ultimate. This, as we have seen, is the equivalent of God in religious cosmologies. In this view, God is as dependent on every sentient being, including you and me, as we are dependent on God. This reciprocal process forms the basis of cosmic evolution. Every one of us contributes to the evolution of God or the Creative Ultimate.

God, therefore, is an ongoing, evolving, neverending creative process.

Bibliography

Blackmore, Susan. *Consciousness: An Introduction.* Oxford, U.K.: Oxford University Press, 2009.

Chalmers, David. *The Conscious Mind: In Search of a Fundamental Theory.* Oxford, U.K.: Oxford University Press, 1997.

Clarke, Arthur C. *Childhood's End.* New York: Del Ray/Ballentine, 2001.

de Chardin, Pierre Teilhard. *The Phenomenon of Man.* New York: Harper Perennial Modern Classics, 2008.

de Quincey, Christian. *Consciousness from Zombies to Angels.* Rochester, Vt.: Park Street Press, 2011.

———. *Deep Spirit: Cracking the Noetic Code.* Half Moon Bay, Calif.: Wisdom Academy Press, 2009.

———. *Radical Knowing: Understanding Consciousness through Relationship.* Rochester, Vt.: Park Street Press, 2005.

———. *Radical Nature: The Soul of Matter.* Rochester, Vt.: Park Street Press, 2010.

FitzGerald, Edward. *The Rubaiyat of Omar Khayyam.* New York: Dover, 2011.

Freire, Paulo. *Pedagogy of the Oppressed.* New York: Continuum, 2000.

Hawking, Stephen. *A Brief History of Time.* New York: Bantam, 1998.

Heidegger, Martin. *Being and Time.* New York: Harper & Row, 1962.

Holmes, Ernest. *The Science of Mind.* New York: Tarcher, 2010.

Libet, Benjamin. "Unconscious Cerebral Initiative and the Role of Conscious Will in Voluntary Action." *The Behavioral and Brain Sciences* 8 (1985): 529–66.

Low, Philip. "The Cambridge Declaration on Consciousness." 2012. http://fcm conference.org/img/CambridgeDeclarationOnConsciousness.pdf. Accessed May 7, 2015.

Nietzsche, Friedrich. *Beyond Good and Evil: Prelude to a Philosophy of the Future.* New York: Vintage, 1989.

Russell, Peter. *A White Hole in Time: Our Future Evolution and the Meaning of Now.* New York: HarperCollins, 1992.

Sartre, Jean-Paul. *Being and Nothingness.* New York: Washington Square Press, 1993.

Simon, Herbert. "Designing Organizations for an Information-Rich World." In *Computers, Communication, and the Public Interest.* Martin Greenberger, ed. Baltimore, Md.: Johns Hopkins Press, 1971.

Tolle, Eckhart. *The Power of Now.* Vancouver, B.C.: Namaste Press, 2004.

Weiss, Eric. *The Long Trajectory: The Metaphysics of Reincarnation and Life after Death.* Bloomington, Ind.: iUniverse, 2012.

Whitehead, A. N. *Process and Reality* (2nd ed.). New York: Free Press, 2010.

Williams, Caroline. "Are These the Brain Cells That Give Us Consciousness?" *New Scientist,* July 12, 2012.

Young, Arthur. *The Reflexive Universe.* Cambria, Calif.: Anodos Foundation, 1999.

Index

About the Author

Philosopher Christian de Quincey, Ph.D., an award-winning author, is an international speaker on consciousness, spirituality, and science at conferences and workshops in the United States, Europe, Australia, Africa, and Asia. He is a professor of Consciousness Studies at John F. Kennedy University, dean of Consciousness Studies at the University of Philosophical Research, and an adjunct faculty member at Sofia University (formerly Institute of Transpersonal Psychology). Before founding The Wisdom Academy (www.thewisdomacademy.org), where he offers personal mentorships in consciousness, de Quincey worked for twelve years as managing editor for the Institute of Noetic Sciences.

De Quincey's books include the award-winning *Radical Nature: The Soul of Matter* (2010) and *Radical Knowing: Understanding Consciousness through Relationship* (2005) as well as *Consciousness from Zombies to Angels* (2008) and *Deep Spirit: Cracking the Noetic Code* (2011). His work on consciousness has appeared in both popular and academic journals, including the *Journal of Consciousness Studies, Journal of Transpersonal Psychology, Cerebrum, IONS Review, Shift, ReVision, Network, Connections, World Futures, Somatics,* and *Tikkun.*

De Quincey earned his Ph.D. in philosophy and religion from the California Institute of Integral Studies and a master's degree in consciousness studies from John F. Kennedy University. More of his writings on consciousness and cosmology can be found at www.ChristiandeQuincey .com, www.christiandequincey.com/iQNoeticNews, and on his Facebook page "Consciousness for Life" (www.facebook.com/ChristiandeQuincey .ConsciousnessforLife?fref=ts).